Acts of Inclusion

Acts of Inclusion

Studies Bearing on an Elementary Theory of Romanticism

Michael G. Cooke

New Haven and London
Yale University Press
1979

Published with assistance from the Louis Stern Memorial Fund.

Designed by Thos. Whitridge and set in IBM Baskerville type. Printed in the United States of America by Halliday Lithograph, West Hanover, Mass.

Published in Great Britain, Europe, Africa, and Asia (except Japan) by Yale University Press, Ltd., London. Distributed in Australia and New Zealand by Book & Film Services, Artarmon, N.S.W., Australia; and in Japan by Harper & Row, Publishers, Tokyo Office.

Library of Congress Cataloging in Publication Data

Cooke, Michael G.
  Acts of inclusion.
  Includes bibliographical references and index.
  1. English literature—19th century—History and criticism. 2. Romanticism. I. Title.
PR457.C6   820'.9'14   78-21909
ISBN 0-300-02303-0

Grateful acknowledgment is made to the museums that granted permission to reproduce the pictures accompanying the chapter titles:
  Chapter 1: William Blake, *Jerusalem* 25D. Courtesy of the Houghton Library, Harvard University.
  Chapter 2: Théodore Géricault, *Raft of the Medusa*. Courtesy of the Musée du Louvre, Paris.
  Chapter 3: Sir Henry Raeburn, *Miss Eleanor Urquhart*. Courtesy of the National Gallery of Art, Washington. Andrew W. Mellon Collection.
  Chapter 4: Goya, *The Colossus*. Courtesy of the Metropolitan Museum of Art, New York. Harris Brisbane Dick Fund, 1935.
  Chapter 5: Théodore Chassériau, *Cossack Girl Finding the Body of Mazeppa*. Courtesy of the Musée des Beaux Arts, Strasbourg.

"The Mode of Argument of Wordsworth's Poetry" is an expanded version of an essay first published in *Romantic and Victorian: Studies in Memory of William H. Marshall*, edited by W. Paul Elledge and Richard L. Hoffman; it is used here with the kind permission of Associated University Presses.

"Byron's *Don Juan*: The Obsession and Self-Discipline of Spontaneity" first appeared, in shorter form, in *Studies in Romanticism* and is included here with the kind permission of the Trustees of Boston University.

Contents

Introduction
Romanticism and the Universality of Art

The most universal quality is diversity.
Montaigne

What can we mean by the "universality" of art? Surely no more than that, with any particular work expressing the power of human grasp and embodiment and shaping, enough is present—and arrestingly enough—so that we desire and think of nothing not invoked or controlled by the matter at hand. We read an elegy and say its sorrow is universal, though it is far from making us think of mourning in a Sherpa village or a Manhattan pied-à-terre. When we apprehend certain lines of elegy by Bion or Milton or Wordsworth, we find something about the lines rather than the subject universal.

We can test this postulate by calling up another universal subject, sex, and we will instantly realize that while pornography is ubiquitous, few examples of pornographic art inspire the judgment "universal." This is because such art is too much merely localized in a Sherpa village or a Manhattan pied-à-terre. Its subject or action may be duplicated everywhere, but that makes it a mere reminder of actuality. In a sense it distracts as much as it attracts, neither satisfying nor fulfilling attention. The universal both enlarges and settles attention. It is answerable without being specific to an interest or a place.

A scene from *King Lear*, say, or a piece of Benin sculpture, or Goya or Utamaro on various incidents of war or travel: these things impress us with their universality by suspending

(1) that natural centrifuge of attention which drives our curiosity about other forms, and (2) that gift and passion for cavil which springs from our steadfast dissatisfaction with ourselves (truly smug people shun art). Universal art-works do not summon but indirectly suppress the rest of the world. In a complex way they substitute for and become the world, for the reader and the duration. Their universality begins as a subjective absorption, and on its heels a saving conviction that their finished quality is capable of possessing as many as come that way. We wish to stay with and repeat the relationship and apprehension, or they tend to stay with us. What Paul Valéry says of art's production in "The Idea of Art" may be applied also to the domain of response: "If . . . *we are compelled or induced to repeat our . . . maneuver indefinitely*, we gradually lose our sense of the *arbitrary* character of our act, and a certain sense of *necessity* is born in us."*

This is not to suggest anything like decadent aesthetics, with art as the ultimate and only good, existing unto itself and giving sole value to life. The individual, absorbed with the work of art, is not absorbed in worship or magical transformation, and does not dismiss the world. Rather, the intensity of his engagement makes a willing sacrifice of the extended awareness that is available to him. He suffers a loss here, but achieves an indirect recovery of this loss by the presumption that other people must come into the same relation to the work and the world. Also possessed, others will be in no position to judge or take advantage of the given individual's departure from ordinary perception and care. The moment of appreciation/possession abides in art, but also is an abiding if oblique possibility in life.

As it gives the possessed individual assurance that his response will find kinship and justification everywhere, the

Aesthetics, trans. Ralph Manheim (London: Routledge & Kegan Paul, 1964), p. 75.

attributed universality of art works to satisfy his peculiar need for substantiation through otherness; personality seeks generality, seeks to flatter and vindicate itself, its perceptions and passions and values, in the world abroad. Perhaps the universality of art need be no more than a stalking-horse for this species of vanity. It does not, at any rate, consider the pragmatic point that the subject (sorrow or sex) transpires everywhere, but rather rests on the notion that the value assigned to a particular rendition will prevail at large.

Joyce Kilmer's "Trees" or William Henley's "Invictus" may help to bring the distinction into clearer focus. The sentiment of piety or indomitability, subjects such as a tree or a poem or God or fate or the metaphor of a ship, all present themselves everywhere, without proving in these cases universal. Universality depends on statement, on articulation and substance, rather than on immediate subject and sentiment. The latter, though *in fact* ubiquitous, are in the form the poem affords them bland and torpid, inducing at best a deadened agreement or acknowledgement. *That* a position is taken is creditable—*how* it is taken and, more to the point, *held*, leaves much to be imagined, everything to be desired. The poems in question point, with a single, blunt, and rigid finger, at what they should bring home, and that in a form articulate, shapely, diverse and coherent as the hand, the place where conception and realization most effectively meet.

If art, as opposed to its subject-freight of sorrow, say, or problems of justice or love, has universality only in effect and by personal consent, it becomes paramount to tell how that effect and consent are achieved. One wishes to know if the effect is legitimate and the consent honorable, rather than a matter of fallacy or indulgence. As long as we recognize that art lacks the simple universality of air or disease, we are in a good position to see that it creates a universality not of presence but of apprehension. This means that divergent needs, values, expectations are satisfied in a single ordering, and our usual harum-scarum apprehension of those matters is composed to reflect the composition of the work. As Harold Osborne observes in *The Art of Appreciation*, "the arts" satisfy not just a "desire for the titillation of pleasurable emotions and sensations, but some deeper impulse for self-fulfillment in the expansion of awareness."* We may say that art is universal when it proves at once sufficient in itself and sufficient for us.

What is involved here goes beyond the conviction that the personal response which proves basic to universality will prevail anywhere. A further sense arises that the response to art can encompass and transcend all local, specific, phenomenal responses in the individual. In the encounter with the work thought universal, this individual's defects are compensated and his excesses tempered, his notion of possibility and his experience of necessity focused and enriched, his dread of monotony lifted and his hope of sensible prediction substantiated. His response becomes a perfect Kantian action, in that he can will it for all people, can universalize it. Unlike a mystic who is absorbed into the universal, he assumes the universal into himself, and, by his response, becomes universal.

How can this be so? What behavior, what elements in a work of art can induce or justify such a response? Precisely its power of incorporation, its ability to thrive on paradox, or rather a state of paradoxy; the work of art realizes the fact that paradoxy is the root out of which the various things we call orthodox have branched. Such paradoxy here has little intrinsically to do with local rhetorical play, or with any local relations of opposition and disparity. It is a term for the basic capacity in universal art to suspend the spirit of denial and dismissal which makes us think ourselves right when we are being merely righteous. We find art universal when it is marked by intensity but also a curious range; when it grapples

*(London: Oxford University Press, 1970), p. 56.

with complexity without sacrificing measure and clearness; when it conveys conviction and yet recalls that all mere dogmas are linked to death as their origin and end; when its beauty and courage enable the participant to stand up under its unbearable force and revelation.

It will be of use, perhaps, to distinguish this state of paradoxy from the taste for irony cultivated by I. A. Richards and made a staple of value by the New Criticism until a decade or two ago. Right off one may observe that irony was a rhetorical ploy of the movement, and one of its central *orthodoxies.* It was a means of protecting a cherished statement rather than a measure for rendering a complex reality. As R. P. Warren avers in "Pure and Impure Poetry," the objective, the ideal was the pure (as opposed to the inclusive) poem, and

the pure poem tries to be pure by excluding, more or less rigidly, certain elements which might qualify or contradict its original impulse. In other words, the pure poems want to be, and desperately, all of a piece . . . there is not one doctrine of "pure poetry"—not one definition of what constitutes impurity in poems—but many.

To produce and, worse, to maintain, such poetry was trouble enough, and so irony was invoked:

The poet . . . proves his vision by submitting it to the fires of irony—to the drama of his structure—in the hope that the fires will refine it. In other words, the poet wishes to indicate that his vision has been earned, that it can survive reference to the complexities and contradictions of experience. And irony is one such device of reference.*

Paradoxy goes beyond this. It involves the claim, to the fullest of knowledge, that the fullest of being is grasped and conveyed, or in other words that universality is afoot. It must happen that the more a given work sustains the individual

Selected Essays (New York: Random House, 1958), pp. 16, 29. See also I. A. Richards, *Principles of Literary Criticism* (New York: Harcourt, Brace & Co., n.d.), passim.

contention of universality, the less it comes to depend on individual contentions as a medium of support, until the quality of universality seems to reside simply in its own substance. But even Shakespeare's universality has emerged in time, and through subjective recognition. That emergence occurred in the romantic period, and it may seem more than accidental that, after being blithely revised in the later seventeenth century and convincingly forged in the later eighteenth century, Shakespeare came into his own just then. For the romantic took a new and explicit interest in the paradoxes of inclusion, that is, in universality.

Where the Augustans upheld what was representative, the romantics pursued what was universal. Kant found the universal ineffable, but speculated that access to it might come through the moment of aesthetic apprehension; his categorical imperative is analogous in the realm of conduct to what I have called the universalizing of subjective conviction in relation to works of art. Hegel in turn made the universal "concrete," and the poets made up for his disparagement of a protean actuality by finding the universal, as synecdoche or symbol, in that same actuality. Universality was more than a fact or a tenet. It became for the romantics a problem and a necessity.

Small signs prove telling here. Johnson objects to the way early seventeenth-century poets compose love poems in a "metaphysical" style, but this, apart from its dubious conception of what moves women, smacks of overcompartmentalism, as though passion and metaphysics *may* not mix because they *have* not done so. By contrast, Coleridge owns in *Anima Poetae* that he is drawn to metaphysical poetry and, even if his private temperament comes into play here, he is reflecting a contemporary interest in what reality can include in a single position. Again, as a small sign: the Augustans favor a *concordia discors*, which entails a compatible combination of varied phenomena, while the romantics rediscover the force of *coincidentia oppositorum*, an identification or inter-presence between phenomena that seem to deny each other.

This is the basis of romantic irony, the swift removal of the veil between aspiration and absurdity, or between magnanimity and fatuousness, or even, as in "Christabel," between charity and disloyal eroticism. The effect of romantic irony is less to undermine faith and romance than to increase awareness of actuality, and thus to suggest a richer, more complex, more challenging ground for a faith that would better withstand its challenges. Frederick Garber, for example, brings out the positive capacities of romantic irony in his acute comments in "Nature and the Romantic Mind: Egotism, Empathy, Irony."* The flash of moonlight in Wordsworth's bemisted, arduous ascent of Mount Snowdon is structurally akin to romantic irony, and works as a corrective, creative obverse of that phenomenon. Wordsworth has been overweening before, in the rowboat episode or climbing the Alps, and has been shocked into humility. Now he is shocked into exaltation. In both cases he comes upon, is swept up into, a more inclusive vision and role. The thing to recognize is not that the romantics included opposites in their work, as dialecticism would suggest, but rather that they proposed acts of inclusion as their ground and goal.

Coleridge gives voice to that mission when he calls for the reconciliation of opposite and discordant qualities, and *multiplies qualities* before our eyes. The qualities become omnipresent and simultaneous, and not sequential as in dialectics. A similar effect occurs in Schiller's description of himself as "a hybrid, between concept and contemplation, between law and feeling, between a technical mind and genius." And it is striking to find Hegel recognizing an essential unity, and not dualism, in Schiller's position; in the preface to his *Philosophy of Fine Art*, he insists that Schiller get credit for "daring

Comparative Literature 29 (1977):207ff.

to . . . [apprehend] the principles of unity and reconciliation.*

Though radical reconciliation is basic to the romantic position, it need not follow that encountering such reconciliation
will prove easy or simple. There can be a readily enlarged
apprehension and appreciation, a positive response, or there
can be bafflement and resistance. It is striking to see Schubert
boggling at Beethoven's measures of combination and reconciliation. He objects in his diary to Beethoven's "eccentricity,"
finding that Beethoven "joins and confuses the tragic with the
comic . . . so as to goad them to madness instead of dissolving
them in love." But perhaps the opposite of this "madness" is
less truly sanity than falsification. We may note that Schubert
himself, while complaining of Beethoven's way with genres,
was as startling and unorthodox in his use of harmonies.
Harold C. Schonberg speaks of him as "the greatest master of
modulation the world had yet known. His harmonies are not
written by the book. . . . [He] had a genius for finding new,
inevitable-sounding combinations. He wanders freely from
key to key with breathtaking surprises en route, swinging
around pivotal harmonies with indescribable touches. . . ."†
The point is that paradoxical combination, reconciliation,
occurs in many guises, as a gift and challenge. It is not comfortable but necessary, and its practitioners may be offended
by it in one guise while being impelled to it in another. Wordsworth's fondness for the concept of his "harmonies" merits
special attention here, and we may recall that in his "mature
style," as Morse Peckham has observed, "the shifts from
one rhetorical mode to another are continuous and striking."‡ What I am proposing here clearly relates to influential
views already advanced concerning romanticism: Lovejoy's

---

*Quoted by Reginald Snell, introduction to *On the Aesthetic Educa-
tion of Man* (New Haven: Yale University Press, 1954), pp. 11, 12.
†*The New York Times Magazine*, 19 March 1978, p. 54.
‡*The Triumph of Romanticism* (Columbia: University of South Carolina Press, 1970), pp. 135–36.

signalizing of "diversitarianism" as a key romantic trait; the principle of "organicism" propounded by Wellek and later reaffirmed with modifications by Morse Peckham; Jacques Barzun's associating romanticism with a "desire and expectation of change." But more remains to be related. Wordsworth arranged his poetry into several categories and still insisted that his poems should each be counted as part of one work—he calls it an unfinished cathedral. Here, finding a diversity along with a sense of integrity and root belonging, we may see an emblem of the fact that romanticism must be construed as more than the presence of divers data and alternative schemes. It entails an impulse and a demand for a principle of comprehension. It takes the form, characteristically, of an act of inclusion.

De Quincey, trying to incorporate opium into the realm of the plausible and to establish its connection with dreams, childhood, and music, is performing a romantic act of inclusion. Christabel, slipping out of the castle gates, is breaching a principle of exclusion that the gate as well as the castle must entail, and tacitly pursuing an act of inclusion. In some ways Byron's *The Giaour* is the most complete attempt at inclusion that the romantic period affords. Its very mode of composition, with pieces accruing ad lib, might suggest that *exclusion* will get no countenance; its chief character is pious and murderous; its philosophy involves stoicism and rampant egotism; its sympathies are split between justification and condemnation of the protagonist. In short, the form, personality, thought, and tone of *The Giaour* become gestures toward inclusion, evidence of the trials met by those who meet the world equally without prescription and without protection.

It is obvious that Coleridge's definition of the imagination makes a principle of the act of inclusion. Coleridge makes the individual human being a surrogate creator, with responsibility to, and for, the totality of the world, though its terms for that individual are difficult, obscure, and incomplete. In certain respects the definition lacks *definition*; it proceeds by anticipation—abstract and not concrete—of factors which are essential to thought and action, and which effectively change their grounds. At bottom it defines an attitude, a readiness to entertain and engage the world as it comes, at once emergent and inclusive. It is notable, too, that Coleridge in his "Essay on the Principles of Method" sees inclusion as an object of the "laboratory" and does not confine it to the imagination. In his view the "chemical philosopher" (the phrase should not startle us in this context) "is instinctively labouring to extract" certain "elementary powers" and "law." And he comments that

> this instinct . . . is itself but the form, in which the idea, the mental Correlative of the law, first announces its incipient germination in his own mind: and hence proceeds the striving after unity of principle through all the diversity of forms, with a feeling resembling that which accompanies our endeavors to recollect a forgotten name; when we seem at once to have and not to have it; which the memory feels but cannot find. . . . So water and flame, the diamond, the charcoal, and the mantling champagne . . . are convoked and fraternized by the theory of the chemist.*

The principle of inclusion is basic to the following study. It might have been explicated in terms of particular texts— Keats's *The Fall of Hyperion* and Goethe's *Faust* afford us all but systematic embodiments of the romantic act of inclusion, its suspect heroism and ennobling defeats. But a different approach, according to generic and thematic and formal issues, seemed to give a better prospect of covering the topic in depth and breadth, inclusively as it were. Some of the topics addressed will appear more glamorous or more massive than others. But the significance of the overall issue of inclusion can be determined only by seeing how it pervades and

*The Friend, in The Collected Works of Samuel Taylor Coleridge, ed. Barbara E. Rooke (Princeton: Princeton University Press, 1969), 1:470–71.

informs not only philosophical positions and cultural values, but also genres and modes, and finally even the way poems are constructed and the voice a poet speaks with. This study then offers itself as a constellation of essays on the variety and complexity of ways in which the impulse to inclusion expresses itself in romanticism.

Morse Peckham, in his study *Romanticism and Behavior*, has developed out of A. C. Bradley's notion that the romantics found themselves without a central coherent philosophy the principle of "explanatory collapse," and has shown how alienation, "cultural vandalism," and "randomization of behavior" result from it as features of romanticism. But more than such reactions occur upon explanatory collapse. Something recreative also occurs, an affirmative response to the collapse as opportunity no less than deprivation. The corollary of this position would be that the edifice of explanation generally enjoyed by an Elizabethan or an Augustan would resemble, to a romantic, more of a prison than a protection. The act of inclusion then works as an avoidance of still and dusty compartmentalization of the honeycomb of experience. Thus my opening chapter, "Elegy, Prophecy, and Satire," is meant to illumine a dominant mode in romanticism—namely, elegy—by showing how it contains and controls modes we usually treat as distinct from it (namely, prophecy and satire). The essay expands to take in classical elegy and in silhouette a history of elegy before romanticism; this, not by a mimic act of inclusion, but as a means of giving a context and measurement to the romantic development of the form.

The second chapter, "The Norm of Consequences," takes up questions that grow naturally out of the condition of elegy. The presence of loss and death are everywhere lamentable, but how they are lamented varies between cultures and periods. I suggest that romanticism treats loss and death as a product of personality, an index of failure of perception and relationship, rather than as a given of any external theological or social system. A regimen based on punishment for specific failures thus yields, in the romantic scheme, to one centering on consequences, on unmanageable revelations of vulnerability and need.

What makes "consequences" an example of inclusion, where "punishment" would not be? In itself punishment seeks to exclude certain forms of behavior and even attitudes. It treats these as formal, isolated, aberrant, working almost exclusively on the relation of behavior and attitudes toward a social complex and authority. Frequently, though punishment has a counterpart in reward, a regimen founded on punishment takes "normal" or "creditable" behavior for granted, thus again excluding a portion of things from essential recognition. The extremes of sanctity and sin, heroism and pusillanimity tend to preoccupy attention under the regimen of punishment.

It is otherwise with consequences. Good deeds, such as Christabel's succoring of Geraldine, seem inextricably to involve the perverse effect and echo of Geraldine's suckering Christabel. An orientation by consequences looks through the transparent ice on which we proceed in a standard punishment scheme, and recognizes the weird and difficult turmoil that streams underneath. It does not neglect social relations, but also does not canonize them at the expense of the relation between definite behavior and the infinite, unpredictable play of the world. In its treatment of consequences (as of elegy), the romantic period achieves a distinction of emphasis and range, which I have tried to bring out by tracing the question back to Chaucer and forward to Ibsen and Conrad. (A sidelight of my research is the contrast between Chaucer's elaborate, almost indiscriminate system of protection against punishment, and Ibsen and Conrad's relentless insistence on consequences.)

The shift of attention from social ordinance to the play of consequences is tied, implicitly, to altered distributions and values and roles in individual life. New terms of relationship,

new opportunities and goals emerge. Nowhere is this more
decisively marked than in the status of women. My third
chapter, "The Feminine as the Crux of Value," takes up this
element of romanticism, again with a comparative survey of
responses ranging from Aeschylus to Virginia Woolf. The nub
of the chapter is that romanticism produces a breakdown in
the grammar of opposites—and opposition—that had defined
the situation of the sexes. In philosophy, as shown variously
by Schiller, Schlegel, and Shelley, in politics, as Mary Wollstonecraft would show, in educational theory, as Rousseau
and Schiller show, and widely in literary romanticism we find
an express movement to overcome the male-*versus*-female
prejudice and cliché, and to institute a male-*and*-female
principle. The crucial, and heady, feature of this principle is
that it does not rest merely on cooperation, on having one
of each in any context (which our own crude and shallow
arithmetic insists on), but rather on interpenetration and
interpresence, that is, on the recognition that male and
female are in complex measures and modes *included* in each
other. It would be sanguine to say that romanticism produces
a solution to the age-old dilemma of sexual opposition, but it
singularly essays one, with a degree of candor, humility,
courage, imagination, and intelligence that cannot be neglected
in these agitated times.

The fourth chapter, dealing with "the mode of argument"
in romantic poetry (especially Wordsworth), seeks to come to
terms with the fact that the act of inclusion—as regards elegy
or consequences or the status of women—entails problems of
legitimacy and acceptance. Argument is at the bottom of the
romantic adventure, and this chapter explores its existence
and effects. It must be kept in mind here that romanticism
involves an argument *with*, using the double force of the
preposition to suggest at once resistance and sharing. If the
romantics resisted dogma as imposition, they shared with the
dogmatist a feeling for truth, albeit an evolutionary one. Put

another way, while Keats opposes Byron's or Wordsworth's or Coleridge's *tenets*, and Byron opposes Wordsworth's (and vice versa), they all share the same *mission*, to reach the most inclusive and answerable position. Again, De Quincey in his *Confessions* does not speak absolutely against music or wine as stimulants or sources of power; he speaks against the tendency to exclude anything but music or wine from recognition, and in short agitates for the inclusion of opium. The significance of arguing *with*, taken all in all, becomes clearest perhaps when we realize that the romantics were facing not just doubts and unfamiliarity from outside, but also their own uncertainties and vulnerability. Argument is intrinsic not only to the statement but to its maker in the romantic regimen. The efficacy of the argument, then, affects internal conviction in the text no less than it does the reader with his "willing suspension of disbelief."

If romantic argument takes up the philosophy of inclusion, romantic epic takes up its pragmatics. My study concludes with a chapter entitled "Byron's *Don Juan*: The Obsession and Self-Discipline of Spontaneity," in an attempt to show how the romantic demand for infinitude was symbolically served by its penchant for fragments, and how ambiguity and irony served romanticism as a way through the Scylla and Charybdis of shapelessness and rigidity. Byron is the arch-representative of a tendency in the romantic mind toward a sort of entropism: everything must have its chance, its day, and while single things hold for the duration they cannot be held or held to, without sacrificing truth or vitality. Disconcerting as it may seem, Byron's wilful shift from "notes that grow too sad" into frolicsome adventure at the end of the Haidée episode says less about his sense of mischief than about his sense of justice and the wealth of reality. Shelley's departure from elegy into prophecy, in *Adonais*, is of a piece with Byron's abandoning elegy for comedy. And both are of a piece with the romantic engagement with the necessary, free act of inclusion.

1

Elegy, Prophecy, and Satire
in the Romantic Order

No, No, go not to Lethe, neither twist
Wolf's-bane, tight-rooted, for its poisonous wine.

Keats

On the question as to which rings truer to romanticism,
melancholy or ecstasy, unanimity is less likely than spirited
debate. Some of the disagreement might spring from individual
temperament, as a factor of what one notices or stresses. But
the basic difficulty resides in the material itself. Is the Haidée
episode in *Don Juan* marked by ecstasy or melancholy? Isn't
The Fall of Hyperion a study of melancholy through ecstasy
and vice versa, as the narrator imbibes his rapturous feast
only to find it contains a radical threat to his existence, while
this in turn opens out onto a radical expansion of his mind?
Arnold in his famous 1853 palinode to poetry accuses
himself of gratuitous melancholy, but the fault could have
been laid off on Byron and Wordsworth, who taught him,
and all the Victorians, to play in this key. And Swinburne
presents himself as a revolutionary rhapsode, but only
after having taken council with his mentors, Shelley and
Blake.

If romanticism prepares both casts of mind, perhaps the
cast of the question—melancholy or ecstasy—is too rigid and
exclusive. As Wordsworth's "Ode: Intimations of Immortal-
tiy" shows, ecstasy and melancholy can be virtual twins,
identical in origin and structure, and differing only as the fat
and lean versions, the fulfilled and unfulfilled states of certain
primary needs and satisfactions. We may go further and say
that there is a restless relationship between the two, that one

2

presupposes and produces the other, not as counteraction but as counterpart.

Byron's *Manfred* would be a case in point, as Manfred's melancholy, indeed all but suicidal gloom over Astarte's death keeps a direct ratio with his extravagant visions of a world they two might have made. Wordsworth's "A Slumber Did My Spirit Seal" is in many ways an analogous document. The ecstasy comes out plainly at the outset: "She seemed a thing that could not feel/The touch of earthly years." But this ecstatic mood of unearthly out-of-touchness is crushingly brought back to reality, and the earth takes possession of her in the grave, where she is, in the grim and grieving lines of the poem, "Rolled round . . . /With rocks, and stones, and trees." Perhaps this kind of movement from ecstasy to melancholy will seem probable as a comeuppance syndrome; it is well to recall that the opposite movement, from melancholy to ecstasy, also occurs, as in Coleridge's "This Lime-Tree Bower, My Prison," or Keats's ode "To Psyche."

The romantic highlighting (it was no absolute discovery) of the interdependence and interpenetration of melancholy and ecstasy may be regarded as an emblem of a prevailing concern with the common ground of divers moods. These moods, of course, have a possessive force and allure of their own, and would seem in a way to have been canonized in genres and modes: melancholy in elegy and tragedy, ecstasy in prophecy, anger in satire, etc. At this more abstract level of genre, the romantic decalendarization of sainted entities appears not just as a fact but as a veritable program. Closet (or introspective and contemplative) drama appears cheek by jowl with lyrical ballads, both representing bold revisions of normal generic conduct and assumptions. Kroeber and Peckham have also pointed out the reconstitution of norms of narrative, and Wilkie the reformation of epic principles. Thus, even if it is true that closet drama occurred in the late sixteenth century, and a remodeling of epic in the late seventeenth century, the romantic period remains distinctive in its catholic or comprehensive approach to these possibilities. The upsurge of medievalism is in this light less a pious recovery than a kind of opportunism and imperialism backwards in time. It should be instructive, then, to consider more closely what the romantic period made of moods of melancholy and ecstasy, and the modes of elegy and prophecy. And it will emerge that these are more than accidentally linked to anger, and to satire.

The clearest exposition of the kinship between cruelty and laughter is given us in Freud's *Wit and Its Relation to the Unconscious*. But that kinship was recognized at least as early as the eighteenth century, when satirists defended their right to make a destitute man—ostensibly a figure of sympathy— the butt of their jokes. Such a man, William Cleland specifically declared in a formal defense of Pope, was fair game by reason of the disguises, contortions, pretensions, and whatever devices he took up, albeit under the pressure of destitution, to keep a decent visage to the world. Laughter becomes possible, even necessary, when the fact of destitution is subordinated into a vague background for the master image of pretension or, as Cleland more forcibly puts it, "malice and villainy."[1]

All comedy, as theorists have long urged, depends on a selective or elliptical focus. Bergson in his essay on "Laughter" calls this "insensibility in the spectator,"[2] but the spectator should not have to bear the blame. The comic work itself insists on insensitivity by minimizing a shadowy association with grief, in the victim, or with cruelty, in the practitioner of the comic action. The cruelty gets little or no direct attention,[3] but it gives a singular tension and resonance to the topos of awareness; it would seem less comic to find pretension in a rich man than in a pauper, because the former would be less vulnerable. Should we then regard comedy as a kind of low-grade tragedy manqué, and should we conversely be prepared to see in tragedy a form of grief-stricken comedy? Is the difference between comedy and tragedy merely a matter of bedecking or unshrouding cruelty and grief? Probably not, and the reason is not far to seek. Both genres involve more than an angle or pattern of attention, more than a technical deployment of material and experience. They necessitate more than formal value, because they intrinsically involve emotional norms. Both tragedy and comedy involve a total emotional complex that rests on a scheme of values as much as on any formal properties, and considerable latitudes—of proportion, compensation, sequence—arise as to the method of establishing appropriate values. One must in fact break the seizure of attention and reflect on its teleology to get a true sense of the difference between tragedy and comedy.

Of radical importance is their treatment of consequences, which comedy minimizes and tragedy intensely scrutinizes. This is formally imaged in the relatively choppy action of comedy,[4] compared with the momentous coherence of tragedy. Aristotle in the *Poetics* speaks of the thin line between tragedy and comedy, but that line must not be taken lightly. Not modification but transformation of feeling and value would be required to convey a single body of material across the line from tragic to comic or vice versa. More than a crossing, a certain transgression is entailed. A narrowing of attention in tragedy will not ipso facto elicit comedy. An expansion of attention, to take in confusion, disease, desolation, will undo comedy, but will not disclose tragedy. We are faced here with the need to confront the fact that tragedy and comedy are not true antitheses, but only contrastive in effect. A fair sense of their relationship is arrived at through the following formulation: comedy contains grief as tragedy contains joy. Without going into the formal and rhetorical demands of either genre, I would like to stress the spiritual impurity common to both, the way they achieve authority by containing—overcoming and yet including—antipathetic elements.

The effect of containment, evident enough in tragedy or comedy, is not merely a feature of literary expression, but a

norm in the psychic establishment of a human being. In order
to apprehend or to relate any occurrence of matter or thought,
it is necessary to shape it for statement and so to take a position concerning it. But every statement, every position preempts other possibilities within that occurrence, and in effect
also other possibilities in the world. One is instinctively
jealous and even afraid of this preemption, in honor of the
vastness and versatility of the world (which is also to say of
our imaginative possibilities therein). Each statement or position comes under the obligation of denying, or placating, or
perhaps buying out the version that might form in spite of it.
And yet the alternative versions are not simply shut out. We
cannot achieve what Leibniz calls true predication, knowing
everything about a substance and all true propositions concerning it; but we can minimize resistance and disbelief, and
curtail the centrifugal impulse generated by the absence of
true predication. The security and cogency of each statement
and position depends on the relationship *of containment* it
contrives with its "rivals." The object of attention in itself is
neutral. In context, it is always bound to an arc of statement
or evaluation which works against the impulse to comprehensiveness in the gift of attention, against potential variety in
the object and centrifugality in the attention itself.

While my main interest lies in this general psychic establishment and its play in romantic poetry, it will be of use to
dwell a moment longer on tragedy and comedy. "All com-
edies," Byron has observed, "are ended by a marriage."
This is more than a shallow barb, it is deep wisdom. The
comedy that is over has also reached its destination, and the
"blocking" figure against whom Frye's springtime "young
man"[5] must prevail is also (1) the instrument whereby he
tests his mettle, and (2) the forecast of what he will become
unless he himself remembers the creativity, and not only the
incontinence and disorderliness, of youth. The freedom of
comedy is Wordsworth's paradoxical freedom; one is "free as

a bird / to settle." The paradox is well caught in the expression "to solemnize a marriage." Here are festivity and solemnity in one, as again in the phrase "marriage license," with its plaiting of responsibility and free play.

In this light, tragicomedy is but a daring amplification of the muted or suppressed term of the dominant conventions of comedy and tragedy. Tragicomedy exhibits amplitude and the *unity of a controlled motion* where comedy and tragedy have intensity and the *unity of a maintained position*. A tragedy like *Romeo and Juliet* may begin in romance and jollity, but even these positive elements have the taint of instability and violence, and the play gathers momentum and gloom together; the Apothecary is too sinister to be funny; the cry "wherefore art thou Romeo?" is too fraught with merciless strife to be charming, and the marriage that should reconcile families and unify the society in happiness is scheduled in a tomb. Dominant tone and controlled proportion are necessary to the establishment of a mode. A change in proportion results in a change in resonance and, before we know it, in quality. This is a danger tragedies as august as *King Lear* run.[6] As Gloucester does not really go over the precipice into disaster, so Shakespeare does not go over the precipice into comedy; but in isolation (if we could, for example, forget those bloody eyes and daughters) a scene like *Lear* 4.6—Lear on the heath— is not unimaginable as comedy, what with its deception, metamorphic fantasy, overschematic diminuendo, calculated teasing ("do but look up"), mooniness, and the king "fantastically dressed with flowers." The raw material of comedy is present without being effectual, and indeed is made to reinforce the themes of horror and indignation, victimization and dispossession that the tragedy embodies. In like manner Polonius behind the arras is a potentially comic figure, and Hamlet's dispatching him so conclusively may be read as a way of saving *his* tragedy from Polonius's comedy.[7]

The psychic principle at work here may be summarized in

the phrase "the convertibility of emotion." It is neatly illustrated in a poem not otherwise remarkable, "Love," by
Samuel Taylor Coleridge. The opening quatrain explicitly
announces its bias toward its paramount emotion:

All thoughts, *all* passions, *all* delights,
Whatever stirs this mortal frame
All are but ministers of Love,
  And feed his sacred flame.
           [Italics added]

But the notion of multiplicity ministering to unity, of one
flame growing from many inflammations, vividly represents
the conversion of other emotions, and thus the underlying
principle of convertibility. Coleridge, with a forgivable care,
marshalls the argument for love. His success settles judgment
for this occasion, even while it sets a form, a foundation for
recognizing another sacred flame, one of whose ministers on
that occasion might be love.

Coleridge's interest in the reconciliation of opposite and
discordant qualities (*Biographia Literaria*, chapter 14) is far
more than the self-protective cathexis of a man who, as Keats
charged, was "incapable of remaining content with half
knowledge," incapable "of being in uncertainties, Mysteries,
doubts."[8] Making whatever room we see fit for personality
in the case, we are still obliged to recognize that Coleridge is
formulating a general romantic intuition/proposition, concerning the mystery of the common origin and common end
shared by separate things. To canonize the particularity of
separate things may only reflect the lack of an adequate level
of conception or generalization. This lack was theoretically
supplied by Burke in *A Philosophical Inquiry into the Origin
of Our Ideas of the Sublime and Beautiful*, where "opposites"
such as darkness and light, disorderly magnificence and
orderly infinity, vast objects and vacuity alike produce the
effect of sublimity; and again biographically overcome by

Wordsworth when he grasped the fact that he "grew up/Fostered alike by beauty and by fear" and knew "universal power" not "alone,/'Mid gloom and tumult, but no less 'mid fair/And tranquil scenes" (*Prelude*, 1.301-02; 2.323-25). Wordsworth does not capture only the reconciliation, the collaboration, and even effective identity of opposites (beauty and fear); he indicates the joining of origin and end, act and goal, parent and child (fostered). It comes down to intrinsic design, "a dark/Inscrutable workmanship that reconciles/Discordant elements, makes them cling together/In one society" (*Prelude*, 1.341-44). The post-romantic Nietzsche enunciates the way wholeness and wholesomeness of mind rest on a paradoxical doubling and conflict; in *The Will to Power* he observes that "every ideal presupposes love *and* hate, reverence *and* contempt" (italics added).[9]

Such a concept must, of course, hold its ground *along with* a Western tradition of dialectical or oppositional thinking (a tradition that is very strong and very valuable, in its place). We find it easier to acknowledge monism or dualism than to entertain what might be termed multeism. Dualism, after all, is disguised monism; it is a one-versus-one system, and holds out the hope of an absolute triumph and resolution. But whether we encounter it in Manicheanism (good versus evil), Zoroastrianism (light versus dark), Kantianism (phenomenon versus noumenon), Existentialism (Kierkegaard's Either/Or), Marxism (privileged versus alienated classes), or even Jakobsonianism (metonymy versus metaphor), it involves the presumption that only two things, in a one-on-one relation, may dominate and exhaust a situation. This will prove true, sometimes. But it can be an unduly possessive formulation, as when it fosters the notion of male-versus-female and thus coerces a copious and joyous variety of individual entities and powers into close conflict in a shared dualistic box whose demarcations have little to do with realities.

What I have called the world's versatility, in moment and

pattern, meets with the mind's adaptability, in sensing and conceiving, to form a world of options. That world is never *actual*, it is a cumulative inference, an abstraction. It is the abstraction which at bottom makes possible every human enterprise. But each enterprise is no sooner there than it finds itself challenged, chastened by other manifestations of the world of options. A central question of authority arises everywhere. How it is resolved in actuality the present essay is neither intended nor, *sit etiam laus*, obliged to investigate. Its pertinence in literary terms has been partially deflected by the canonization of genre and mode, as we have taken a gross material authority for an intrinsic dynamic authority; we say *King Lear* is a tragedy not a comedy, or *Don Quixote* is a novel not a play, and do not really give much thought to the cryptic comic possibilities of the former, or the cryptic scenic properties of the novel Cervantes abandoned the drama for. Tragedy and fiction have the authority of "immediate revelation."[10] The question of authority has been further allayed by the Coleridgean critical injunction to "that willing suspension of disbelief . . . which constitutes poetic faith" (*Biographia Literaria*, chapter 14). But the net effect is to gloss over, rather than to gloss the crux that is manifest when the comic trespass is nullified and made to reinforce the tragic possession of a work.

The question of authority, in literature, is always necessary, but becomes urgent when standards of acceptance come into question or forms of representation diverge drastically from a "convention." Such a state of urgency arises in the romantic period, with its bold dissolution of genres, its freewheeling reconstitution of terminology, and in general its persistent reformulation of the terms of value. It is important to keep in mind, however, the fact that the romantics freely appropriated elements of forms they officially denounced, as it were returning the elements to the realm of options and ordaining them in a new character. A kind of moodiness or seemingly random changefulness may appear (as in Byron's *Don Juan* or Coleridge's "Eolian Harp"), but the basic effect is a more explicit, a fuller, a better controlled melding of ostensibly divergent elements.

The romantic mind sets itself in opposition to mere opposition, making as Coleridge would say distinctions without contradistinctions, driving heartily toward singularity and at the same time toward synthesis. The romantics' plunge into the "abyss" of the human mind was neither desolate nor headlong, but a finely calibrated, even analytical adventure. It was a way to chart and to honor that diversity and complexity of psychic and material experience which I have roughly sketched above. It was a way to face what De Quincey found, that opium leads equally to heaven and to hell. The effect in literary terms is no wild transmogrification; still there are epic and elegy, still couplet and sonnet. But these forms persist with a difference: the epic becomes subjective, the sonnet—"bound with garlands of her own"—a gracious version of the self-crowned Napoleon who yet has no special freedom, since *bound* suggests confinement as well as honor. As Leigh Hunt observed, poetry plays "between nature and convention."

I would like to investigate how the turbulent complex (potential chaos) of the *psyche* was given shape and status by a vibrantly complex *techne*, and how this *techne* manifested and exploited elements which tended to go hidden under the solidity of traditional forms. Our attention is to be centered on elegy, prophecy, and satire as sharing a common psychic origin and representing, for all their formal and modal integrity, alternatives of one another. More than this, elegy, prophecy, and satire may be, on pain of becoming depleted, one another's nourishment, and in that sense recognizable in one another. The act of "reconciliation" depends on the art of incorporation, or to hold the metaphor a moment longer, effective digestion. By this approach it will be possible to show how elegy or prophecy or satire gains or loses depth and reticularity as it succeeds or fails in this regard. And it will be possible to shed new light on the problematical persistence of satire—conventionally identified with the eighteenth century—in the romantic period, frequently characterized in terms of elegy or prophecy. There is too much ground in experience, in imagination, to be covered by the Horatian precept: "Sit quodvis simplex dumtaxat et unum." Unity, for the romantics, becomes a factor not of simplicity but of integration.

We may advantageously begin by observing that elegy, though occasioned by death and loss, does not deal so much with the dead as with the effect of their death upon the living. By the same token it concerns not the past but the future. The condition of elegy arises from the revelation, through the life that is no longer available to a given subject, of the life that is no longer possible for the survivors. It is their reflected loss, their own loss ineluctably to be experienced, that they mourn.

Christ facing his crucifixion points to this conclusion when he urges the women "Weep not for me, but for your children," and Phaedo at Socrates' deathbed says he "wept broken-heartedly,—not for him, but for my own calamity." In a more literary vein, Wordsworth plainly expresses the self-mourning function of elegy in his characterization of Collins's ode on the death of Thomson as the utterance of one who "Could find no refuge from distress/But in the milder grief of pity" ("Remembrance of Collins," ll.15–16). Finally we may recall Thomas Tickell's pre-gothic image of the dead blocking the living in the poem "To the Earl of Warwick on the Death of Mr. Addison":

That awful form (which, so ye heavens decree
Must still be loved and still deplored by me)
In nightly visions seldom fails to rise,
Or, roused by fancy, meets my waking eyes.
If business calls, or crowded courts invite,

The unblemished statesman seems to strike my sight;
If in the stage I seek to soothe my care,
I meet his soul, which breathes in Cato there;
If pensive to the rural shades I rove,
His shape o'ertakes me in the lonely grove;
'Twas there of just and good he reasoned strong,
Cleared some great truth or raised some serious song;
There patient showed us the wise course to steer,
A candid censor and a friend severe. . . .

[67-80]

For the purposes of elegy, then, the victim's life is over, once and for all; the survivor's life is in principle denied, now and forevermore. One need not be a Christian or a nihilist to see that the force of the elegy corresponds to the force of the denial, and that the force of the denial provides the measure of the loss. Otherwise, the loss is taken with some equanimity. To illustrate: if Mao Tse-tung had died two decades earlier, the denial to his people would have seemed incalculably greater, and the state of elegy correspondingly magnified; if John F. Kennedy had died two decades later, the denial to his people would, from all we are learning, have seemed much slighter, and the state of elegy likewise diminished. A single death bears into elegy when it powerfully stimulates, symbolizes what Paul Ricoeur calls *"the pathetique of 'misery,'"* the radical condition "of man's precomprehension of himself as 'miserable.'"[11] Shelley conveys the impact of such a death in the elegiac conclusion of "Alastor"; a surpassing Spirit, taken off, "leaves"

Those who remain behind, not sobs or groans,
The passionate tumult of a clinging hope;
But pale despair and cold tranquillity,
Nature's vast frame, the web of human things,
Birth and the grave, that are not as they were.

But if elegy is generated for the *loss of the living future*, it revolves from specific lament into a mode of thwarted aspiration. The potentialities for resentment in elegy seem at once acute. What would be the object of this resentment? Equally the world, for being as it is; the self, for being taken in by the world and exalting the victim; and the victim, for being part of the world after all and for dying. The subsistence of elegy furnishes an environment for satire, and a presentiment of it.

This is not to give temporal or spiritual precedence to elegy, but only to recognize that where elegy actually presents itself, satire will not be far removed. The converse would also hold good. A psychic kinship exists between elegy and satire, a kinship that emerges graphically if we acknowledge that, as elegy answers to the loss of the living future, satire reacts to a *dread for the living future*. As elegy responds to the loss of a heroic or at least an elevated personality, satire with its slightly higher degree of critical generalization concerns itself with the loss of the ideal and objects of elevation. Both make the same fundamental postulate: the present state (a death, a degree of vice) precludes the living future. At the same time elegy and satire move in distinct modes and directions off that postulate. Elegy implies that within known terms nothing can be done about the case—few of the dead revive—and the only thing left is to grieve. Satire adopts the attitude that with so much to grieve over something had better be done about the case, before a state of deathliness overtakes us all. It has been observed that "the satirist . . . has usually little hope of reform through literature; his purpose—or his compulsion—is to unmask, to reveal men to themselves and to their souls as they are, not as they pretend to be,"[12] Though thus working in anger more than in hope, satire must be credited at least with a sort of thwarted anticipation. If elegy lacks resilience, satire lacks a certain realism. Elegy takes a declarative stand that we can summarize in Wordsworth's phrasing: "The things which I have seen I now can see no more." The satirist takes a speculative stance: the things which I desire and am supposed to see, I mean to see, or else. We can see in Kernan's description of the actual world of satire how compatible its specifications are with the actualities of elegy: "Society is transformed into a mob ruled only by strength and cunning, the city becomes a wasteland, the sheep changes to the wolf and the vulture, while the garden reverts to the jungle."[13] The preferred world of satire never really exists; it amounts to a heroic (i.e. glamorized) past, or a wholly regenerate—and hence implausible—future. Satire arises as a bold attempt to fill the vacuum created when social forces and moral prescriptions prove incapable of checking human wildness/wickedness.

To advance this much is to recognize that satire, as it enunciates vital undertones in elegy, requires prophecy to give voice to its own inner needs and concepts. The world that satire cannot find prophecy makes. The latter, whether it fulfills itself or not (for there we are back in actuality and out of its emulous surrogate, literature), fulfills a tendency in satire to dismiss rather than save the world, fulfills its shy and surly vision of the better world.

Prophecy, of the three modes in question the most abstract in being least bound to specific phenomena for its fulfillment, modifies the attitude and content of satire and likewise of elegy, by its conjuration of the better world. As far as the here and now are concerned, it agrees with elegy that nothing can be done about diminishment or decay. Even so it agrees with satire that something needs urgently to be done, without, however, getting materially trapped in the here and now. Having the need but no locus of action, it makes its own locus, as it were realizing the unknown wish of elegy as well as the unknown impulse of satire.

Do elegy, prophecy, and satire become, then, interchangeable? Clearly not. They represent three modes of one act of recognition and evaluation: the world has gone foul, dismal, to the spirit no less than to the senses. The primary content of the three modes is in this sense identical. They are not interchangeable, but implicit or diffusely present in one another. Perhaps we could find a useful analog to this situation in the triple-goddess of Greek mythology; we immediately recognize Hecate or Artemis or Selene by their concentrated presence, but we simultaneously know that the focal figure is always associated with the "absent" pair and in the course of things likely to yield place to them.

It may seem problematical to ascribe the same content to elegy, prophecy, and satire when they obviously depart from one another in form—after all, what was once a contention of Croce's has become a cliché of criticism: that content and form are indivisible. But it is possible without iconoclasm to observe that this saw works by virtue of a neat tautology; the sentence on the page is at once form and content, which means that the sentence (form) cannot with impunity be separated from the sentence (content). As Robert Plant Armstrong says, "works of art are physically identical to their 'meaning'."[14] But if we take content in a larger or more abstract sense than "what is presented" or "what is said" in actual explicit phenomenal terms, the conclusion is not so pat.

Let us, by way of illustration, take three comparable phrases:

(1) Hail, fellow! Well met.
(2) Good morning.
(3) Hi!

Clearly these phrases differ among themselves in far from negligible ways, ranging from archaism to slang, from a fairly elaborate grammar to a minimum ejaculation. Each conveys different information about the user and the audience and the context. A difference in content appears to reflect a difference in form. But there remains a deeper level of identity; we recognize in each what Michel Foucault calls "the same nucleus of meaning."[15] All three phrases involve a greeting, a social convention of civil encounter. Or again we may take three phrases of abrupt dismissal:

(1) Avaunt, thou miscreant!
(2) Get away, you reprobate!
(3) Beat it, creep!

The essential content—greeting or dismissal—may be variously presented and is bound to no organization. The formal content—the phrases—is as it is presented, and is usually what we think of when making pronouncements on "form" and "content." In music, somehow, we are more comfortable with the "same" tune in a "different" form, as anyone will recognize who plays "Spring Is Here" or "What's New" in popular-ballad renditions, then as jazz pieces by Miles Davis or Zoot Sims.

It would be worthwhile, at least to avoid any ambiguity in the use of the word *content*, to set up in place of "form and content" the locution "act and mode," taking the act as essential or abstract, mode as formal and particular. This is a distinction (without contradistinction) that sensitive people experience every day, as they are being seated in restaurants or interviewed for a job. Statistics or history will show they have eaten or had the interview—the act has occurred. But it may have occurred as brusque insult, as solicitous honor, or as accidental farce. The mode saves the act from amorphous generality; it determines not the act but the value of the act, and its effect, for the occasion. We experience the act in its mode, while we only conceive of the act in itself.

The proposition I am making boils down to this: elegy, prophecy, and satire are divergent modes of the act of acknowledging ineluctable weakness and mortality in the world, modes of measuring our failure to sustain or even realize goodness and grace. That act as against, say, dining out or looking for a job takes on incalculable weight and depth because its modes are not accidents of the given scene but *permanent* and *intrinsic to the situation and thus to one another.* As Descartes long ago observed, it is natural for man "to have several volitions about the same thing." A veritable ring of modes establishes itself around the point of weakness/mortality; adjacent positions represent at best shades of psychic difference, and apparent conceptual extremes turn out to resemble each other closely in their psychic functions.

The accompanying diagram (figure 1) should afford a convenient image of these relationships. The radiation of responses around the hub of mortality does not pretend to be exhaustive.

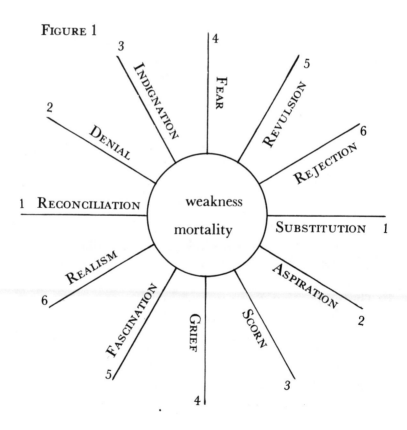

Figure 1

The cardinal point is that all the responses interact vitally with one another, and all occur freely, perhaps inevitably, within one mind. Two sets of terms, in an obverse relationship, may be identified (as shown in figure 2). The set

Figure 2

One

a) realism
b) fascination
c) grief
d) scorn
e) denial
f) reconciliation

weakness
mortality

Two

a) rejection
b) revulsion
c) fear
d) indignation
e) aspiration
f) substitution

numbered *One* marks positive or objective behavior toward the problem of mortality, the set numbered *Two* marks negative or subjective behavior. The difference between the corresponding positions in the sets springs not from opposition but from emphasis; as in the flight-or-fight reaction in physiology, the essential act and goal is the same, to cope, or restore or enhance the experience of life. Thus "denial" and "aspiration," to take the pair most likely to give trouble, yield the same result—an escape from the threat by defusion (denying that it is so bad) or removal (aspiring to an alternative order). Reconciliation, which we might attain by religious faith or by stoicism, consummates this escape as decisively as substitution, which we would recognize in prophecy. For reconciliation confers a new character on mortality, cancelling its negation, and investing it with opportunities for strength and poise.

There remains a danger of mistaking the relationship among the array of responses to mortality, in the very gesture of setting up pairs of terms. The habit of oppositional thinking is vitally embedded in the economies of the Western mind[16] and exercises itself all too readily where sets or pairs occur; thus Roland Barthes in *Writing: Degree Zero* speaks of "singular-plural, preterite-present," as "polar" oppositions.[17] Indeed it is a hypothesis of structuralism that "binary oppositions" give an image of the intrinsic constitution of the mind, and amount to a category of thought. Lévi-Strauss in anthropology and Jakobson in linguistics both maintain this view. But Lévi-Strauss in a moment of reflection seems to suggest that oppositional thinking may be a habit that results from a hasty gesture of giving possession of the mind to the terms of the moment, the gesture of canonizing *actual* terms as authoritative or exclusive.[18] Such a gesture does an instant injustice to the real continuum of possibility; even "presence" and "absence," which might be offered to redeem the honor of oppositional thinking, are part of a continuum that we cannot deny, though we also cannot experience it. The friend who is "absent" here is, no less than a comet lost to view, "present" elsewhere, and even after death is "present" in altered terms. Further, it would be impossible to refer to them as absent without thereby making them present in mind. The ancient Egyptians rightly held that "to speak the name of the dead is to make him live again." Modern philosophers and psychologists such as Nietzsche, Silvano Arieti, and John Weir Perry have recognized the positive aspect of apparent negation and rejected the impulse to privilege that leads to rank oppositions.[19] And of course Freud in delving into dreams as a basic act of the mind has discovered that ostensible, analytical "opposites" substitute for one another or serve but as sides of one actual relationship. The intensity of our reaction to altered states expresses itself, too dramatically perhaps, in the imposing logic of opposition. The altered states themselves belong in a continuum of matter and mind. We may let Byron, in "The Dream," speak for his age: "Sleep hath its own world,/A boundary between the things misnamed/Death and existence."

Even the reaction to death, where the immediate spectacle of opposition is most graphic, reveals a continuum of alternatives rather than any arrangement of self-obliterating pairs. The position is rather one of evolving recognitions, a play of prospects and choices that we experience as single and stable because a given personality and philosophy effectively composes the other—abstractly equal—possibilities under its recognizable mantle. The two sets of responses to mortality in this light should be seen as valid without being definitive. More basically the terms move off and among one another, in a dynamic continuum, a non-vicious circle as it were (see figure 3). We may speak of the positive and negative *arcs* (rather than sets), and it will not be difficult to locate elegy, prophecy, and satire along the arcs. Appropriately, as they are more active modes, prophecy and satire occur along the positive arc, elegy along the negative. But it will be apparent that elegiac reactions are capable of recoiling into their positive counterparts, and prophetic and satirical reactions into their negatives (see figure 4).[20]

The veritable clustering of elegy, prophecy, and satire underscores the psychic kinship already predicated of them. This kinship is of course perennial. But is seems to have taken the romantic period to highlight it by resorting to all three modes and interanimating them not only in one period but in individual poems. Perhaps this reflects, in romantic literature, a degree of freedom from generic sanctions and from the proprietary power of found conventions—a freedom ironically promoted by Dr. Johnson,[21] the giant "of the last classical generation," through his support for tragicomedy as a genuine form in itself and not a mulish hybrid.[22] To bring out the special properties of the romantic development it will be

FIGURE 3

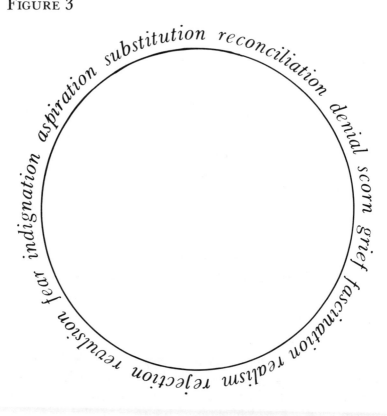

useful to proceed by comparison between romantic poems, elegy in particular, and late Renaissance and Augustan works in a like vein. The differences are not abrupt, since the triple impulse at the root of elegy certainly evinces itself before romanticism; but they appear decisive, and underlie John Hollander's remark that in neoclassical poetry elegy is defined "metrically" and "entails a longish poem in couplets. . . . It

FIGURE 4

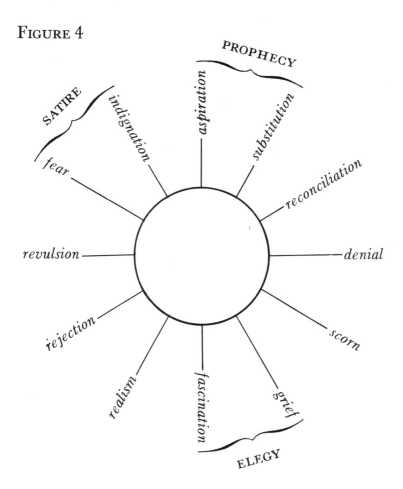

is only toward the end of the eighteenth century that 'the elegiac tone' is defined as a mood rather than as a formal mode."[23] For the purposes of the comparison, two pairs of poems prove especially instructive: Milton's "Lycidas" and Shelley's *Adonais*, and no less tellingly Pope's "Elegy to the Memory of an Unfortunate Lady" and Wordsworth's "She Dwelt Among the Untrodden Ways."

Pope's "Elegy to the Memory of an Unfortunate Lady" has been touted as a forecast into the mainstream of romanticism. Certainly there are elements in the poem that acquire in the romantic period a prominence they do not enjoy in the Augustan age: its melancholic strain, the ghost in dappled moonlight, the "visionary sword," the aspiring soul, the speaker's undying devotion. But there is need to question whether these elements occur in a mixture or an environment that fosters a romantic character, or whether they are but piquant topoi in a basically Augustan scheme. The "Elegy to the Memory of an Unfortunate Lady" shares many features with Wordsworth's "She Dwelt Among the Untrodden Ways," and comparison between these poems will go a long way toward classifying Pope's "Elegy" as well as establishing some of the earmarks of romantic elegy.

Within the poems, a major parallel appears in the social neglect suffered by the subjects. Wordsworth's "maid" has "none to praise" and "very few to love" her. Pope's "lady," with her "fate unpity'd, and . . . rites unpaid," seems as badly off. Another lesser parallel may be recognized in the use of heavenly associations to point up the subject's distinction and value. Wordsworth draws on the analogy of a fair and singular star to make the maid's isolation not so much privative as striking, luminous, and admirable. Pope has his lady "snatched . . . to the pitying sky," as a mark of favor and exaltation: "As into air the purer spirits flow,/And sep'rate from their kindred dregs below. . . ." On closer inspection, though, these parallels prove somewhat specious. The neglect suffered by the lady is circumstantial, a reaction to a specific departure from an implied code of behavior; the neglect of the maid is radical, an expression of the order of things in the social scheme. But we readily come to realize that the neglect of the lady is simply suffered whereas the neglect of the maid is in a sense the reflex of her detachment from the ways of the world and so, implicitly, is suffered with a certain indifference. It is factual rather than material to the conduct and temper of her life. Even their titles corroborate the difference in vulnerability and character between them. The "lady" is by her title assigned a social condition (with punitive as well as privileging propensities, as her story shows); the "maid" is identified by her title as possessing a natural-symbolic state. It might be said that "quality" for the "lady" is predominantly social, for the "maid" predominantly personal and intrinsic. The speaker in the "Elegy" opposes this definition of the lady's quality, but without establishing another, except in terms of his individual sentiments. The speaker in "She Dwelt" opposes *the restriction* of the definition of the maid's quality, and the poem becomes a cryptic argument bent on showing the society at large the justice of his cry: "the difference to me!"

The relation to society and its values is crucial in both poems. This relation centers on a question of privacy—emblematized in the namelessness and concealed identity of the women who have died.[24] Here again, surface likeness masks critical dissimilarities. The fact that the lady dies by suicide, the maid by that "nature" whose bidding the lady does not wait for ("Elegy," 23) has some influence on the terms of privacy adopted, but Pope is not really covering up the suicide; rather he fits it into Augustan mores as an act of honor, "a Roman's part." What Pope's speaker is concealing is the very thing Wordsworth's avows, the vital, paramount relationship with the woman. Nothing but such a relationship appears to account for her coming to him after death, or his keeping her in memory until death. It seems likely, from the last lines of the poem, that he is involved in her committing suicide,[25] that she is sent to "foreign" climes as a means of keeping them apart and cooling her passion for him; the cure not only fails, but drives her to the distracted gesture of putting a dagger into her heart. This conclusion is likely, rather than positive, because the speaker of the "Elegy" does not acknowledge his connection with the lady until the end: "Then from his closing eyes thy form shall part,/And the last pang shall tear thee from his heart" (79–80). It is as though he will not acknowledge the relationship in life, but only on his deathbed; and even that acknowledgement comes in the guise of poet rather than man, and in a discreet third person ("his") rather than in the first person ("my steps," 2) with which the poem commences. Privacy is verging on aggravated reticence here.

It is odd, in retrospect, that the speaker fails to recognize the lady—coming to him as a ghost, *in spirit*—at the outset of the poem: "What beck'ning ghost . . . ?" Perhaps he is affected by shock, but that alone cannot explain his distancing her. The epithets he resorts to when he realizes that "'Tis she!" seem at once to gloss over her dire fate ("ever beauteous") and to play down the element of personal involvement ("ever friendly"). The lady is cast as a revenant counselor: "tell,/Is it, in heav'n, a crime to love too well?" This elegy is cast in a mold of grave general reflection, and drawn away from the issue of personal grief and death. Pope constantly shirks or subordinates personality—the only force that makes death terrible, *deadly*—in favor of sententious generality. Even the fierce lines accusing the lady's uncle-guardian of heartlessness and threatening him with retribution for her death stiffen into moralism: "Thus unlamented pass the proud away . . ." (43ff.). Since "Poets themselves must fall" (71), and the lady herself has been carefully reduced to "a heap of dust" (65–69), we seem to be in a mini-version of the climactic annihilation of book 4 of *The Dunciad*; the moral vision of *The Dunciad* is also scaled down to the truism: all men shall die. The indiscriminacy of death, which leaves "the proud" and the lady alike in a heap of dust, distracts the poet from his service to the lady, and makes him betray her singularity and worth. The "Elegy" accordingly lacks the personality that is the hallmark of the romantic, lyrical modes; in typical

Augustan fashion it converts the elegiac situation, with its preoccupation with personality, into an occasion for elegiac, moralizing rumination. The poet paradoxically buries the lady, in the ground (a heap of dust) and in his "heart," rather than saving her from mortality. Even where he strives, with signs of springtime nature ("tears" of morning, "with rising flowers . . . drest"), to offset the lack of emblems of her exalted station ("weeping loves," "Hallow'd dirges"), an artificiality of troping gets in the way of conviction, and the introduction of "reliques" suggests a confusion between canonization and naturalization as an *antidote* to grief. The elegy, as eloquent as its parts may seem, remains subdued, without a clear antagonist,[26] since "the proud" are not properly defined, and without a clear alternative because life itself, the love of which generates elegy, is but "idle business" (77).

The quantum revelation of integrated personality, which Pope so veils and displaces with generality, is the sine qua non of Wordsworth's, and of the romantic, way with elegy. The matter of privacy in "She Dwelt Among the Untrodden Ways" does not weaken this point, for Wordsworth qualifies the mechanical social sense of privacy and makes it a dynamic bonding-point between personality and generality. Where Pope in the "Elegy" (and often in his satires and moral essays) gives in to the interest of generality and makes the individual a "ghost" of a self, if not "a heap of dust," Wordsworth seems to promote a new relationship or negotiation between personality and generality. One may say that romanticism offers not only a reincarnation of the individual disembodied by Augustan general principles, but a reincarnation of generality itself.

At bottom "She Dwelt Among the Untrodden Ways" is less concerned with privacy and grief than with a new form of value and vision. The privacy and grief—"the difference to me"—are clearly intensified by the signs of new value and vision; the unnoticed beauty of the violet and the brilliance of the lone evening star neglected by those who keep their gaze to the earth leave no doubt that she deserves and *has* to be missed, even if she happened to have lived largely unknown, unloved, and unpraised. But in that very intensification a kind of obverse image is created: privacy becomes uniqueness, grief a measure of excellence (and here it is fair to observe that neither uniqueness nor excellence is substantiated in Pope's "Elegy," rather to the contrary). Thus as the speaker's evocative vision of violet and star becomes the reader's revelation and revision of the "maid," the neglect that has encompassed her redounds rather to the reader's discredit than to hers. Obliquely, but cogently, Wordsworth sets forth a critique of social fashion and vanity—the belle who is abundantly loved and praised belongs to "trodden" ways and is less than a "maid." Wordsworth in effect creates a triple strength of feeling and principle, in his crypto-satirical treatment of the world and its trodden ways, his crypto-prophetic invocation of a world where violet and star will be properly appreciated, and his overt lament for someone whose privacy he preserves (the difference *to me*) while yet he establishes dearness, and indeed a standard of dearness in her. The subject and emphasis of the poem qualify it as elegy; the power of the elegy, its resonance and depth, arise from its containment of potential satire and would-be prophecy.

What I have called a quantum revelation, or articulation, of personality may be taken as the basis of the complex of elegy-prophecy-satire in the romantic order. It is personality that releases the writer from the bonds of convention, while holding him to the centripetal line of psychic freedom-and-coherence. For Pope, whose "pitying sky" might have modulated into prophecy, and whose "false guardian" might have provoked satire, the sententiae of elegy and the topos of death's homogenizing omnipresence have a deep authority that, we might say now, preempts the subject and the terms of elegy. The poem is about death, not life, about the extermination rather than the oppression of life. Pope harks back, though he holds aloft identifiable signs of things to come. Pope in fact stands in a midway position between classical elegy, with its formal-technical requirements,[27] and romantic elegy, with its intimate concern for personality and the quandary of death.

This is not to say that Pope lacks personal sentiments, or the sentiment of personality. Rather it would seem that his response to personality, as to nature, was circumscribed by a certain formal policy or perspective; he works in a flat-earth rather than a Columbian vision of personality, and his "unfortunate lady" is as firmly recalled into its grid as his Eloisa, after her momentary ecstasy in nature, is drawn back into her convent. The constraints of convention are more apparent in Pope than in Wordsworth, who all but explicitly pits personality against convention.

Dryden, it is interesting to observe, works in Pope's vein. His elegy "To the Memory of Mr. Oldham" subordinates the person to the satirist, in Oldham's case, and to the critic in Dryden's. The poem presents two contradictory images of Oldham, as a relative stranger ("too little and too lately known") and as an *alter ego* ("souls . . . near allied" and "cast in the same poetic mold"). The elegy might have bridged the gap and settled decisively in the field of a lamented friendship. Instead it declines into criticism and the same pessimistic view of time that occurs in Pope's "Elegy." The sense of the lost future, so indispensable to elegy, is counteracted by a sense of time's futility:

O early ripe! to thy abundant store
What could advancing age have added more?
                 . . . maturing time
But mellows what we write to the dull sweets of rhyme.

This not only makes it seem just as well that Oldham has died

young, but also a source of slackening and specious ease that
Dryden has lived long, since he is the same kind of writer as
Oldham. Maturity and mellowness, if they bring a gain in social quality, do so at the cost of dullness or loss of intrinsic
quality. The poem lacks a future, not only in the redeemed
terms of prophecy or the rectified terms of satire, but also
in the bereft sense that should be overt in elegy. If nature is
disregarded in Pope's "Elegy," it actively withholds benefits
in "Mr. Oldham," not giving fluency "to the young" and
making fluency a "dull sweet" in the old. The poem is solid
and correct, but too knowledgeable and reconciled to enjoy
the power of its mode. It seems more than incidental that
Dryden ends, as Pope begins, with an important personality
vanishing into a ghostly shade: "Thy brows with ivy and
with laurels bound,/But Fate and gloomy night encompass
thee around."

The substance and flavor of personality in romantic elegy, as
well as its triple bond with satire and prophecy, emerge
graphically if we consider Shelley's *Adonais* in conjunction
with a "classical" elegy with which it shares many significant
features and which yet fails to break through the bonds of
formality and convention, namely, Milton's "Lycidas."
Intense as it is in voice, "Lycidas" represents not an out-
burst of mourning but an *obsequium*, a pious performance
of duty for the dead. Starting from the same ground as Dryden, with the premature demise of a kindred poet, Milton
constructs an elaborate memorial wreath of *curriculum vitae*
and pageant, pastoral and natural landscape, natural and
mythic sea, Cambridge and Paradise, British lore and classical
mythology, Christian and pagan symbolism. This wreath he
largely imposes on the occasion. Its elaborateness obviously
measures his skill, the wealth of his resources. As a measure
of how much he cares, though, it is contradicted by the
seeming reluctance with which he enters the elegiac setting

and the blitheness he shows in leaving it. The poem comes to seem opportunistic, exploiting the conventions of elegy rather than directly participating in them. Thus it leaves genuine questions as to whether the conventions that foster a work may not end up preying on it.[28]

The signs of reluctance in the opening lines of "Lycidas" are frequent enough to suggest a state of coercion, where a free surge into elegy might seem in order. The description of his "forced fingers rude" (4) and the acknowledgement that "Bitter constraint . . . Compels" him make no bones about his reluctance. The very initial words of the poem, "*Yet* once more" (italics added) imply a degree of weariness and resistance, as opposed to, say, the "again" and "once more" ringing eagerly through the first lines of "Tintern Abbey." Logic ("Who would not sing for Lycidas?") and duty ("He must not float upon his watery bier / Unwept") motivate him, in place of the quickness of grief. Though the speaker and Lycidas "were nursed upon the self-same hill" (22), and grew up "together" (25) and shared a common "song" (36), the speaker has to overcome a tendency—neatly foisted off on the Muses—to "denial vain and coy excuse" (18). He wishes for Lycidas, deceased, "*some* melodious tear" (14; italics added), and does not easily express his own. It is not surprising in this light that the "I" of the opening lines gradually loses connection with Lycidas, being predominantly self-concerned by the time Phoebus "touched my trembling ears" (77), and distances into a detached third-person "he" in the concluding section. This shift from first to third person in the speaking voice has an exact parallel in Pope's "Unfortunate Lady," and the same effect of subduing, if not dismissing involvement.

And yet it is clear that Milton begins with a certain involvement in the poem. That involvement seems elegiac, but the elegy is a pretext for, rather than the center of, a personal quarrel with time and fame. Milton's involvement with

Lycidas/King stimulates and gets engulfed in a deeper involvement, with poetry and fame and his own place in the scheme
of things. Thus "Lycidas" is crammed with questions and
sources and practitioners of poetry, and with the traditional
content of poetry, myths, and gods; and again, instead of a
funeral procession, it offers a procession of "poetic" figures.
The obvious exception is "The Pilot of the Galilean Lake,"
Saint Peter, with a "dread Voice" that contracts and intimi-
dates the representatives of classical mythology. The place of
Saint Peter in the poem has exerted magnetic force on
criticism. Its immediacy, realism, spirit make it seem the best
poetry while being the least "poetic." Milton's involvement,
in his attack on the Church, is patent and pungent. It is also
heavy with ambiguity.

We may note first of all that Saint Peter represents the only
power in the poem capable of having rescued Lycidas, and
was himself the beneficiary of such a rescue when Christ
walked on water and stilled the sea. Even so, while he is
described as bearing the keys of the kingdom of heaven he is
presented in the throwback role of sword-wielder, satirically
lopping off the ears of the corrupt clergy (118 ff). King,
combining in himself the double meaning of pastoral—as
cura, and as *poesis*—gives Milton the excuse for this attack on
the "shepherds" of the Church.[29] Isabel MacCaffrey sees the
poem as a basic confrontation with a "disruption of macrocosmic decorum," and Douglas Bush insists that "we cannot
understand" the poem "unless we realize [Milton's] Christian
premise, that no sparrow falls to the ground without God's
will."[30] And yet the immediate data of the poem suggest a
radical uncertainty in the relationship between man and any
presiding order. It is ironic that the very "shepherds" Milton
attacks are the honored and successful personages he aspires
to number himself among through poetry, and ironic too that
"all-judging Jove," the counterpart to Saint Peter in the
mythological domain, offers the true dedicated poet scarcely

more assurance of good in eternity; Phoebus leaves ample room for zero fame when he remarks, "As he [Jove] pronounces lastly on each deed,/Of so much fame in heaven expect thy meed" (83–84). One is tempted to conclude that, in addition to the element of justice in Milton's strictures on the clergy, there is an element of envy and the sort of opportunism which leads to the theological fault-line of Saint Peter implicitly challenging the ordination of King's death.

Just as the elegy for King is displaced by poeticization and impersonality, so the satire for King is debilitated by its arising so incidentally, and by its ambiguities and ironies. In either case the overt intention suffers at the hands of an implicit motive, which is, I think, to work through an ambivalence toward poetry and its vocation. Milton is devoted to poetry, lives *for it*, and yet wants it to do *for him* something which signifies and justifies his devotion. What he gets is the fact of his alter ego poet, Lycidas, dead, and the friable assurance that he himself will be rewarded "as [Jove] pronounces lastly on each deed." That leaves a lot of room for anxiety. Perhaps it is a mortal's modesty, but it looks like preoccupation with his own fame that keeps Milton from touching on King's "meed" in heaven.

A potential for prophecy exists in the poem, in the correspondences of returning spring and resurrection, but this potential, like the voice of elegy and satire, participates in the prevailing condition manqué. The spring does not bring back a conviction or possession of life, but the accoutrements of death: "every flower . . ./To strew the laureate hearse where Lycid lies" (148–51). It affords a momentary palliation of grief, whereby "our frail thoughts" may "dally with false surmise" (153). The resurrection does better, but oddly only on the surface. The poet, Lycidas, is in a realm of poetry, but in the capacity of audience now and not participant. He "*hears* the unexpressive nuptial song," and all the saints (isn't he tacitly one?) "sing" to "entertain him." The most troublesome note in this choir of celebration occurs in the phrase "wipe the tears for ever from his eyes." Is there one gesture of wiping that eternally precludes the possibility of tears, or is it that Lycidas/King has tears in his eyes forever, and is being ministered to forever with saintly solicitude? The explicit prophecy of the poem—"Henceforth thou art the Genius of the Shore" (183)—honors Lycidas but only in a way that assigns him a convenient role and disposes of him. The implicit prophecy of the poem then has nothing to do with Lycidas; "Tomorrow to fresh woods, and pastures new" is a renewal of faith and conviction in the speaking poet, who no longer has Lycidas to grieve over, though he may owe him thanks for bringing him to, and through, his crisis of vocation. "Lycidas" is a rare example of the reluctant and grateful elegy.

One senses in effect a treacherous disequilibrium between the intention and the destination of Milton's eloquence, as though the plane of intention precipitated him into a position that becomes acceptable as fait accompli, while remaining problematical as idea. Without agreeing with Richard Lanham that "the only thing one can do about the dead" is "to forget them," one sees through Milton the face of Lanham's general conclusion that the subject of elegy can become "man's tremendous resources of verbal pleasure, his endless ability to metamorphose one emotion into another by means of the word. . . . Man can interpose words between himself and death, make of death a pleasure and finally—his self transformed—*enjoy* it."[31] The problem is that "metamorphosis" proves forgetful, being so fascinated with its moments. There is an alternative, a continuous manner of changing that keeps what it changes from, by incorporating it into what it turns out to be. This I have described as the convertibility of emotion. Milton does not practice it, is not really concerned to do so. Nor does he, in fairness, so much practice as fall into the art of metamorphosis. He is not enjoying death, he is enjoying the art of poetry: eloquence itself. King's death enables, perhaps obliges him to confront himself in relation to that art, and the technical "elegy" slides toward a dramatic meditation on the collision of poetry and death. The death of King does not stimulate what Toni Morrison in *Sula* calls "a fist-shaking grief," but something inferior in the way of an obligation to say something, do something, feel something about the dead." That "obligation" meets and gives way to the passion for poetry, thus leading Milton to discover, in place of an elegiac future that is unlivable, a plausible future marked by an almost Byronic élan, whereby one twitches one's mantle blue and decides: "Tomorrow to fresh woods, and pastures new." This is the true prophecy of the poem, a prophecy-as-project that eliminates every consideration but the poet's own burgeoning ("fresh," "new") career. So much for Lycidas, so much for elegy.

A final reversal of grief is, of course, part of the convention of elegy from its earliest known occurrence. I have proposed that such an act of reversal implies not an inconsistency but a fuller recognition of the nature of a human situation and the human actor than any single line of expression, confined to one direction and one dimension, can convey. For elegy, grief is genuine, but not exclusive. Complexity and freedom mark a vital, as opposed to a mechanical, response, and by the same token energy and change, rather than persistence, mark a vital form.

The question concerning *Lycidas* does not stem from an absence of complexity, freedom, energy, and change. If the problem were that simple, it would long ago have been solved with the poem's descent below the horizon of esteem. The question really has to do with the internal coherence, the integrity with which Milton manages the complexity that is proper to elegy; and this means the integrity of his relation to his conventions.

It will be useful here to keep some basic features of the

life-history of a convention in mind. Every convention is sustained by acts of discovery, by infusions of singularity. After all, convention arises where one man's singular manifestation proves personally advantageous or appealing to many others: the lisping of a Castilian prince determines the pronunciation of the standard Spanish *z*, Laurence Sterne's sentimental mode becomes the ideal of Germany, Christ's capacity for forgiveness undermines the edifice of retaliation that Western culture inherits, and so becomes an abiding value.

In a sense it is odd to consider elegy as having a comparable origin. All people die, from Socrates to Lucy or Felix Randal, and survivors grieve. Elegy would seem to be immemorial and ubiquitous. That it is not already points to a departure from mere naturalism, a quantum of singularity that I have tried to show is indispensable to the growth of a convention. From the outset, in Bion's *Lament for Adonis*, elegy singularizes the conception of death by holding before the face of settled mourning the startling image of curative time and recovery to joy. With elegy, in effect, the possessiveness of the emotional moment is consciously challenged by the continuity *and the multiplicity* of experience. No longer is there grief and then, as a distinct phenomenon, an end of grief. Instead the end of grief becomes the revelation of the presence, within that state, of self-qualifications and self-reversals that bring into question the discrete interpretation of experience.

But the departure from naturalism in the *Lament for Adonis*—that departure which means the beginning of elegy— entails basic problems of conventionalization for the poet coming after Bion. Actually the subject of Bion's *Lament* is removed from the human orbit, whether as immortal god (Adonis)[32] or as perpetual nature (the recreative cycle of seasons). With Bion, the naturalism of death yields to a myth of immortality, but this myth means for the human celebrant a gain in recognition—Adonis only seems dead, he *is* immortal —and not a pathway to participation. The truth about Adonis or nature is at best an inviting speculation for humankind. To learn that truth, when for a while Adonis seems lost for good, alters our stance toward life, but in no way increases our distance from death. The basic ingredients of elegy— desolation, complaint, analysis, new recognition, recovery— are proffered by Bion, and his successors seem to have the means of reproducing his achievement. But they lack Bion's subject, the personality that invites elegy, and might thus seem to have the ingredients without the vessel for elegy. The difficulty with the convention is not that it gets "removed from the province of realism,"[33] but rather that it must accommodate itself to realism with the promotion of the human subject.

In Moschus's *Lament for Bion* two devices appear calculated to meet this emergency in the form. To begin with, metaphor supplants myth ("no more must the honey be gathered, now that thy honey [Bion's poetry] has perished"). The effect of the metaphor is to elevate sympathy toward identification, rather than basing identification on causality, as in the case of Adonis's death and the onset of winter. Even more important, specific divinity (Adonis) yields to a sort of general human dignity as the basis of grief: "we, the great, the mighty, the wise men . . . die [and] sleep in the hollow earth, a right long sleep without end or awaking."[34] In Moschus's vision, the unfruitful time of the earth and the death of a lamented person occur together, but they do not, as with Bion's *Lament for Adonis,* appear as one. While death is "without end" for the mortal Bion, the bees will hive again. Moschus avoids the embarrassment of claiming more than is plausible *for* Bion by a clever metonymic definition *of* Bion as a generator of "song." It is not in himself that Bion is immortal, but through song. With this one stroke Moschus establishes the propriety of devoting to humankind the elevated lament that consti- tutes elegy, and he also uses the matter of song to introduce into elegy the intimate celebrant's voice that gives the surviving speaker a stature virtually equal to the deceased. "I am heir," says Moschus, "to that Dorian Muse which thou [Bion] didst once teach thy pupils and with which thou didst endow me, leaving thy wealth to others, but *to me the heritage of song*" (p. 39; italics added).

The point can promptly be made that whatever special life is available through the metonymy of song resides with Moschus, the speaker of the elegy, rather than with Bion, its subject. The tacit motto frames itself: the poet is dead, long live the poet, with immortality inhering in the function and not in the personality. The corollary also promptly comes to mind; Milton is to King as Moschus to Bion. Why then should Milton prove liable to strictures for occupying the center of *Lycidas*, instead of leaving it to King?

Seeing Milton's technique in this light makes it less abrupt, less original perhaps, without making it less questionable. Milton does not say: King is dead, long live King-Milton (that would be the equivalent of what Moschus says). He does not really hold King in very high esteem as cleric or poet, and is not recognizing, through the barrier of his actual death, the essential immortality that Moschus ascribes to Bion. Even after death Bion seems to Moschus to keep singing like Orpheus (p. 40); by comparison Milton diminishes and silences King, as we have seen. It would be odd to invoke tradition in Milton's defense when, especially in relation to his subject, he seems so ambivalent about belonging in the tradition (as Isabel MacCaffrey notes, Milton does not "explicitly take his bearings in the tradition of pastoral elegy," and ultimately writes "a poem about poetry *and* about human life—about . . . man's vision of himself and the mirror of art in which he sees the vision").[35] Somehow King and his death have trailed away from what the poem is "about"; the technical complexity of his elegiac performance may outdo, but not cancel the perfunctory character of his elegiac responses. The intimate voice that Moschus introduces into elegy is a voice *in relationship*; with Milton that voice becomes somehow a voice *for dissociation*, since Milton does not allow King a genuine share in the "heritage of song," let alone any power to participate in its opposition to death.

Like "Lycidas," Shelley's *Adonais* deals with the collision of poetry—as a consummate expression of human reality— with death. There is evidence, as Leslie Brisman observes, that Shelley makes a "confrontation with Milton part of the subject of the poem,"[36] and Seymour Reiter gives a neat summary of the "paralleled conventions" between the two poems.[37] Still it seems necessary to ask how profound is the confrontation, and how deep do the parallels go? Is Shelley desperately facing a challenge of preemption by Milton, or only using him as a foil, a convenient way of setting off (and setting off on) his own distinctive course? Is Shelley sustaining under bond the tradition of classical elegy, or is he breaking publicly with that tradition, fulfilling its possibilities perhaps, but substantially altering its actualities? To address these questions, it will be advantageous to take up a few of the salient connections between "Lycidas" and *Adonais*.

One is struck at once with the economy—that feature Freud uses to characterize wit—with which both Milton and Shelley fuse Christian and classical values at the base of their poems. Both in fact resort to puns. Milton, as already pointed out, achieves this fusion by invoking the double meaning of shepherd and pastoral: *cura* and *poesis*. Shelley creates the fusion in his title; Adonais combines Adonis and "adonai," the classical fertility god and the "Lord," Christ. Milton's pun is marked by a certain opportunism; the joint between the aesthetic and the ecclesiastical shows enough so that the reader is aware of King's being dropped in one capacity and brought forth in the other. It is otherwise with Shelley. As Spenser's Georgos evolves into Saint George without dropping his experience, his susceptibilities, or his commitments, so the gored Adonis-figure of the opening stanzas evolves into the Adonais of the final stanzas.[38]

The difference goes beyond the fact that the "religious value and meaning that Shelley comes to [in *Adonais*] are a revelation radically other than Milton's."[39] There is, after all, as the Cambridge Platonists show, a sublime arc linking Milton's Christian with Shelley's platonic vision. What puts Shelley in another sphere than Milton is the way he involves his speaker's consciousness radically, problematically in the poem's action, so that where Milton seems to bank his Christian vision until the strategic moment for bringing it to light, Shelley presents a struggle, filled with grief and rage and dubiety, toward (and *not* to) his platonic vision. There arises thus a momentous continuity and positive growth from stage to stage of *Adonais*. The poet learns and earns his way by stages, with a degree of uncertainty dogging him to the end. One feels a genuine encounter between a mode of writing and a force of experience, between elegy and grief. Each alters in the encounter, with reference to the other (whereas with Milton one may recognize the imposition of a mode on matter and emotion not altogether appropriate for it).

It is important to notice, too, that the poet in *Adonais* is presented as a genuinely independent figure, rather than being a simple medium or spokesman for Shelley. In "Lycidas" the poet and Milton work effectively as one, but Shelley displaces and transcends himself with a true *persona* poet, who is thus at large to discover the conditions and powers residing in the elegiac situation, rather than in Shelley's immediate interests and hopes. *In propia persona* Shelley cuts a figure of pregnant failure, at once special for having "gazed on Nature's naked loveliness," and forlorn, "astray with feeble steps o'er the world's wilderness" (xxxi). Not only does paradox characterize him in that he is "a Power/Girt round with weakness" (xxxii), but he also gives rise to paradox: the other

mourners "at his partial moan/Smiled through their tears";
finally he is stranded in paradox, unable to resolve the question whether his "branded and ensanguined brow" is "like
Cain's or Christ's" (xxxiv). This figure places himself and
belongs on the fringe of the elegiac situation; he presents
himself with the accoutrements of elegy—pansies overblown,
faced violets, cypress, ivy—but his chaplet and wand become
on one level silly affectation and on another sad dissimula-
tion, since the chaplet seems meant to cover up the mark on
his brow. On the fringe he both embodies and blocks development of the danger in elegy that it might soften into solipsistic
melancholia.

The poet in *Adonais* is if anything in danger of being too
heartily involved in the shock and reverberation of the
elegiac fact: "I weep for Adonais—he is dead!" The distance
between him and the "Lycidas" poet in this respect can be
gauged in the parallel lines:

Where were ye Nymphs . . . ?   ["Lycidas," 50]

Where wert thou, mighty Mother . . . ?   [*Adonais*, st. 2, l. 10]

Milton, to be blunt, does not mean the question. As he says
himself, "what could that have done?" (57). The nymphs
have nothing to do with Lycidas, and are powerless anyway.
Milton goes even further and observes that one far greater
than they, Calliope, could have done nothing for "her
enchanting son," Orpheus, who is of course a far greater poet
than Lycidas. An assumption in favor of a reconciliation to
death informs these rather knowing lines (50–63), even though
they seem to express a wild question and lament.

If he is working in the same convention, and with the same
device, Shelley infuses it with a new tension and complexity.
His question is not what could have been done, but what
should have been done. And this question is addressed to
Urania, thus directly reaching the level of Milton's Calliope

rather than the ancillary nymphs, and reaching also a degree of relationship, mother to son, that Milton puts beyond the pale of Lycidas's death. This gives both elevation and involvement to *Adonais*, for Urania is brought down, mighty power and all, into the throes of the elegy. She is an actor here, not just a numinous myth and Muse. So much so that we know exactly where she was, and find in the "explanation" of Adonais's death a tacit charge against Urania:

> With veiled eyes,
> Mid listening Echoes, in her Paradise
> She sate, while one, with soft enamoured breath,
> Rekindled all the fading melodies,
> With which, like flowers that mock the corse beneath,
> He had adorned and hid the coming bulk of Death.
> [st. 2, ll. 13–18]

An unalert Muse and Mother ("with veiled eyes") is the least that Urania may be called here. Her unalertness stems from her absorption with the past; she sits surrounded by Echoes, trying to recapture the warmth of old, "fading melodies." Surely we must see an irony in her posture—the living who need her attention fall to death while she lives on the insubstantial vestiges of times past. The fact that Urania is a practical failure—and not like Milton's Christ a savior—has much to do with the character of *Adonais* as elegy, since it gives death an authority absent from the Christian scheme, and forces the poet to make a radical confrontation with that authority in the scheme of reality. In short, the elegy is intenser for it, and its resolution more indigenous.

That Urania has interests and flaws in the overall design of *Adonais* needs to be candidly recognized. She is not a spiritualized, transcendental Venus, as critics like Notopoulos and Wasserman have argued. As Shelley weaves the myth of Venus and Adonis into his elegy of Keats's death, Venus's name is changed and her relationships altered, without any clean repudiation of her venereal attributes. Shelley's Urania suggests a "heavenly muse" *in potentia*, but she retains in memory and gesture the imprint of a sensual, if also heavenly, lover. Entitled the "mighty Mother," she yet gravitates toward the outdated role of the mistress while her "youngest, dearest one" perishes (vi). The root of her unalertness, the thing that "veils" her eyes is the thickening effluvia of passion. The evidence lies plain before us: the Echo's "soft *enamoured* breath," the way old melodies are *"rekindled"* (ii; italics added). There is a perverse synaesthesia in the use of melodies to hide "the coming bulk of Death,"[40] but it is a perversity practiced with Urania's hearty cooperation; she closes her eyes to confess and also increase the musical affect, so that the melodies may the more readily overcome her and leave her blind to present, and imminent, reality.

Urania begins as a Mae West of the mythical domain; it becomes a vital corroboration and measure of the grievousness surrounding Adonais's death that her reverie can be pierced by Misery. In a sense she is more saved than saving. She is a "fading Splendour" that might have imperceptibly vanished away but for the abrupt shock of recognizing her final loss—without Adonais, she is a "childless Mother" (xxii). Even so, Urania does not simply assume the role of mother. Her grief contains reminiscences of her amorous days and a conscious wish for dissolution that makes her earlier unalertness seem ominous indeed. "Stay yet awhile!" she cries to Adonais.

>   . . . speak to me once again;
> Kiss me, so long as but a kiss may live;[41]
> And in my heartless breast and burning brain
> That word, that kiss, shall all thoughts else survive,
>
> . . . .
>   . . . I would give
> All that I am to be as thou now art!
> But I am chained to Time, and cannot thence depart.
>   [xxvi]

These lines express a triple relationship and character: bereft mother, bereft lover, and despairing person with a private dream of annihilation. Urania almost seems a triple goddess here, with overtones of Persephone (longing for death) added to the conventional Venus and Urania properties already suggested. But still she is a figure in process, and neither a source, as Muse, nor a goal, as spiritual love and beauty, of the poem's action. In fact Urania has played her part here and the poem goes on without, and beyond, her. The meaning of her helpless cry "I would give All that I am to be as thou art!" is greater than she knows, for it takes death as a simple cessation of being, when it is only the ultimate question about being. Hers is the view of someone "chained to Time," and seeking escape instead of transcendence.

The poet is the one who fully faces what it means when one "would give all to be" as Adonais is. Urania carries him to the farthest reaches of lament, and herself remains blind to anything beyond; indeed she shows to the last her penchant for going back to the past, since Adonais's impossible "kiss" would only supersede the "melodies" that arrest her life.[42] The poet looks into the void. He is stimulated by Urania's yearning for Adonais's state ("as thou now art"),[43] and perhaps also by her remonstration against the fact that Adonais had gone to "Dare the unpastured dragon in his den" (xxvii). But where she leaves the investigation of metaphysics and society, he picks it up and carries it to satirical and, ultimately, platonic vision.[44]

The satire on the critics is no less striking than Milton's attack on the clergy in "Lycidas," but differs from that in being thoroughly integrated into the poem's action. The critics make up the environment in which Adonais has lived, and represent the principle of death—"Envy and calumny and pain and hate," "unprofitable strife . . . fear and grief"—if they do not actually "kill" Adonais. There is no transfer of attention from King-as-poet to King-as-cleric, nor any dubious impulse to substitution such as Milton betrays in wishing other people dead instead of King. The attack on the critics is an attack on Adonais's enemies and destroyers, and emerges as a natural recoil of concern for him, in a continuous powerful motion. Similarly within the attack there crystallizes an awareness of the debased, savage state of ordinary life, with two divergent effects: (1) the poet wants the critics to live (not to die, as in Milton), so that they can experience the horror of their own natures: "But be thyself, and know thyself to be!" (xxxvii); and (2) the poet begins to apprehend a latent but ample definition of life, beyond the ordinary.

The satire thus occurs in a pivotal position in *Adonais*. It springs spontaneously from the base of lamentation and gains a countervailing perspective, or vision. It becomes inappropriate to "weep" as soon as one sees that the subject of lamentation "is fled / Far from these carrion kites that scream below" (xxxviii); and it becomes possible to observe that

'Tis we, who lost in stormy visions, keep
With phantoms an unprofitable strife,
And in mad trance, strike with our spirit's knife
Invulnerable nothings—*We* decay
Like corpses in a charnel; fear and grief
Convulse us and consume us day by day,
And cold hopes swarm like worms within our living clay.
                                        [xxxix]

A fearful battle wages in these lines between love of life—self-preservation—and love of good—self-respect. The two had seemed one until the shocks of Adonais's death and its enforced reappraisal of the terms of life. The repellency of the last image ("cold hopes . . . like worms within our living clay") leaves an invincible sense that life is death, and the corollary forms in a trice: to get away from it is to live, "'tis Death is dead, not he [Adonais]." This of course amounts to an emotional or sensuous logic, a kind of argument to which there clings the satirical and elegiac hysteria of its very origins. Argument by assertion ("He is made one with Nature:

there is heard/His voice in all her music") alternates with argument through images ("The splendours of the firmament of time [like Adonais] /May be eclipsed, but are extinguished not") to hammer home the necessary point—ordinary life being unlivable, its opposite, death, must contain or conceal true life. But that point has a further logic of its own. Conviction calls for action, though it is conviction about the unknowable. The poet has not solved the problem of death with his new vision; he has but posed it for himself.

The question is posed within a statement of prophecy, a *speaking beforehand* of what does not have available existence. It is to be stressed that the poet speaks in response to a complex psychology and logic of grief and rage: "The One remains, the many change and pass" (lii). He is not stating an idea but a commitment to become "What Adonais is" (li), since the prospect of escape from "the world's bitter wind" and joining "the white radiance of Eternity" is so inviting. And yet—and herein lies the genius of Shelley's giving the *persona* poet the freedom of the action—there is "fear . . . to become" like Adonais (li). Irony abounds. The immortal Urania misconstrues what Adonais is and finds it attractive but ineligible; the mortal poet comes to a profound conception of Adonais's state and finds it both compelling and frightening.

Within the poet's personality and psyche the elegy has modulated through satire into prophecy, and yet the prophecy contains satire's cousin, irony, and a plangent new source of grief, the poet's mortal weakness and indeed weakness for mortality: "Why linger, why turn back, why shrink, my Heart?" (liii). And irony and elegy penetrate even into the enraptured moment of identification with Adonais:

I am borne darkly, fearfully afar;
Whilst, burning through the inmost veil of Heaven,
The soul of Adonais, like a star,

Beacons from the abode where the Eternal are.

[lv]

Borne (or born) into Eternity, man experiences darkness, fear, estrangement; as Emily Dickinson puts it, "The Maker's cordial visage,/However good to see,/Is shunned, we must admit it,/Like an adversity." Thus, though a personal star guides the poet's way, it is through a veil which is not rent; no apocalypse is achieved. The poem ends with an expression of absolute essence, "the Eternal are," which represents a quantum advance over the exclusion of Urania and the initial retreat of the poem from Adonais's essence ("as thou now art," "what Adonais is"; xxvi, li). Still no "fellowship with essence" materializes. The poem ends in the region between cold mortality and cold eternity, aglow with hope and fear.

With all the variety of its voices, *Adonais* has a decisive continuity and integrity, from the first active "I weep" to the final passive "I am borne." The dominant voice is elegy, in that the weeping for Adonais does not absolutely cease but instead blends into and amplifies the notes of satire and prophecy. The poem does more than show the radical kinship among the three recognized modes; it tends to demonstrate that each mode by itself entails denials and suppressions of feeling and psyche that make for "purity" at the expense of authenticity. Perhaps this underlies the modern sense that pure satire, like Pope's or Juvenal's, is an insufficient form. And yet it is clear upon reflection that Pope is not without a prophetic strain. In book 3 of *The Dunciad* he holds up false prophecy to ridicule: "from the straw where Bedlam's Prophet nods,/He hears loud Oracles, and talks with Gods"; the third book is largely given over to the Sage's fatuous but also terrible forecast of "all the Western World" coming under the sway of Dulness, thus bringing about "a new world, to nature's laws unknown." This displacement of prophecy into the dark-souled Sage is in keeping with satire's negative use of the form—what is foreseen must be forestalled. But *The Dunciad* carries satire's dread for the living future to such a pitch that it imagines its worst fears realized. The end of book 4 offers prophecy as the actuality of final doom. Still it would seem that the corrective impulse of satire mingles with the admonitory function of the Hebraic prophets; if Pope has brought upon the reader the moment of doom, his satire seems to suppose that the helicopter can be invented between the plunge into "universal Darkness" and the contact with nothingness.

To recognize the interpresence and interdependence of elegy, prophecy, and satire, whichever proves the dominant mode, is to allay misgivings about the variable style of a satire like Byron's *Don Juan*, and to highlight the variety which has never been adequately focused in a prophecy like Blake's *Jerusalem*. A brief comment on these two illustrative poems will help to round out this discussion. The presence of elegy comes hard on the heels of prophecy as *Jerusalem* begins, and in fact the elegiac strain seems more explicit and substantial than the prophetic. The latter amounts to a summons and pointing to a new and larger life: "Awake! awake O sleeper of the land of shadows, wake! expand!" By contrast, the scope and terms of mourning bear in directly on everyone:

In all the dark Atlantic vale down from the hills of Surrey
A black water accumulates, return Albion! return!
Thy brethren call thee, and thy fathers, and thy sons,
Thy nurses and thy mothers, thy sisters and thy daughters
Weep at thy souls disease, and the Divine Vision is darkened.
                                            [1. 9–13]

And yet the brief intimation of prophecy ("awaking to Eternal Life") informs and governs the elegiac description; the poem moves "*through*/Eternal Death" and "*to* Eternal Life," and death, having no dominion, cannot establish a hold for elegy as a primary mode. The element of elegy underscores the necessity and the allure of prophecy. Jerusalem and the Daughters of Albion—the immediate family as it were—are the principal bearers of the elegy (1.5. 62–65), but Los shares materially in it as Albion's champion and the clearest pursuer of visionary hope.

Los heard [Jerusalem's] lamentation in the deeps afar! his tears fall
Inversant before the Furnaces . . .
. . . he labours and he mourns!

[1.5. 66–68]

Los's involvement in fact reaches into every dimension of the poem; besides "hearing" what Albion misses or ignores, and "labouring" where others fall passive, and mourning as intensely as any, Los analyzes and interprets and strives to condition the action in the "furnace" of his heart, mind, and spirit. He embodies the fullest implications of the prophecy and in himself expresses the triple root of the form. Again at the outset of the poem (for Blake is carefully setting up the terms of necessary response) we can find Los in the midst of "his tears" resorting to satire and envisioning the world redeemed. "Comfort thyself in my strength," he advises his adversary, the Spectre of Urthona, "the time will arrive / When all Albion's injuries shall cease, and when we shall / Embrace him tenfold bright, rising from his tomb in immortality" (1.7. 54–56). But the basic assurance of this prophecy is not something he can live by—the state of elegy is founded in part in Los's own weakness, and not solely in Albion's disorientation. It is, as already pointed out, the internalization and generalization of the evil that befalls another that makes for elegy. And Los reacts characteristically to the shortfall of prophecy and the presumption of elegy: he evinces a denunciatory "wrath" of a distinctly satirical cast:

O that I could abstain from wrath! O that the Lamb
Of God would look upon me and pity me in my fury.
In anguish of regeneration! . . .

O holy Generation (*Image*) of regeneration!

. . . .

Hand sits before his furnace: scorn of others & furious pride!

. . . .

Rose up against me thundering from the Brook of Albions River
. . . but when he saw my Mace
Whirld round from heaven to earth, trembling he sat: his cold
Poisons rose up: & his sweet deceits covered them all over
With a tender cloud. As thou art now; such was he O Spectre
I know thy deceit & thy revenges, and unless thou desist
I will certainly create an eternal Hell for thee. Listen!
Be attentive! be obedient! Lo the Furnaces are ready to receive thee.
I will break thee into shivers! & melt thee in the furnaces of death;
I will cast thee into forms of abhorrence & torment if thou
Desist not from thine own will, & obey not my stern command!

                              [1.7. 59-73; 8. 1-12]

This is a sort of descriptive satire of Hand, within an avowal of Los's own disposition to satire or corrective "wrath," and with a summary of the function and motive of satire in relation to the Spectre: "I will cast thee into forms of abhorrence & torment."

In *Jerusalem* an explicit conversion or containment works to give the prophecy authority over its marked elements of elegy and satire. The elegy is converted into compassion, a feeling of one's own desolation into an act of sympathy with the desolation of another and beyond that into a position of sacrifice for their good: "O what shall we do for lovely Jerusalem?/To protect the Emanations of Albion's mighty ones from cruelty?" (1.11. 17-18). By the same token satire is converted into commitment—the satirist assists and sets an example for his subjects with his "sublime Labours" (10-65), rather than leaving them to understand and apply his concepts on their own. Ultimately satire is modified into a promise of acceptance and mercy, instead of keeping an austere, impregnable countenance: "Obey my voice . . ./And I will be merciful to thee" (10.29-30). The point is that, as prophecy looks toward the millennium, it intrinsically proffers mercy and grace in the way of the Hebraic Hosea; but in relation to the millennium actuality is always at year one, and so remains susceptible of the minatory severity of a Jeremiah or the scalding lamentations of a Job. *Jerusalem* draws on the full diapason of responses that its dominant voice of prophecy allows.

The question of tone and consistency in *Don Juan* comes readily to the fore, and has been continually commented on. It bears emphasizing that Byron is not only testing the possibilities of epic in the poem,[45] but also giving free play to the possibilities of satire. Though Byron's posture as a satirist varies from pounding severity to disarming whimsicality, satire is a constant in *Don Juan* and is announced as the keynote in the very "Dedication," with its crescendo of attack on those who oppose the freedom and plenitude of life, from Wordsworth to Southey to Castlereagh. When Byron finds occasion for the elegiac note (at Haidées' death, at the destruction of the Tartar Khan), it enters as an amplification of the grounds of the satire. This is especially important to observe when he shies away from mourning Haidée ("But let me change this theme which grows too sad," (canto 4, st. 74). Contrary to first appearances, Byron is not just playing the "capricious elf" (ibid.), but wresting himself away from an indulgence of grief that all but imperceptibly competes with and undermines the mission of satire. Grief has its need, but for the satirist it has also its limits. It is equivalent to "seeming touched" (ibid.) to forget that mission—satire is a way of keeping sane in a maddening environment.[46] And indeed the poem pulls away from Haidée and her "immedicable" world to the picture of Juan "Wounded and fetter'd, cabin'd, cribb'd, confined" (75), a picture the very antithesis of the freedom and mutual generosity Byron espouses. From this point to the aftermath of the Siege of Ismael in the Empress Catherine's court, the satire builds in explicitness and vigor; the decision to "change this theme" constitutes a careful and effectual pivot in *Don Juan*, from the lamentable local effects of Lambro's tyranny to the insufferable vision of public

tyranny that escalates beyond Lambro to Gulbeyaz and on to
Suwarrow and the amorously bloodthirsty Empress Catherine.
Haidée's elegy is highlighted as an instance of the world that
demands satire, but as an instance must yield to the larger
"theme."

As the lost love of Haidée calls the elegiac strain into the
satire, so the potential love of Aurora Raby prompts Byron
to introduce a prophetic air. Anti-uniformitarian, anti-institu-
tional, anti-collectivist, the satire in *Don Juan* has as its undertone a longing for the freedom and plenitude of life, and
seems to envision this freedom in terms of personal love. Thus
Aurora "renew'd / In" Juan

> some feelings he had lately lost
> Or harden'd; feelings which, perhaps ideal,
> Are so divine, that I must deem them real: —
>
> The love of higher things and better days;
> The unbounded hope, and heavenly ignorance
> Of what is call'd the world, and the world's ways;
> The moments when we gather from a glance
> More joy than from all future pride or praise,
> Which kindle manhood, but can ne'er entrance
> The heart in an existence of its own,
> Of which another's bosom is the zone.
>   [16, sts. 107–08]

Where in Milton personal virtue surpasses heroism, for Byron
personal love ("another's bosom") surpasses heroism (the
"pride or praise" of "manhood"); more, it has visionary
reaches, and gives one access to the "reality" of the "divine."
Of course a relationship between Don Juan and Aurora Raby
may seem rather speculative than strictly prophetic. The
vision of a future they might share is offset by the present
"apparition" of the Duchess of Fitz-Fulke in Don Juan's
chambers. Still the speculative prophecy does occur, and
compellingly enough to strengthen the satire on lower things
and worse days. It even forms a basis for an oblique satirizing

of Don Juan himself, in that he not only fails to pursue prophetic "joy" but evidently falls below a certain level of "manhood"; the Duchess of Fitz-Fulke presents him with an opportunity "to show his strength/Moral or physical," and he emerges somewhat less than triumphant, "Being wan and warm, with eyes that hardly brook'd/The light" (17–22, 24).

The principle of triple-rootedness in elegy, prophecy, and satire has general application in the romantic order. It speaks to the quality of visionary poems like Keats's *The Fall of Hyperion* and Wordsworth's "Ode: Intimations of Immortality" and Coleridge's *Kubla Khan* and Byron's *A Vision of Judgement*, and to satirical works like Shelley's *Peter Bell the Third* and Blake's *An Island in the Moon*. The depth of its influence can be appreciated if we consider how it resonates in the silences of that stunned elegy, "A Slumber Did My Spirit Seal." Wordsworth departs from the usual form of prophecy in that he does not deal with redemption from a fallen condition, but a prophetic dimension occurs in his sense of exemption from such a condition: "She seemed a thing that could not feel/The touch of earthly years." The exemption extends to the speaker by association: "I had no human fears," and the relation between "him" and "her" comes to embrace the paradox of presentness and unearthliness. It is of course a specious prophecy of exemption, a fact which gives rise to what I regard as the self-satire of the poem. The speaker has been a blithe fool, a dupe to his own wishfulness. His astonishment at her death—the keynote of the poem—is a mark of his bereavement, and implies his backward satirical judgment on himself for infatuation (and, akin to that, fatuity). This latent satire exacerbates his grief no less than the overt prophecy; the satire and prophecy are intrinsic to the speaker's relation to the subject of the elegy, and intrinsic to the elegy itself.

But the value of the principle of root combination in the distinct growths of literary elegy, prophecy, and satire goes finally beyond romanticism. Matthew Arnold tacitly recognizes this principle when he writes to J. C. Shairp that he has given so much attention to the "idyllic side" of "Thyrsis" that "the whole prophetic side" gets shut out. Combination and containment are a signal of the integrative power over diversity in any worthwhile literary document, and no less a signal of the susceptibility of inert material to diverse modes of *poesis.* Much of the difficulty critics and students have been experiencing with, say, Northrop Frye's theory of genre-and-myth criticism stems from the disparity between *its* analytical exclusivity and the multiplicity of the *necessary text.* Frye himself remarks that "while one mode constitutes the underlying tonality of a work . . . , any or all of the other four *may* be simultaneously present."[47] Perhaps rather it is necessary to avoid such strict distinctions, even if urged "to recombine" the modes. For the modes are not separate strands, cleverly plaited. They are intrinsic possibilities of any situation, and *will normally* be "simultaneously present" in a text, and be given certain relative values. The dominant "tonality of a work" requires a vigorous, precise grasp of the modes, and also a specific response involving sensitive balance and tact. It is well to be told that *Antony and Cleopatra "is* high mimetic"[48] and then advised that it is in significant ways also ironic, low mimetic, romantic, and mythic. It would have been better to be shown how the high mimetic contains and exploits the other modes to establish itself, how in effect the modes naturally play among one another. Much of the difficulty in sustaining analytical along with generic criticism dissolves when we respond to the combinational integrity of texts, and recognize the privilege of critics and students to enjoy at once a consistent and efficacious theory and the vital properties of texts that obey and yet hold surprises for known categories.

2
Christ or Prometheus?
The Norm of Consequences
in English Romanticism

To forgive is human, to be forgiven divine.

Anon.

In *The Phenomenology of Mind* Hegel works, with great candor and discernment, through all the tangled questions of identity and substantiation that Descartes slashes by in his famous formula "I think therefore I am." Hegel articulates what he calls "The Freedom of Self-Consciousness," showing how "the subservient consciousness" or the dependence of consciousness on something outside of itself need not require the formulation: *I recognize myself through the other, therefore I think I am.* As Hegel puts it,

the subservient consciousness as such finds these two moments fall apart—the moment of itself as independent object, and the moment of this object as a mode of consciousness, and so its own proper reality. Since, however, the form and the self-existence are for us, or objectively in themselves, one and the same, and since in the notion of independent consciousness the inherent reality is consciousness, the phase of inherent existence (*Ansichsein*) or thinghood which received its shape and form through labour, is no other substance than consciousness. In this way, we have a new attitude or mode of consciousness brought about: a type of consciousness which takes on the form of infinitude, or one whose essence consists in unimpeded movement of consciousness. It is one which *thinks* or is free self-consciousness. For thinking does not mean being an abstract ego, but an ego which has at the same time the significance of inherently existing in itself; it means being object to itself or relating itself to objective reality in such a way that this connotes the self-existence of that consciousness for which it is an object.[1]

This notion of "independent consciousness" with a capacity

to take on "the form of infinitude" and to enjoy "unimpeded movement" presents itself in many guises in the romantic period. It appears as the motivating force in Goethe's *Faust*, where the protagonist is not so much interested in encompassing all knowledge as in knowing all compass for his thoughts and impulses. It appears more coolly, as a principle, in Schiller's *Letters on the Aesthetic Education of Man* and in Fichte's espousal of the absolute Ego. It occurs, in however thwarted a form, in Byron's *Manfred* and Coleridge's *The Rime of the Ancient Mariner* and Keats's *The Fall of Hyperion* and in Wordsworth's fascinated, reverent image of Newton voyaging through "strange seas of thought, alone."

It need occasion no surprise that the most influential critics have signalized one manifestation or another of the independent consciousness as basic to romanticism. E. E. Bostetter in *The Romantic Ventriloquists* locates this independence in the domain of elocution, with the major figures multiplying their voices to maintain the unanimity of the self. M. H. Abrams turns to the domain of illumination, in *The Mirror and the Lamp*, with the lamp representing the self's radiant capacity to manifest and determine the world. And Morse Peckham, in both *The Triumph of Romanticism* and his recent study *Romanticism and Behavior,* concentrates on the domain of substitution in which the self becomes its own myth to make up for the disorder into which hereditary myths (or "explanations") had been thrown.

In all of these theories one must recognize an element of *performance* as well as inviolable existence for the self, an element which puts the authoritative self in a decidedly uncertain relationship with the very situations in which it would manifest authority. To put it another way, its authority has continually to be discovered and even established; this is what Coleridge's definition of the imagination declares, rather than the importance of "understanding the metaphysical process . . . [and] comprehending and explaining metaphysical behavior."[2] We may look upon the interpresence of elegy, prophecy, and satire as a caution against canonizing any condition of the self, or any stage of its *existence*. For in *performance*, stages evolve, revise themselves, merge, and the self is left with the ultimate task (if also the ultimate tool) of imagination, to cope with an emerging and enlarging and complicating whole.

It is of greatest interest, then, to see Morse Peckham, who has been concerning himself with the issue of behavior since *Man's Rage For Chaos*, bringing it forward as a cardinal matter in *Romanticism and Behavior*. Peckham has motivation and, above all, "explanation" in mind, and assigns the "self" a positive scope and value in a situation of social and political and philosophical "collapse." There remains, however, considerable room for misgiving about the adequacy of the "self" in performance and in relationship with what Peckham calls "the other" and "the object." A certain precariousness, even a kind of circumstantial treachery can be discerned again and again in the romantic situation. The performance of the self, its acts, and enactment as it were carry the self beyond its original dimensions and meaning. It is a question whether the self or the context proves to include more than was foreseen or bargained for. But that uncomfortable inclusiveness emerges as a key feature of romanticism, and may with profit occupy our attention.

Within the plain descriptive surface of Wordsworth's "A Slumber Did My Spirit Seal" there are unspoken conditions and references that I have synthesized in the phrase "stunned elegy." The two stanzas of the poem play between fantastic presumption and unthinkable reality. The precise nature of the connection between the two remains unarticulated. If either the presumption (an untouchable person) or the reality (an unfeeling person) has special implications, these remain unconfessed. Even the implications of the opposed states (seeming imperviousness, actual annihilation) are not broached. But the connection and the implications demand our attention. It is crucial to recognize that under the poem's surface of plain description there lies an area of silence, and to recognize also that within this silence is enshrined a conviction of responsibility, of guilt for a failure in perception at the first level, and beyond that for a want of providence. "A Slumber Did My Spirit Seal" is almost about its silence, which seems both psychologically and spiritually capable of interpretation in terms of the problem of guilt and consequences.

We may first recognize in the poem the horror of a fulfilled vision. Lucy, who has "seemed a thing that could not feel / The touch of earthly years," has indeed become such a *thing*, "Rolled round in earth's diurnal course, / With rocks, and stones, and trees." But the fact involves a sinking under rather than a rising above the terrestrial order. Lucy "*is*," as Hartman observes, "what she seemed to be,"[3] and yet what she is understood to be has changed drastically. When the poet calls her "a thing," it is because no other term will do; she is beyond category, beyond identification, beyond understanding, and we may regard his "slumber" as the corresponding state of one who cannot identify or understand. But his is something beyond the corresponding state—it involves a special participation. As he has no "human fears" about her vulnerability to "the touch of earthly years," he also is absolutely without human fears in himself. Her seeming immunity extends to him by association. By the same token, when he wakes to the fact that Lucy, far from enjoying transcendence, is one with "things" like rocks and stones and trees, his own vulnerability is at issue. And the features of that vulnerability include the way he has tended to apotheosize her. He experiences the temporality of consequences; one is punished for hoping good can last eternally. For good is the experience of freedom from mortality's defects. Psyche, in the classical myth, intuitively appreciates what this involves for a mortal. Divinized to rival Aphrodite, she knows what she has coming to her and, as Erich Neumann points out, bows to it.[4]

Thus one must also recognize the paradoxical metaphor of death in the opening line: "A slumber did my spirit seal." It is customary to think of the death in the poem as Lucy's, but this phrase suggests for the speaker a state akin to death, where to "seal" implies an airtight, decisive shutting of the "spirit" and an impressing of "slumber" upon it, and "slumber" implies a state of thorough quiescence. The intimated death in the opening stanza confirms itself in the reality of the second, and may be construed as blindly foretelling it— the poet sleeps through his inward knowledge of death, only to be awakened—too late—by the fact of it. As a result a psychic (as opposed to a social) sense of responsibility makes its way into the second stanza: "No motion has she *now*" (italics added). This can amount to no more than a speculative responsibility: *what if* he had been alert? But it involves real guilt, for someone who has moved above and beyond the touch of earthly years is reduced to a passive and indiscriminate state of being "rolled round . . . with rocks," *on the heels of the speaker's slumber*. No more is necessary to the logic of guilt, which refers itself not only to what has been done, but also to what has been lost in our lives. The fact that *"the poet expresses no shock at finding his illusion . . . betrayed"*[5] should not mislead us. He is too stricken to speak. The poem, occurring at the point of amazed discovery, is prereflective, but we can, as I have tried to do, closely infer the content of its repressed reflections.

A third feature of the latent reflections can be outlined when we consider the statement "She neither hears nor sees." For it is the only point where any concrete or specific human action comes to bear on Lucy—everything else is either abstract (motion, force) or impersonally distributed (rolled round . . . with rocks) or preternatural (a thing that could not feel). That she might hear and see humanizes Lucy. The line serves as a downward pivot between her exaltation and her dissolution. The speaker's thinking of her, after all, as capable of hearing and seeing conveys a belated recognition of her humanity, as well as an intimation of desire for her to hear and see *him*, for him to deal with her on a human level.

"A Slumber Did My Spirit Seal" secretly enshrines not just an elegy for a relationship that has not been, but a sense of guilt for that failure. Lucy's death is associated with the speaker's dehumanizing idolatry (though obviously not caused by it). On the other hand the loss of Lucy is caused by the speaker's "slumber," his neglect of action, his deadly presumption of an exemption from the terms of life. The same association between a state of fascination and the imminence of death appears in "Strange Fits of Passion," but "A Slumber Did My Spirit Seal," for all its surface reticence, affords a telling insight into the domain of responsibility and consequence where that fascination is concerned.

There emerges in "A Slumber Did My Spirit Seal" a sense of something at once fated and courted. The effect of the poem strictly conforms neither to moral-theological punishment for wrongdoing nor to classical *ananke*, suffering that occurs in the fatal course of things. Lucy's death and loss may seem inevitable; the speaker's sense of punishment may seem understandable, but neither gives a sufficient account of the action. The impact of the poem arrives with the fact that the burden of her inevitable death comes abruptly and fiercely on the speaker because of his fascination with her. That fascination accounts for his intuition of consequences. We may well ask whether the one is adequate to the other. A certain disproportion can be felt here. But the problem of consequences in disproportion is not peculiar to this poem, or even to Wordsworth. It appears continually in the romantic period (and may ultimately represent an unexplored facet of romantic irony). Coleridge virtually sums up the issue of disproportion and the dread of losing, through it, a "substratum of permanence, of identity, and therefore of reality." In the conclusion of *Biographia Literaria* he writes:

> It sometimes happens that we are punished for our faults by incidents, in the causation of which these faults had no share: and this I have always felt the severest punishment. . . . There is always a consolatory feeling that accompanies the sense of a proportion between antecedents and consequents. The sense of Before and After becomes both intelligible and intellectual when, and *only* when, we contemplate the succession in the relations of Cause and Effect, which, like the two poles of the magnet manifest the being and unity of the one power by relative opposites, and give, as it were, a substratum of permanence, of identity, and therefore of reality, to the shadowy flux of Time.

One may observe in romanticism a fairly constant relation between fascination—any state of absorption with the self *through another*—and disproportionate consequences. The fascination—of Lycius with Lamia or Christabel with Geraldine or the Keats poet with Moneta or Shelley's poet with the Spirit of Solitude or the Knight with the Belle Dame sans Merci—holds out a promise of transcendence but emerges as a form of transgression. It is no accident that removal and crossing of boundaries is a universal motif in these stories. One notices too that the phenomenon of silence, already identified in "A Slumber Did My Spirit Seal," occurs invariably in the material of fascination. It is not the silence of incomprehension, but of unmanageable comprehension, of seeing the full import—the consequences—of what one has wanted and done.[6] Even in *The Fall of Hyperion*, where the poet rises to the occasion and gains from every adversity that stems from his self-indulgence, a negative temper affects the silence:

> Without stay or prop,
> But my own weak mortality, I bore
> The load of this eternal *quietude*,

The unchanging gloom and the three *fixed* shapes
Ponderous upon my senses, a whole moon. . . .
                    [1.388–92; italics added]

The silence of an utter metaphysical astonishment is most marked, and somehow most telling, in Coleridge's *Christabel.* That silence is so intense as to force itself at times even on the highly garrulous narrator. He is a proud spokesman for family history (the background of the action), individual psychology (the Baron's behavior), and formal theology (the intercession of the saints and the Virgin's protective presence); but his speech operates within the canons and confines of the known, and the action is basically running beyond him into transcendence/transgression.

Much attention has been paid to the omens of the poem— the owl, the shroud-conscious mastiff bitch, the wan dull moon, the "dreams" Christabel has had, the oak tree with its suggestion of primitive religion and rites. These are important as an environment for her behavior, but her behavior is independent of them. The fact that Christabel goes beyond the castle precincts is paramount in itself. This gesture first signifies the claustrophobic incapacity of the castle-world to sustain her spirit or meet her needs (the description of the castle, from "toothless" watchdog untimely "fast asleep" to the Baron sleeping and "weak in health," suggests a deteriorated husk of a system). It also signifies in Christabel an intuition of and an impulse toward dimensions of the world beyond her world. Herein lies the crux of the poem. There is traffic between the two dimensions—Christabel can go out, and can bring Geraldine in—but there is also deep contradiction between them. The charity that Christabel exercises beyond the castle is both genuine and, in effect, perverse. The conduct of Geraldine within the castle both reflects and desecrates the relationship Christabel bears to the two people dearest to her, mother and lover. Definitions collapse and decay, nature itself seems confused when to save a desolate maiden is to be possessed for unspeakable acts, and when a stranger takes the place of mother (301) and lover (233 ff.) in a situation—the bed—where their roles could not normally be combined. In effect, Christabel must either remain unrealized within the castle, or venture beyond it to be undone.

Christabel is replete with symbols and a philosophy of being "free from danger, free from fear" (144). These are ironic. They represent the ideal of the poem, where its actuality demonstrates how limited and imprecise they are. The poem basically brings into common ground two intensely incongruous systems. Or rather Christabel, implicitly seeking a *fuller* world, unwittingly introduces a *rival* one into her wanted sphere. She finds indeed that there is more, but it proves conflictive, even oppressive. She declares that she has unwittingly "sinned," but sin would fall within the castle-world, and could be repented, confessed, atoned for. No such option is open to Christabel. Instead she is arrested in a kind of unconsciousness and silence. The silence speaks volumes. It is accounted for as a "spell" cast by Geraldine (276–78). This is in keeping with the paraphernalia of primitivism and paganism that bedeck the poem. At a more radical, timeless level, it pertains to an astonished sense of what our innocent, even our virtuous, acts may entail. Far from being "free from danger, free from fear," we prove weirdly vulnerable, within and without, to our best selves, and we paradoxically wed ourselves—as Christabel carries Geraldine over the threshold—to our bane. At bottom Christabel cannot speak because she dares not speak, dares not even acknowledge the force of incongruity, the degree of vulnerability in her experience.

It trivializes the poem to read it as a treatment of a sexual taboo (lesbianism) or as a canvassing of a theological infraction (non-conjugal sex). The sense of evil pervading the poem is primary; it is the evil of being mortal, uncertain, inadequate. Christabel is not punished—to the extent that she *is* punished

—as one who harbors hot thoughts of her lover, or even as one who should have known better the bounds of "love and . . . charity" (277). She suffers the consequences of a simple metaphysical inadequacy. The unredoubtable castle and all its doubtful accoutrements might almost be taken as an emblem of the individual life, within whose limits is no satisfaction, while still transcendence of those limits is always transgression, leading to the satisfaction of principles beyond our control or bearing. Silence then would seem to be the consequence of acknowledging what is indescribable or unspeakable, in the sense that it cannot be brought within the grammar of normal understanding and conduct. It is the negative idiom of astonishment at the trespassing self and the invading world. Only once does it occur divorced from pain, where Keats's "stout Cortez" stands "Silent, upon a peak in Darien." He too has transgressed the bounds of the known and accepted, and his followers, who "look at each other with a wild surmise," remind us of what in himself he masters, the dread and violation that romantic silence implies.

None of the foregoing discussion of fascination and silence is meant to suggest that romanticism invented or preempted the phenomenon. It is a perennial occurrence that comes into high relief in romanticism, by virtue of the way romantic writers alter the underlying structure of consequences. They in effect negotiate a shift from specific infractions of specific ordinances, with specific sanctions and within a "comprehensive" framework, to what may be called generic violations of recognizable presumptions within an evolving, eventualist framework of discovery and accommodation. It will be useful here to trace the outlines of this shift.

It is hard to imagine a man more single-minded and self-convinced than the puritan general Oliver Cromwell. Guided by his inner light, he stood willing to affront an age-old theory of kingship no less than the immediate biases of pleasure. He may have been the first to espouse the idea of unvarnished candor, without respect to consequences, in human portrayal. His instructions to the painter John Lyly include the following severe warning: "Paint my picture truly like me, and [do] not flatter me at all; but remark all these roughnesses, pimples, warts, and everything as you see me, otherwise I will never pay a farthing for it." If consequences of his radical departure from the norm enter his mind, they do so negatively, in relation to Lyly, not to himself. We may for contrast consider Cromwell's contemporary John Aubrey, who implored Anthony á Wood to take "the naked and plain truth, which is here exposed so bare that the very *pudenda* are not covered," and "make a castration . . . and sew on some fig-leaves—i.e., to be my *Index expurgatorius*." That is a long way to go to achieve the proper self-image. And yet it is Cromwell, the apostle of the unretouched image, who urged his rival Sir Henry Vane before the assembled Parliament to hold off from opposition and consider that he "might be wrong." Cromwell is in effect implying that the consequences will be on his opponent's conscience, as well as on his head. That he himself might have been wrong seems not to have crossed Cromwell's mind. He professed a love of toleration, but he was in effect arguing toleration of himself and his values and ways *by others*. He proved an inspired and brilliantly unyielding man.

In his presumption of his own integrity and his apprehension of error as possible *in others*, Cromwell gives a classic delineation of the conflict between our singular inner constitution and every outer circumstance. Such a conflict manifests itself aboriginally. As Adam and Eve show, even a message from God, to the effect that something is likely to happen that is not good, can fail to overcome a self-contained code of personal conviction: we feel otherwise in our bones, and our palpable promise of pleasure makes warnings merely abstract, if not inconceivable. Perhaps the justice of the warning remains inconceivable even after the experience of miscalculation and pain. As even Saint Augustine, contemplating virtue, said to the Lord: "not just yet a while." Some spiritual prophylaxis blocks in our minds the embodiment of mortal justice that would reduce a forthright person to a helpless bundle of dread. To put ourselves in the gravitational field of justice is to make it the center of our lives, and as Cesare Beccaria in his study *Of Crime and Punishment* recognized, "Every man tends to make *himself* the center of his whole world." We grieve to find we have erred, of course; we repent our ways. But is this to restore a safe relationship with the universe, or to recover a free and credulous relationship with ourselves? To be freed from guilt is to be free to be guilty again.

Because of the double-edged conviction of the self, the human demand to be saved proves insatiable, the need for consolation unabating. Nietzsche in fact roots this phenomenon in nature itself; in his "Meditation on Schopenhauer" he declares that "nature, with her compulsive need for redemption, wishes to make existence explicable and meaningful by the production of the philosopher and the artist." Here is, perhaps, too much emphasis on the "explicable and meaningful" where questions of value seem uppermost, and too much focus on "the philosopher and the artist," considering that all humankind is actively, personally impelled toward belonging in the light. This is what gives power to the Christian myth of redemption, and in particular to the Roman ceremony of confession. We confess to be told still again that we can be saved from all (and for all) our errors and failings. We confess to be salved for the injury we do ourselves—in conscience, in self-regard, and public opinion—through the injuries we inflict on others. Only helplessly do we confess sorrow for what we do; the unspoken word is of regret that it is so, as we are so.

A major discord then arises between the two terms "to forgive" and "to save"—despite their association in common understanding. To save is to furnish means of getting away from the finally punitive bounds of personality;[7] to forgive is implicitly to reinforce those bounds, to suggest that it is possible to get away with what they entail. Jupiter, the supposed tyrant, may be due some sympathy for his position toward Prometheus; given that *saving* the Titan is out of the question, forgiveness would have no point, and attrition—rather than contrition—would emerge as the only eligible course of action.

A condition of distress in the relation between two authorities—that of an individual act and that of prevailing circumstances—results from the human capacity for error. But the capacity to act takes priority over the capacity for error, though the latter comments ironically on the former. Too faithful an anticipation of that irony is tantamount to paralysis, itself an occasion for irony and so on in constricting bands of doubt and inaction. And yet the blood finds channels, the heart pounds, and, without believing it makes sense or hoping to be surprised, one continues to act. Existential angst and alienation are both genuine and implausible conditions of modern experience; they deny themselves by the very act of confession, and move, while claiming the empty uselessness of moving, into a charming paradox: a community of alienation. Chaos is as much our convention as order was the eighteenth century's. "We move," as Lewis Mumford says in "The Little Testament of Bernard Martin, Aet. 30," "in spite of Zeno!"

One acts as one is. But if the indispensable integrity of action ends in pitfalls, and irony in a kind of annihilation, where do we turn? Quoi penser, quoi faire? This quandary has necessitated various images of immunity, from the Christian saint, converting punishment into opportunity, to the Stoic sage, reducing punishment to insignificance. By guaranteed action or guaranteed endurance the bugaboo of punishment is exorcised. But in its more practical forms, a solution seems harder to come by. Saint and sage stand as strenuous ideals, while the living picture presents itself with dynamic uncertainty.

The problem of consequences—of effects that seem so much a delayed embodiment of an agent's status as to become metaphysical, and not merely customary or logical—needs a dynamic interpretation, and an economy of consequences needs to be set up. Is prayer or a donation to charity a form of bribery (buying off), and is bribery an analog of redemption (buying back)? What attitudes can be taken toward liability and what value can be given to self-conviction? Each of us knows something like the inexplicable moment where, before all is darkness, one blows out a lamp and the whole house tumbles down; but we do not have an actuary of the spirit to work out a formula for the relation between indignation and submission, nor yet a philosophy that explains the responsibility of surprise. Terms like "Freudian slip" and "accident prone" find favor by playing on our faith in intention, but they do not abolish the question we ask, with an equal faith in accident, "Why me?"

The modern temper is especially prone to cathexis on a state of suffering, and prone to block off the question of consequences—of the relation between suffering and something antecedent—that might alter at once the experience and the perspective of suffering. This may be a gain over the superstitious sense of consequences exhibited by the medieval mind—for which nothing was accident, and everything somehow deserved. But a corresponding loss also appears, in that the modern has no way out of a suffering which looks both causeless and aimless. A sense of randomness worthy of Democritus and a sense of the agnostics of causation worthy of Hume keep the modern not so much free as disconnected. The contemporary position resembles nothing more nearly than a loopy Faustian bargain in which a quest for knowledge —of the moon or Mars, of bioengineering or mind-reformation

—is supposed to have no cost to speak of, because the cost is classified, taboo. As it happens, though, there is more to being modern than skill in accountancy and management of the press. Where science and social science detail the forms and processes of our human nature, it remains for art, and especially literature, to articulate the experience of being both vehicle and authority for those forms/processes.

Modern literature gives cogent evidence of an apprehension of consequences[8] that is at once material and intuitive. Dmitri Karamazov affords a good example of the case. Dostoevski portrays Dmitri in a legal situation that is not only a shallow version of consequences, but also a false one; "successfully" prosecuted and convicted, he has actually not killed his father. But if one regards the legal framework so as to register not what is within but what is around it, one recognizes it as a deep if crude analog of justice for Dmitri. Though he is not specifically involved in killing, he is everywhere involved in mortality, in acts of gaming and drunkenness and borrowing and rage and even sacrifice that attenuate and threaten the existence of others, as well as his own. Furthermore, he is guilty by sympathy with the damned. Dmitri accepts the verdict of the law not for its justice but for its aptness, and its aptness is of course to his condition and conviction of himself. As Mikhail Bakhtin observes, "that 'truth' at which, having explained events to himself, the hero must . . . arrive can be for Dostoevsky essentially only the truth of the *hero's own consciousness*."[9] Dmitri is conscious of vicarious guilt, a state in which the innocent recognize what is impossible for them (freedom) and what is incumbent upon them (submission) as a result of another's action. The suggestion that he might abscond from punishment cannot be dismissed; he could steal off to America, the land without a past, and so without consequences; and yet this is tantamount to saying he will, when at last his spiritual eyes are opened, steal from his own spirit. The spirit of Dmitri's acceptance is lucidly summarized in Dostoevski's *Notes from the Underground*:

The enjoyment [came] from feeling oneself that one had reached the last barrier, that it was horrible, but that it could not be otherwise; that there was no escape for you; that you *never could* become a different man; that even if time and faith were still left you to change into something different [the American dream?] you would most likely not wish to change; or if you did wish to, even then you would do nothing; because perhaps in reality there was nothing for you to change into.[10]

Perhaps it will help us to understand Dmitri's submission, even his cleaving to punishment, if we recall another problematical innocent of just about the same vintage, namely Henry James's Isabel Archer.[11] Both characters pass up handy and not dishonorable instruments of "freedom," and thus take on a lifetime of self-confinement and alienation. In both, it is important to realize, the act of submission constitutes a *new* statement of self-will, and serves as a vital correction, a counter-*deliberation*, of the more selfish and impetuous expression of self-will each has made. Dmitri Karamazov and Isabel Archer are, in short, both involved in the ambiguity of self-will, that power which is the sine qua non of our individual existence and which proves equally the fons et origo of our liability to consequences.

A fault-line in the relation of law and consequences is continually explored in literature since Dostoevski, with comparable metaphysical overtones. In Richard Wright's *Native Son* Bigger Thomas seems, from a technical standpoint, more truly "guilty" of taking a life than Dmitri Karamazov. And yet the law fits his case as awkwardly, and reduces itself to an instrument of metaphysical opportunity as decisively as with Dmitri. Mary Dalton dies at Bigger's hands by accidental homicide, but by the time the deed reaches the public it has taken on scandalous and gruesome proportions, with the dismemberment and partial cremation of the body in the home furnace, and with the fierce conviction that Bigger, a black man, had raped the white heiress Mary. Just the opposite has been the case—Bigger acts to stifle any least suspicion of rape in a situation that clamors of the possibility (he has brought Mary, helplessly drunk, back to her room, and her blind mother comes to her door). The law is interested in him as a sort of beast of rapine, according to the prosecution's version, or a victim of ineluctable forces, in the defense attorney's plea; but he emerges as a sort of independent Coleridgean entity, capable of echoing the divine "I am" in and through his deeds. Bigger brings out the principle, tacit in Dostoevski and James, that it is not what we do but what we accept that establishes our being.

It is a grim paradox of his experience that he develops, from the unintentional killing of Mary Dalton to the more calculated stuffing of her body into the furnace and beyond that to the carefully wrought murder of his girlfriend Bessie Mears, the gifts of self-consciousness and self-control. It is a compounding paradox that, in the fearful act of destroying the two women (symmetrically, one black and one white), Bigger destroys his fear of non-being and so destroys his capacity for treating others as non-beings, as disposable objects. The punishment for being black and for killing is execution, in keeping with the self-defining programs of society and the law; but the consequence in the self-discovering domain of Bigger's experience is the assumption of independent personality and character, evincing philosophy and philanthropy even on the brink of death.

In a sense Bigger's killing of Bessie is a consequence of an accident (namely, Mary Dalton's death), and is as exorbitant in its negative way as Bigger's self-respect growing positively from his having killed. The evidence of disproportion right and left in the matter of consequences is a salient phenomenon. It runs close to the core of the modern situation, which seems either to cultivate an improbable impunity, as in Norman Mailer's *An American Dream*, or to set off a relentless train of dire effects from a slight flick of the wrist, as in Ibsen's *Ghosts*.

With Ibsen, the question of consequences is all but explicit, and yet the framework of consequences is uncertain, unpredictable. Where Hardy, for instance, suggests a notion of doom encompassing and invading human affairs, Ibsen conveys a sense of doom lurking in human purpose and gesture, working closer to the open as we work harder to keep it confined. Dostoevski is taken as a seminal modern figure, but he has this peculiarity, that along with recognizing the centrifugal swing of our lives and minds, he continues to propound the maintenance of the edifice of ancient refuge.[12] In opposing wanton personality to traditional values he is too formal and analytical to be fully modern; the modern dichotomy is not anarchy or individualism versus order, but atomism versus identity. Captain Ahab, Meursault, and Kurtz are our brothers, Alyosha Karamazov our nostalgic saint.

Ibsen appears to carry us entirely into modernity. Born in the same decade as Dostoevski, he lived into the first years of our century and began on the so-called social plays on which his fame principally rests only in 1877, four years before Dostoevski died. The first to "reverberate across the roof of the world"[13] was *A Doll's House*, written in 1879. Ibsen outlived Dostoevski by twenty-five years, but he was inactive for the last six years of his life; in effect he may be said to have used the years leading into the twentieth century (his final play, *When We Dead Awaken*, was produced in 1899) to lead in the twentieth century.

A Doll's House constitutes a modern inquiry into the domain of courtly love. It suggests at a minimum that courtly love was a device for warding off the ills of chattel marriage and the evil of dishonesty; in Nora's case, of course, the dishonesty is financial and not sexual. The play denies the efficacy of the courtly love scheme and meets Nora's twin difficulties head on. There is almost a classic confrontation of traditional organization and new energy as Torvald Helmer and Nora exchange philosophies in their final colloquy: "One doesn't sacrifice one's honor," Torvald intones, "for love's sake." And Nora responds: "Millions of women have done so." In other words passion, private feeling, is frankly acknowledged as an undeniable ground of action, and the sense of worth placed above the enjoyment of reputation. The trick of courtly love was to have it both ways, as the lady was elevated by consensuality, protected from harm by a love convention that opposed the marriage convention. With his simple claim for "love" over against "honor," Ibsen brings us far beyond the medieval attachment to convention and abstraction. And as the case of the Master Builder strikingly attests, the overthrow of the forms for a personal "idea" is no mere feminine trait. We may argue that utter personal sacrifice has a classic precedent in *Antony and Cleopatra* (to say nothing of Dryden's *All for Love*). But we are also far removed from *Antony and Cleopatra*, since Nora's private choice is not glorified, or even sacrificial; it is a practical business. And Ibsen goes even further. *A Doll's House* ends with a choice, a point of some significance considering that the universe of the play has been essentially one without choice, as Mrs. Linde vehemently reminds Krogstad: "I *had* no choice, I tell you" (act 3). *Ghosts, Rosmersholm, Hedda Gabler,* and *The Master Builder* effectively represent the universe of choice, giving unretouched pictures of its origin and consequences.

Ibsen himself seems to have conceived of *Ghosts* in this framework. He comments in a note for the play: "Marriage for external reasons, even when these are religious or moral, brings a Nemesis on the offspring."[14] Perhaps, though, more is involved than a nemesis on the offspring. There is in logic nothing to safeguard marriage entered into for "internal" reasons from like disaster, and there is, in the play, some basis for being uneasy with this view of Oswald—not only has he been much the freest and happiest of the characters, but he is obviously unaware of the visit of nemesis upon him. Rather it would seem that the play's central thrust is toward Mrs. Alving's full realization of all that her venial choice of comfort and respectability has entailed. Oswald's demented looking for "the sun—the sun" has density and force because of her intolerably lucid looking at him, her "son." The stage direction, "in speechless terror," is really superfluous. We know. And with all due deference to the Victorian strain in Ibsen's anti-Victorianism, it does not appear that her terror has much to do with "marriage for external reasons" and "a Nemesis upon the offspring." More fundamentally it seems to spring from the utter failure of her efforts to manage and control her existence, and that of people around her, at least in the public eye, and the stark recognition of how she herself has imparted to circumstances the inertia which has become a juggernaut aimed at her dear son, and at herself through him.

The independent and relentless inertia of choice: this seems focal in Ibsen's vision in the social plays. But *The Master Builder* and *Hedda Gabler* distinctively also evoke the humble, if not frivolous, origins of choices implicitly tending toward a form of "speechless terror." Natural pregnancy, or unnatural fastidiousness, in Hedda Gabler are certainly the ostensible cause of her tragedy; the cause of Halvard Solness's tragedy is that fear of strangers and of competition which has as its compensation his overweening possessiveness and need for a "kingdom." Both are guilty of hubris, à la Pentheus or Doctor Faustus; both would tool the universe to their own specification. But now hubris and pathos are virtually interchangeable. At least, neither Hedda Gabler nor Halvard Solness relates to any cosmic power; neither substantially conceives of one. They do not seek to be gods, but adequate people, pathetically and perhaps pathologically struggling against unworthiness, staving off the threat of being all too human, or of being swamped in the tides of humanity.

It is Ibsen's distinction to have enunciated a thoroughly naturalistic order of consequences, marked by limitless liability for the most limited of venial, if not innocent, acts. Other modern writers convey a similar sense of the individual's vulnerability to consequences in his pursuit of security or adequacy. Conrad's "Mistah Kurtz" is more successful than Hedda Gabler or Mrs. Alving in this struggle, but while his success spares him "speechless terror," it only brings him to "The horror! The horror!" By the same token, Winnie Verloc in *The Secret Agent* embodies the low-class, crime-bound version of Mrs. Alving, making the compromises that promote destruction in the guise of love and protection. Neither the sense of "absolute safety" nor intrinsic "vigilance" nor finally the intimations of something "providential" about Adolf Verloc can save "poor Stevie." Indeed, these very factors make for the catastrophe. The eagerness of Winnie and her mother to secure Stevie in Verloc's good graces practically inspires Verloc to use Stevie to blow up the Greenwich observatory. As Conrad chorally intones: "There are circumstances when the disposal of a few tables and chairs, brass bedsteads, and so on, may be big with remote and disastrous consequences." Perhaps the ultimate expression of this syndrome occurs in *Waiting for Godot*, which presents a set of pernicious consequences searching for a cause.

The modern cathexis on suffering stands in harsh contrast to its historical background, the Western Christian inheritance of a cosmos of redemption. The medieval situation, for instance, departs from the modern in two directions: its concept of punishment is more elaborate and specific than today, while at the same time it offers no less elaborate and specific means of getting away from punishment. Even suffering, a more amorphous form of punishment, admitted of a positive construction; it was undertaken (not, as now, undergone) for the good of the individual soul or the social order. The lengths to which medieval forms could go to uphold this supervening good can readily be measured in the works of Geoffrey Chaucer.

The opening of the "General Prologue" to the *Canterbury Tales* resounds with accents various enough to generate two common images of Chaucer: that of an ingeniously naive, proto-modern naturalist, and that of a thoroughly conditioned, subtle medieval allegorist. But the tension between nature and piety, after all the qualifications and retardations of the first great periodic sentence of the "General Prologue" to *The Canterbury Tales,* seems to stabilize itself within piety's gravitational field. The needs of the body and those of the spirit are both alike helped by the "holy blisful martyr"; *he* does not puristically refuse miracles to the flesh, just because the soul happens to be his metier, and nor does the average pilgrim hold himself to exquisite standards of preparation before heading Canterburyward. It may be only speculative criticism, but it would be fair Christianity to surmise that the Pardoner, even as he goes dispensing false relics from his professional bag, travels with the deep-down hope of replenishing his personal bag. As Blake observes "To the Public" in plate 3 of *Jerusalem*: "he who waits to be righteous before he enters into the Saviour's kingdom, will never enter there." Furthermore, we must remember that "the pilgrimage is a kind of pattern and image of man's uncertain but lively progress through an infinitely various world toward a destination which would be presumed the same for every Christian [i.e., for every] traveler."[15] Thus to acknowledge the body as Chaucer heartily does is hardly to deny the spirit, for the body too, and sometimes first, must be saved. There is in the body a sort of *sermo humilis*; the irregularity and deformity of experience in the world is made up, as Erich Auerbach reminds us, by the divine mind, unifying and perfecting all meaning.[16]

A concern with salvation as a primary or indiscriminate idea pervades *The Canterbury Tales*. It is manifest in a fair number of tales which have been termed "pathetic" and which have been classified as "tragedies of victimization," that is, tragedies modulating into a "final joy" under the aegis of "divine love and justice."[17] Even a tale of damnation, such as the Pardoner tells, works as a caveat, and effectively bears toward salvation. But it is finally the less obvious instances that enable us to see how easily Chaucer's mind moved in the structures of redemption. Tales which are ostensibly social rather than religious in temper prove to be *structurally* redemptive. This is not to say, à la Robertson, that they embody Christian allegory. To the contrary, the terms of *Christian* salvation would seem to have lost much of their specificity in these tales, and the idea of salvation remains as a formal pattern or structure which Chaucer uses impartially for one kind of tale or another.

The Nun's Priest's Tale comes immediately to mind. Its celebration of animal spirits makes it settle for a simple restoration of the status quo, Chanticleer being rescued rather than redeemed. But that deviation is very much to the point: a comedic sense finally composes the ominous centrifugal flutter of the tale, which retains the general outline of fall and redemption as (to borrow an image from Coleridge) an eggshell pricked and drained retains the form of an egg.

A more complicated example of the structure of redemption offers itself in *The Franklin's Tale*. This tale has been often construed as "a kind of resolution to the problems of the Marriage Group";[18] but it is rather a *continuation* of them, in a new dimension, and comes to serve as a sort of revelation of the vulnerability of the happy marriage. It should be particularly noted that the tale begins where the

Wife of Bath's marriages and her own tale culminate, in a perfect union of mutual humility and assurance and devotion, with two people enjoying ultimate freedom within marriage bonds.

Wommen of kinde desiren libertee,
And nat to been constrained as a thral—
And so doon men, if I sooth sayen shal.

In a way, marriage is less the subject than the environment of the tale, less what it focuses upon than what it arises from. Its general outline is as follows: happiness → anxiety → eccentric hope → despair → submission → recovered happiness.

Specifically this outlines the career of Dorigen, but it is notable that while she is its focal figure, she participates only indirectly in the development of the pattern. She is a virtual spectator, and less active or resourceful than Chanticleer even; he at least uses motherwit to extricate himself from the difficulties he lets himself in for. Dorigen by comparison seems very passive, a creature of charming petulance who almost gets involved in a sordid or perverted tragedy of victimization, but that the world harbors enough *gentilesse* and *freedom* to protect her.

Given these romance terms, *gentilesse* and *freedom*, no one need quarrel with the outcome; that is the way romance goes. But the tale is at pains to suggest that it is more than orthodox romance. Such actors as a "lusty squier" and a "Briton clerk" are not likely embodiments of romance. Indeed there could well be a strict psychological realism in the denouement, if three suppositions hold up: (1) that Aurelius the lusty squire thought better of having to do with a woman who would tell her husband everything, and who had such an exquisite formalist for a husband; (2) that the nameless clerk, who explicitly wishes to emulate his social superiors in "magnanimity," frees the squire of his crushing debt as a way, perhaps, of indulging scholarly loftiness toward money and mere social station; and (3) that Arveragus the husband is a master strategist who can count on things to turn out right, as R. E. Kaske says he does.[19] This last possibility obviously bears looking into, as being to all intents and purposes gratuitous. What we may say is that, whether Arveragus knows or not, the story knows, and thus that the happy solution inheres in its nature as a Breton lay. Certainly the narrator refuses to let Dorigen's real dilemma—namely, that she will be guilty of adultery with *her husband's* *"magnanimous" consent*—take hold in our minds. He hurries to give away the ending, assuring us that Dorigen will enjoy "bettre fortune" than we think. The tale ceases to be even a good story of suspense, as its oblique analog in the story of Abraham and Isaac, can be; rather the energy of suspense is released to give an impetus to the abstract momentum of salvation.

The point should be made that what is saved is not a perfect marriage, but the idea of salvation itself. The marriage takes up very little of the actual story, and gets described in conventional terms; it is not realized or dramatized. Even Aurelius's passion, which receives good space, is conventional. The real relationships in the tale are those the characters bear to abstract ideas; these indeed, in the version by Boccaccio on which Chaucer drew, are the primary object of the story. Arveragus responds to "trouthe," not to Dorigen; Aurelius, who has in a formal if heated way responded to Dorigen, subordinates his emotional interests and needs to Arveragus's abstract principle, and the magical "philosophre" does the same, at one remove. It is important to recall "Gentilesse," a key term in the tale, implies not only "refinement" and "graciousness," but also "grace." The tale effectively becomes an example of medieval realism, where ideas predominate over phenomena, and where accordingly problems of appearance and chance make life piquant, without making it intrinsically dangerous. In the final analysis, chance and magic and even lechery, all ostensible enemies of a virtuous wife and of the virtue of "trouthe" (meaning the marriage bond as well as the bond of honor), actually conspire to spare Dorigen pain. Because of her preoccupied, casual remark to Aurelius, because of his passion and, pursuant to it, his special contract with the "philosophre," the rocks which are really the only thing she has to worry about vanish from sight.

The substance of the story, as opposed to its structural tendency, is strangely volatile. The lamentations of the excitable bride appeal to our sympathies; the sea represents, outside of "a small, luminous area" of civility, what A. D. Nock calls "the *viboumene*," the uncertain vastness of the world,[20] and incites Dorigen's fear of the domination and casuistry of nature. But her lamentations, suggesting that with the rocks on the coast of Brittany God has created Hell on earth ("feendish, grisly, rokkes blak"), contain sacrilege. Her devotion to her husband is delightful, and dangerously exorbitant—the mark of its going beyond the bounds becomes plain in that she would need to betray her husband in order to save him for herself. She has no malice, really no mischief in her, but it makes no difference. The fact that she is a passionate girl playing the faithful, thoughtful wife beyond her philosophical depth calls down a train of consequences that in a naturalistic dispensation would simply crush her. The medieval tenor of the tale precludes this, though. In the structure of redemption which I am suggesting organizes Chaucer's mind, Dorigen's dilemma becomes the occasion of a pervasive play of "trouthe," and the practical, psychological, and moral issue is subsumed in a religious ordinance.

The Franklin's Tale modulates from dread, the anticipation of things we cannot cope with, to shame that we can cope with by simply keeping mum.[21] In a sense it modulates from the sublime to the gratuitous. Man may fall, willy-nilly, but he is saved by the grace of God, or other sufficient principle.

In a sense, as the *Canon's Yeoman's Tale* shows, there is no alternative for someone who remains in society—one must go off into bizarre solitude and esoteric mazes to escape being somehow saved. Within society the principle of salvation may itself reach bizarre lengths, as it does in *The Merchant's Tale*. The January-May relationship is so riddled with sensuality and deceit that the very gods intervene to mete out punishment. And yet all ends status quo, as divinity cancels divinity and personality is saved its worst consequences.

Thus we find a *double* nullification of consequences; January and May both escape the fruits of their errors. The fact that the nullification is in the hands of the gods should remind us of *The Knight's Tale* and establish a formal as well as substantial kinship with that work. This is not to minimize the nasty atmosphere and actions of *The Merchant's Tale*. Rather I would stress that the structure of the tale and the split deus ex machina it finally employs assure that no harm will come of the nastiness. We may boggle at the fact that January and May are "saved" without adopting new principles or modes of behavior, but this in no way distinguishes them from Dorigen and Arveragus. Perhaps the ultimate proof of the structure of redemption is its neutrality or indiscriminacy where we would draw the line, its capacity to embrace even such as January and May with their venereal folly and lechery. As D. W. Robertson observes of medievalism, its "Divine Order includes the sinner as well as the saint; it contains ample provision for both."[22] Both the charm and the severity of this principle emerge in a story concerning the Dominican Vincent Ferrar, a popular fifteenth-century preacher who attracted large crowds wherever he went and who invariably moved his audiences to tears. "One day," as Johan Huizinga reports,

while Ferrar was preaching, he saw two persons, who had been condemned to death—a man and a woman—being led to execution. He begged to have the execution delayed, had them both placed under the pulpit, and went on with his sermon, preaching about their sins. After the sermon, only some bones were found in the place they had occupied, and the people were convinced that the word of the saint had consumed and saved them at the same time. [23]

But Chaucer evinces something subtly at odds with a "confident acceptance of a Providential order underlying the apparent irrationality of the world and its inhabitants."[24] His stories take advantage of an *irrationality in Providence*, an abstract bias in favor of waywardness, in *The Franklin's Tale*, and wantonness, in the *Merchant's Tale*. Providence is not a principle, it is a commodity.

Such an ordinance persists comfortably into the Renaissance, but there grows up beside it in this period, in the notion of the immortality of art, an alternative structure that obliquely challenges the centrality, if not the source, of redemption. It is no paradox but a logical necessity that the formalization of this challenge in the Interregnum and Restoration should have produced the fullest artistic definition of the structure of redemption, in Milton's *Paradise Lost*. And it is appropriate that luxury, and in particular aesthetic luxury, should appear in book 11 of that poem as a great stumbling block to redemption in the post-lapsarian Adam, just as the intoxication of a putative personal independence tripped him up in his innocence. These are the innovations of the Renaissance that make redemption seem a sidelong issue. But the Middle Ages, Huizinga reminds us, constituted an era of "blood," with a "violent tenor of life," and with the Dance of Death as its characteristic cultural symbol;[25] drawing and quartering made up the punishment for theft; failure to support the Christian faith or the Western economy led to "persecution and slaughter." The idea of redemption was a present consolation, as well as a psychological reaction to such a world.

The Renaissance concern with consequences and redemption is manifest from first to last. The Elizabethan drama begins with revenge and ends with romance, begins by insisting on consequences and ends by dissolving them. It may be observed that a spirit of redemption is abroad where it is least expected, as in *King Lear*.[26] By the same token a punitive spirit crops up where redemption seems paramount. In *The Winter's Tale*, for example, we are plainly given a prolepsis of naturalistic doom in the stage direction "Exit, pursued by a bear." A. Bartlett Giamatti has shown how thoroughly the issue of redemption informs Marlowe's *Doctor Faustus*, actually his work overall,[27] and Middleton's *The Changling* and Webster's *The White Devil* and Ford's *'Tis Pity She's a Whore* can be cited here as well.

Still, two significant new developments can be observed in the Renaissance. The first is that the pole of damnation, a spirit of pessimism or cynicism, appears more strongly than in Chaucer, not to represent doubts concerning the principle of redemption, but—as it were intensifying *The Pardoner's Tale*— to exhibit the consequences of a challenge to that principle. Pessimism is the proof, the wages of separation from the world of grace. The second is the possibility that redemption (though never condemnation) may be arbitrary in the Renaissance. The judgment of Lovewit in *The Alchemist* is undisguisedly biased in Face's favor, though at some cost to his "candour" (5.5.160). A direct line can be traced from an overmastering "trouthe" in Chaucer to a topical and urbane "candour" in Jonson, but a certain degeneration is occurring. Face unabashedly appeals to audience sympathy rather than perennial principle for his salvation. Dramatic "decorum" (5.5.167) and public opinion assume the standard of judgment. "Gentilesse" (or spiritual decorum) and "freedom" accordingly suffer some loss of ground. An aesthetic bias, something which in *Volpone* ensnares us into a perverse and in retrospect shameful fondness for Volpone and Mosca, and the very thing which Giamatti represents as the ultimate danger to the Elizabethan world picture, is beginning to be projected across the stage.

Even in Marlowe's *Tamburlaine* an aesthetic bias may be discerned, if we keep in mind the aesthetics or spectacularity of power. In this respect Tamburlaine anticipates, in a positive vein, an attractive feature of Satan's behavioral mode, namely, attachment to grandeur and power. Tamburlaine's imperialistic behavior is more genuinely than Satan's a matter of necessary self-establishment. As a shepherd he is lost in the landscape no less than in pastoral convention, and it is to redeem himself from that possession that he proceeds to the domination of others. But we can see this as a false foundation for the self. He thinks by bringing the mighty down to raise himself, and by reducing others to effective nonentity to confirm his true being. This involves a degree of imaginative ignorance, though it is intrinsic mortality rather than a perpetually subject state that he fails to take into account. Tamburlaine is not condemned, but denied, by death. He is punished from within, by self-exhaustion. Like *Volpone*, *Tamburlaine* has an action that succumbs and can succumb only to an internal entropism. The play boasts an elliptical and obsessive pattern of action, with two signal effects: (1) it affords Tamburlaine no adequate adversary, so that his triumphs remain pale, and (2) it affords the reader no adequate authority, so that Tamburlaine's doom remains cold. The aesthetic bias of the play impedes both consequences and redemption, without achieving a substantive and separate aesthetic order.

The aesthetic bias perhaps culminates in Restoration comedy and heroic tragedy, but it is so at home there, in the elegant impunity of the court and the outlandish ostentation of the Almanzorian battleground, as to have lost its active meaning and relation to the audience and to history. The work which most resolutely celebrates the aesthetic bias is instead the proto-Paterian *Antony and Cleopatra*, with its conviction that "to burn always with [a] hard, gemlike flame, to maintain this ecstasy, is success in life."[28]

Where "trouthe" and "gentilesse" are the attractive principles of *The Franklin's Tale*, "measure" and "honor" and
"nobleness" are typically repulsive principles of *Antony and
Cleopatra*. But not simply so. A redefinition of the area of
value develops explicitly through the play. Antony professes:
"The nobleness of life/Is to do thus" (1.1.36–37), what he
wants with Cleopatra rather than what is expected in Rome,
and he stuns us no less with the narrow finality of "Here is
my space" than with his grand claim that he cannot be
encompassed save in "new heaven, new earth" (1.1.34, 17).
Antony is here a dramatic John Donne, concentrating the
whole cosmos into himself and his lover, and occupying the
whole cosmos between them. But unlike the case with Donne
the public situation is unfavorable to his vision, which seems a
heady mixture of verbiage and bravado. Personality is pitted
against society and morality, and the question of the play
becomes whether, as Janet Adelman suggests, "the claims of
the language" can stand out against the realities of "the
action."[29] Can Antony and Cleopatra, beyond proclaiming
new values, substantially communicate them? The striking
feature of the play is that it makes this question plausible. As
I have observed, the Renaissance tended to treat an ultimate
commitment to the power of language as a disorder and an
impiety. And today we are so far from giving room to any
such individualizing formulation as to give society the deter-
mining role in the constitution of reality; Peter L. Berger is a
most eloquent spokesman for this view, in *The Social Construction of Reality* and elsewhere. But the fact remains that
Antony and Cleopatra not only makes it a real debate between
social norms and idiosyncratic turns, but seems to cherish
and even justify a deviation that cannot be coopted by society
as a way of maintaining hegemony. Of course the consequences of deviation are not, as in *The Alchemist*, spared
Antony and Cleopatra, but paradoxically the lower they fall
in social and moral terms, the higher they rise in personal

existential terms. It has been argued that "the desire to judge and be judged correctly is one of the dominant passions of the play," but it would seem rather that its basic impulse is to challenge and even transcend the forms of judgment. The fact that "the very process of judging is unreliable"[30] seems designed to prepare us for this transcendence.

There is no institutional embodiment of the salvation of Antony and Cleopatra. Against the institutionalized magic of kingship they pit the personal magic of words. They are saved in consciousness; their triumph is conceptual, not material. By the same token, there is no institutional term for their triumph, no word like *measure* or *honour* which could become canonized and make a public pattern "from above." They get away with being *sui generis*, rather than merely unique. The drama, though crowded with actions, is ultimately a drama of language,[31] the drama deriving from the fact that it is a language without a pat idiom, without shibboleths of value; its situation is argumentative, not axiomatic, its object to create and reside in its own authority. In a sense *Antony and Cleopatra* captures in miniature the whole Elizabethan movement from revenge, an ambience of rigid principle and action, to romance, a state founded on the transmuting word.

We have to be convinced that Antony and Cleopatra, who are so vulnerable to accident and change and appetite, can do, or rather be, that which "shackles accidents, and bolts up change,/ . . . and never palates more the dung" (5.2.6–7). And we are convinced, in spite of the remorseless course of the action, by nothing less than the power of language to incarnate its subject out of nothing. Such a use of language does not smack of damnable arrogance, because the creature is not designed to oust the creator. The creation, here possibly the Roman order, is not now basically threatened. We can render unto Caesar the world that is his, without derogation of his rivals; Antony and Cleopatra come to occupy a world elsewhere, or nowhere, save in the mind.

The principle of power yields to the power of principle. Thus an apotheosis can take place. The crucial passage is of course Cleopatra's colloquy with the helpless Dolabella:

Cleopatra. I dreamed there was an Emperor Antony.
. . . .
> His face was as the heavens, and therein stuck
> A sun and moon, which kept their course and lighted
> The little O, th' earth.

Dolabella.   Most sovereign creature—

Cleopatra. His legs bestrid the ocean; his reared arm
> Crested the world: his voice was propertied
> As all the tuned spheres, and that to friends;
> But when he meant to quail and shake the orb,
> He was a rattling thunder. For his bounty
> There was no winter in 't; an autumn 'twas
> That grew the more by reaping: his delights
> Were dolphin-like, they show'd his back above
> The elements they liv'd in: in his livery
> Walked crowns and crownets; realms and islands were
> As plates dropped from his pocket.

Dolabella.   Cleopatra—

Cleopatra. Think you there was, or might be, such a man
> As this I dreamed of?

Dolabella.   Gentle madam, no.

Cleopatra. You lie, up to the hearing of the gods.
> But if there be, or ever were, one such,
> It's past the size of dreaming: nature wants stuff
> To vie strange forms with fancy, yet t'imagine
> An Antony were nature's piece 'gainst fancy,
> Condemning shadows quite.

                    [5.2.76–100]

Ventidius has found in Antony's name a "magical word of war"; here Cleopatra finds in words a cosmic and magical power to create what is the quintessentially real form of Antony. In a sense she is inventing him with words, but in another sense she is imprinting him on language and on our minds. The dream gives here uninhibited access to reality, and so she starts with it. But reality—not everyday actuality which as she says "wants stuff"—reality contains images of bounty (realms . . . as plates), of sportive transcendence (dolphin-like), of order and also mystery (the heavens, with harmony and ability to inspire awe), of ceremony and power (in his livery walked crowns) that go beyond dreams. Antony is the consummation of these images, of reality itself.

Not practically available, this reality is ontological and stands without the verification of the senses or of history, just as it stands beyond the value systems of Enobarbus or Caesar. A singular conception, a conception of something singular emerges as the predominant reality in *Antony and Cleopatra*. The measure of its viability lies in the readiness of its two participants to suffer its consequences, and in their capacity to transmute these consequences, that is, their official debasement, into the precious metal of spiritual triumph. The area of transmutation is the consciousness, Antony and Cleopatra's of course, but the reader's also in an almost constitutive way; and the instrument of transmutation is language.

Some emphasis must be put on the way redemption is abstracted in language and interiorized in consciousness. For as we go beyond the aestheticized Restoration and the relatively didactic and centripetal Augustan age, the possibilities of redemption seem increasingly elusive, and the arena of consequences increasingly inward. We do not quite encounter gratuitous guilt, but the origin of guilt, as in Christabel or the Ancient Mariner or Manfred, grows obscure and narrow in relation to its fierceness and scope. In turn, even while assorted agents of redemption (including a mother in heaven for Christabel) grace the scene, the resolution of guilt seems left to the processes of the individual mind. Where the mind is possessed, in Christabel for example, resolution becomes impossible, notwithstanding Bard Bracy and his ministrations; where it can find relief, but not true recovery, there emerges the Ancient Mariner's helpless alternation of calm and nightmarish reenactment; but where, as in Manfred, it reaches a new peace, the resolution appears problematical, because it remains so much merely in the mind.

To trace the change one can do nothing so constructive as study the status of consequences in the romantic period, which is a veritable watershed between the medieval and the modern order. For the romantic period recapitulates the former and adumbrates the latter. It shows less formal theology but not less religious conviction than the Middle Ages. It experiences less passive bewilderment than modern times, but not less suffering. In effect, the romantic period, breaking the dam of orthodox or established principles that had held through neoclassicism, produced a rush of independent projects and formulations which in turn produced ample occasion for grappling with any variety of consequences. And again, as the period was singularly invested in the open processes of man's assuming his fullest being in the world, it readily lent itself to revealing both the formal and the spontaneous patterns of consequences. Basically, there is a transition from formal to spontaneous contexts in romanticism, a revision rather than a rejection of the phenomenon of consequences. The figure of Satan in *Paradise Lost* occurs as a favorite in romantic thinking on consequences, and can serve as a model of the redefinition of consequences in the period.

Though theology has long maintained that the fall of man is perfectly suited to the transgression of eating the forbidden fruit, something too all-embracing and harsh about the effect sticks in the throat. "And just for that," we can image Eve saying to an incredulous Adam, "He's vexed." A sense of disproportion in the case has been difficult to keep separate from impiety, since it always seems to imply a challenge to the model of creation: if He made man that way something's radically wrong with the production, and we can't even hope for a trade-in. But it is idle to remonstrate with God, and possible that scrutiny of what man has created will reveal the grounds of a better understanding.

God as impregnable punisher and Satan as incorrigible culprit may be taken as a mythic utterance, in dualistic terms, of a prime crux in the human self-image. God would stand as a projection of omnipotence, of our intuition that somehow we can or might be fully adequate and free at any moment, and Satan as the projection of incompetence, of simultaneous intuition that we will somehow manage to misconceive and mishandle even the moments we fashion for ourselves. This double force of self-conviction is caught in a clear endless antagonism which has all the grandeur, and the tedium, of whatever is capable of neither interruption nor change.

The relationship that evinces life as opposed to fixity, and courage as opposed to stubbornness, is the one between Satan and man. This relationship has little to do with the dynamics of temptation, but rather with the dynamics of imaginative identification. Satan is our proleptic substitute, our stalking-horse in the field of self-enactment. The profile of his act and its consequences is, in the purest undisguised form, ours.

Two ways of accounting for Satan's fall are common in criticism of *Paradise Lost*. The first is of course theological, involving the cardinal sin of pride: Satan would occupy God's place, and hoist himself against nature to the top of the chain of being. His overweening ambition carries with it also a negative strain which is summed up in the Satanic motto *non serviam*. That is to say, he will not be a creature in relation to the Creator—hence, ineluctably, his expulsion and fall. This much is strikingly present, in both the narration and the initial colloquy of the poem's first few hundred lines. Satan considers it "Better to reign in Hell, than serve in Heaven," and as the narrator says,

... hee it was, whose guile
Stirr'd up with Envy and Revenge, deceiv'd
The Mother of Mankind; what time his Pride
Had cast him out from Heav'n, with all his Host
Of Rebel Angels, by whose aid aspiring

To set himself in Glory above his Peers
He trusted to have equall'd the most High.
[1.34–40]

Later in book 5 a second motive—on one level subordinate to the first, but also in many ways independent—is divulged; this motive may be called psychological. God announces, to the "circuit inexpressible" of the heavenly host, that he has "begot" his "only Son" as their "Head" and "Lord." As Milton says, "All seem'd well pleas'd, all seem'd, but were not all." The key exception is the quondam Lucifer, who "wak'd . . . fraught with envy" and "thought himself impair'd." A great deal may be made of the fact that he officially loses "his former name" and becomes Satan here and now in the poem; the "begetting" of Christ is counterbalanced but not counteracted by the "becoming" of Satan. Although his feelings are riddled with pride, it is not the same pride as his wanting "to have equall'd the most High." Rather, it is almost a pride of love, or wanting not to be excelled in the esteem of the most High. In this light, Gabriel's biting reminder that Satan more than anybody else had "Once fawn'd, and cring'd, and servilely ador'd/Heav'ns awful Monarch" has a poignant undertone; Satan had been happy, pleased with himself and his place in the "happy Realms of Light." And it may be as much to repair his image of himself—the psychological factor —as to wrest the chain of being into his own hands—the theological issue—that he undertakes his grand impiety.

Both these ways of accounting for Satan's fall revolve around questions of purpose, specific judgments and decisions which culpably violate the clear, given order of things. Both imply a proper manner of fitting into the universe, and a universe centered on God. A third way of accounting for Satan's fall having to do with his intrinsic state of being needs also to be recognized. It is effectively enunciated by Satan himself, in his very first utterance in Hell, and may be called the ontological explanation of the fall (Satan opportunistically wants to adopt it, but Milton exposes it as a fabrication of inflamed impiety). The point occurs where Satan, acknowledging how much "the stronger" God has shown himself "with his Thunder," goes on to make a wryly bitter reflection on the way he had gotten himself embroiled: ". . . and till then who knew/The force of those dire Arms?"

The surface idea here, especially in light of the question whether God's "high Supremacy" had been "upheld by strength, or Chance, or Fate" (1.131-32), is that God had not really shown his hand—or Arms—before, and thus had suckered Satan in. This presupposes a universe not of orthodoxy, but of possibility, a system somewhere between chaos and definitive creation, and one therefore vulnerable to political takeover. Satan evidently does not subscribe to what Honderich calls the prerequisite to any system of punishment: "considerable agreement as to what constitutes a harm." The poem may see, in Honderich's terms, "(i) a certain offence, (ii) the grievance to which it gives rise, and (iii) the penalty that would satisfy the grievance."[32] Satan sees (i) an opportunity, (ii) an undermining of that opportunity by the late revelation of its dangers, and (iii) a considerable to-do over his miscalculation. But his vision, or version, of things is clearly defective. He interprets the situation not in terms of what is there, but, as Byron says, according to "what he wants to see." But once we allow for Satan's tendency to shift blame away from himself, what essentially emerges is a twofold confession. He is confessing (1) a blithe ignorance, unaffected by a sense of anxiety or any intimation of potential surprises and consequences, and (2) an imagination which cannot conceive that its private universe may not be practical or real. His position is one of ontological blind-spotting, or, perhaps better, imaginative ignorance, combining a strong freedom with a deep vulnerability. It is at once perilous and piquant:

what power of mind
Forseeing or presaging, from the Depth,
Of knowledge past or present, could have fear'd
How such united force of Gods, how such
As stood like these, could ever know repulse?
For who can yet believe. . . .?

[1.625-31]

Lacking such imaginative ignorance, good angels like Abdiel deserve our commendation, but do not particularly earn our interest. Our interest in Satan, in some ways to our detriment in reading the poem, rests implicitly on the naked ontological component in his conduct, and tacitly sets a low value on its theology and psychology. After all, theologies may alter, or disappear with the disappearance of their gods; and Satan's experience of being flung "confounded" into a vast void to know a "dismal Situation" appears by now independent of any special psychology. We call it the human condition, taking a naturalistic rather than a theological view of the universe (it is noteworthy that naturalism, though the world—being more than Arnold saw—does have occasional joy, love, light, certitude, peace, and help for pain, follows a pessimistic bent). What remains, through various cultural environments, is the ontological component, the imaginative ignorance which seems indispensable to our confidence and fruitful engagement in the world, but which gently leads us on until we find ourselves in a living hell. Imaginative ignorance saves us from the paralysis or paranoia of our mortality, but only to betray us into weird fields of consequences.

Imaginative ignorance has a definite interest for what it tells us about the world, or its conditions; but a deeper interest attaches to what it may reveal about the nature of the individual actor. Something in Satan (belated prudence? nostalgia?) causes him to wish he had known better, but that very wish reinforces his defection by suggesting that he might have *done* better, and done God in. Every nuance of repentance in the poem is drowned by crescendoes of re-crimination in Satan. He thinks of himself for a moment as faithful, and promptly imagines someone else rebelling, thus reinstating himself in essence while hiding himself in person. This is but a tactic for evading consequences without confronting causes. For the cause is the very self whose nonexistence (or existence in any other quality) Satan finds so unimaginable. Unlike God, he can readily imagine a change in God, or in the universe, but not in himself. Here, in a nutshell, is a crux for finite human existence: what will give in the encounter between it and the world? And where does one find oneself between the poles of implicit redemption from our natures and acts and of limitless liability for them?

These two resolutions can best be understood in relation to Christ and Prometheus as paradigmatic figures in paradigmatic schemata. Each is exempt from mortal limitation and accident, Christ being the Son of God and Prometheus the Titan whose special attribute was, as his name reveals, forethought. Both function to redeem man, Christ with his blood from a state of sin, and Prometheus with fire from a state of savagery. Both can also be associated with the creation of man, Christ as God's coequal and Prometheus (in one version of the myth) fashioning man from mud under authority from Jupiter. But neither power nor their goodness can spare either of them agony, and it may be inferred how inexorable man's suffering will be if he is so weak and so fallible. This holds good in a Christian or in a Promethean universe, though Christ—fulfilling the old order by changing it—exists in a universe of conciliation and forgiveness, while Prometheus—acting within the given order by violating it—operates in a system of defiance and punishment. It is notable that Christ goes voluntarily, but not eagerly or uncritically, to his cross: "Eli, Eli, lama sabacthani"; and notable too that he is redeemed from suffering in the very act by which he redeems us from our sins. Suffering is not absent, indeed it is ineluctable, but it is also by covenant transitory, and is succeeded by progressively glorious manifestations: Resurrection, Epiphany, Ascension, Second Coming. Paradoxically, Prometheus goes unwillingly but enthusiastically to his suffering, and it lasts aeons. Not redemption but retaliation marks his world.

Though Prometheus shares with Christ the role of benefactor to mankind, it is proper to observe that he has intrinsically a different temper from Christ. Prometheus clearly does not make his large and basic gifts to man the end of his being; those gifts seem conceived as incidents in his relationship to Jupiter. The universe in which we see Prometheus lacks the intimacy, the human identification, and completeness of the position Christ takes. Prometheus identifies with neither man nor Jupiter; Christ is identical with both man and God. The endless confrontation of Prometheus and Jupiter then expresses the quality of a universe informed with division. The temporary estrangement (death) of Christ conveys the underlying principle of reconciliation and unison in this domain of thought. As paradigmatic figures, Prometheus and Christ are obviously not confined to a grammar of mythology or religion. They are a way of giving shape and tendency to the manifold terms of human engagement: psychological, social, political, as well as spiritual and cosmological. It is in this larger and more adaptable sense, rather than a rigid institutional one, that these two figures are invoked here.

In this larger sense, the issue seems to come down to the difference between an ordinance based on guilt, where reparation of a broken compact is available, and one based on denial and defiance, where nothing but resumption of a status quo is offered after disruption occurs. Transgression in the case of Prometheus is a personal transgression of the boundaries of power; in the case of Christ it is an assumed transgression, and that of the order of being (which for the self-aggrandizing culprit, man, is always imaginably fuller). In spite of the possibility of transgression, Prometheus is found in a universe of crushing fixation and repetition, as in the rock and feeding eagles; energy is always exerted in relation to and in the interest of the past, the status quo. Even change reinforces the conditions of the past. As god succeeds god, authority repeats authority, and the very gods prove subject to this principle of power. This is Jupiter's anxious recognition, that his rigidity may be as vulnerable to another as Prometheus is to him; he apprehends that it is power that enjoys permanence, rather than he. To make matters worse, the victim knows the weakness of the victimizer, and aggravates it by the gifts to man no less than by withholding from Jupiter the name of the goddess/mistress (Thetis) who will bear him the son more powerful than Jupiter himself. The degree of Jupiter's rage is measured not by that ominous prospect alone, but by his present loss of perquisites in a period where his lusts are countermanded by his lust for power; he dares not philander when any paramour may produce his downfall. The very fact that Prometheus can hold out against him gives proof of a curtailed power and a foretaste of supplanting.

But supplanting in fact is personal, not philosophical, and sustains the status quo under the guise of change. This stands in direct contrast to the change-as-fulfillment of the Christogenic world. For all the order of being, energy is directed in the universe of Christ toward the future, and evinces potentiality and progression. Or, of course, regression. But here is the cardinal symptom of the way of Christ: regression, or guilt, remains oriented—if somewhat perversely—toward the future. For guilt basically impairs the future, as the expunging of guilt essentially restores the future. It is worth stressing that guilt pertains less to what is done than to what is lost, and represents credulity as to what has become impossible out of the range of desirable things one has known.

It would be false, by opposing Christ and Prometheus, to leave the impression that they, as it were, compete for disciples. But it is striking that where the image and value of Christ's way is strongest, in the Middle Ages, Prometheus is visited with general neglect and is relegated to obscurity, and that where Prometheus swings to the forefront, in the romantic era, Christ's way diminishes and grows somewhat perverse, as in Coleridge's *Rime of the Ancient Mariner*, or is stated elliptically, problematically, as in Shelley's *Prometheus Unbound*. In moving from Chaucer to the present, we are moving in a parabolic pattern from Christ, or a creative morphology, to Prometheus, or a rigidity of supplanting. And, as has been suggested above, we eventually move to a position beyond Prometheus, one that might be called Janus-faced. On the one hand corrosive suffering exists, but there is no Jupiter—no power recognizable as source or orderer or defender of suffering—and on the other hand flagrant crimes occur, but there is no real consequence, no sense that the doer is identified with the deed and intrinsically bound to it, root and ramification.

Focusing on the romantic situation we may observe a decided interest in what may perhaps be called the personality of suffering, as opposed to its *physique*. Rather than torture, as something external, there is torment, and rather than exile, bewilderment. The case of Christabel readily shows this concern with inner personal states. Both torment and bewilderment are caught in her simple cry "Sure I have sinned." The maximum outward sign of what she undergoes is in the brief distortion of her face, but that very distortion serves as an emblem of her inner dislocation and distress. By the same token the fact that her formal protections are debilitated (watchdog, father) or foiled (mother, patron saints) or powerlessly intuitive (Bard Bracy)—all of this amounts to an index of the poem's central event, the disintegration of her command of the way she identifies, remembers, expresses, and chooses for herself. When the narrator describes her as "dreaming that alone which is," he refers to a correspondence between a private spontaneous state and some element or event from objective actuality (in fact, the obscure possession by Geraldine); but the correspondence is ominously unequal. The traffic goes only one way, with Geraldine coercing Christabel both physically and spiritually, and Christabel "spontaneously" dreaming in such a way as to perpetuate the coercion. Unable any longer to act on the outside world, even in her tentative and oblique sally beyond the castle precincts, Christabel is effectively thrown inward; and it is a measure of her tragedy that the "last place of refuge, [her] own soul" is invaded and defiled. Coleridge is of course focusing on the person wronged, rather than on the culprit, but the *personal* nature of the basic situation is clearly summarized by Schopenhauer in *The World as Will and Representation*:

The will of the first [individual] breaks through the boundary of another's affirmation of will, since the individual . . . compels the powers of that other body to serve his will, instead of serving the will that appears in that other body. Thus if from the will, appearing as the body of another, he takes away the powers of this body, and thereby increases the powers of his serving *his* will beyond that of his own body, he in consequence affirms his own will beyond his own body by denying the will that appears in the body of another. This breaking through the boundary of another's affirmation of will has at all times been distinctly recognized, and its concept has been denoted by the word *wrong* (*Unrecht*). For both parties instantly recognize the fact, not indeed as we do here in distinct abstraction, but as feeling.[33]

Even Byron, who seems to show such relish for the *physique* of suffering in *The Giaour*, say, or in *Mazeppa*, emerges decidedly on the side of personality. In the latter poem the pageboy Mazeppa is found out in his forbidden liaison with the wife of the blood-proud Count Palatine, who can think of no more terrible punishment for the boy than to have him lashed to a powerfully wild black stallion, and so shaken and battered to death. Surely this must seem as palpable a form of punishment as can be devised; the living horse and its wildness will probably come home to most readers with a keener sense that it could be happening to them than any iron maiden or guillotine or even hangman. And yet the executionary horse is at once more fearful and less sure than more conventional (and hence imaginatively more domesticated) instruments. The execution fails, and the reader is kept in no suspense about this fact. Thus already the authority of physical terms is put into the shade. The interest falls not on the originality or mercilessness of the Count's revenge, but on the peculiarity of what the boy Mazeppa suffers, that is to say, not on outward fact but on inward effect. Indeed, the horse comes to stand as an analog to Mazeppa's inner state: intense, fractious, guided by local impulse, intolerant of duties or curbs, full of impetuous power but lacking in civility or judgment or grace.[34] A major feature of the tale is its study of the contrast in character between Mazeppa as impetuous boy and venerable Old Man. In his latter avatar he is rational, disciplined, and considerate in his treatment of the horse he has ridden in battle, rather than confounded, victimized, and possessing useless gifts and strengths. A small detail may help to confirm the basic concern with personality, with the inward condition before the physical phenomenon, in the tale. To the end, across the five decades of his life from twenty to seventy years of age, Mazeppa harbors his love for Theresa, his hatred for her husband, the Count Palatine. This inextricable conflict of feeling ultimately outweighs the showier *physique* of the poem, and is a signpost to its essential interest in the actions and indestructible consequences of personality.

With *The Giaour* it is easier to see that the emphasis falls on personality, as opposed to paraphernalia—the harem-girl and her illicit love affair with the Giaour, her execution by drowning in a sack, his confrontation and destruction of her

Turkish master, and the Giaour's own withdrawal into a monastery and mysterious gloominess. The very style of narration, with its rapid cuts and cryptic bursts, tends away from the solidity and coherence of its own sensational *physique*; thus the description of Leila's drowning, the very pivot of the action, is by itself obscure and, even with the "Advertisement," surprisingly oblique and unemotional. The tale becomes less a matter of recounting the Giaour's deeds than of accounting (or failing to account) for his state of mind. The reader is not invited to witness an action, but to divine, from the slow mosaic composition, the quality and worth of a personality. Unlike Mazeppa, the Giaour escapes punishment for his "crime," but he does not escape its consequences. That crime, compounded by his revenge on "Black Hassan," has as its consequence his brooding isolation within the community of monks, just as the consequence of the poem is our brooding on him in his isolation. For all the sensational action, we should see brooding, the preoccupation of personality with itself, as the hallmark of the poem.

A movement away from the *physique* of punishment can be observed at large in the romantic era. Perhaps it is anticipated as early as the outset of the eighteenth century; certainly Swift in *A Tale of a Tub* implicitly comes out against the excesses and ruthlessness of punishment when he comments, on the story of the flayed woman, "how much it changed her for the worse," and later, in *Gulliver's Travels*, when he exposes Gulliver's fascination with war and mayhem as a kind of moral pre-adolescence. It is true that even in the romantic period public punishment was made into a form of entertainment (which, one would have thought, until the recent Gilmore case, was soon to die out for good). But the barbarities of punishment, even in the hidden form of incarceration,[35] were increasingly recognized and opposed. Beccaria's influential arguments for measure and compassion in *Of Crime and Punishment* were crucial in the developing change, but

Beccaria represents a spearhead of that "humanitarian altruism" which, as Carl Woodring says, crops up often in the romantic period and which is "epitomized by John Howard's report on prisons."[36] Clearly Beccaria and Howard are dealing with refinements of justice in action, but they are intrinsically also concerned with justice to individuals, and thereby with the sacred intangibility of personality. Thus poets like Byron and Wordsworth, in *The Giaour* and *The Borderers,* respectively, convey indignation and consternation at the excess and potential error of summary physical justice.

But it is important to acknowledge that the poets go beyond the reformers and carry their work decisively out of practical administration and into the realm of spirit. For all his enlightenment, Beccaria remains occupied with modes of punishment and does not really raise questions as to the principle thereof. His is the view summarized by Hegel in *The Philosophy of Right,* that punishment exists as the only instrument for "annulment" of a crime; the "point at issue," Hegel emphatically declares, "is wrong and the righting of it." This is powerful, but does not rule out awareness of the intricacy of a "wrong," and the injury done to the person and consciousness of the wrongdoer in his very performance of his misdeed.

The basis of the romantic preoccupation with the personality of suffering is not far to seek. Where suffering appears in most ages associated with retribution or repentance (or subrogation of the innocent for others who in principle or in fact seem ripe for retribution-repentance), in the case of the romantics it is distinctly connected with what I have called recognition. That is to say, it affects the sufferer's relation to himself and his conception of how vulnerable and treacherous his actions and even his presumptions can prove.[37] The element of transgression then involves the crossing of the boundaries of one's own competence; indeed, the whole question of thresholds in romanticism, so fruitfully taken up by Thomas Weiskel,[38] demands to be studied from the stand-point of consequences. The traditional "crossing" was from freedom to prison, say, or from sanity to an asylum, or from acceptance to coventry—all visible social changes. The typical "crossing" in romanticism is from one state to another in the economy of the self. Thresholds, as in Wordsworth's *The Borderers*, may retain a trace of the old dispensation, with features of social hovering or even actual crossing. But *The Borderers* itself amply shows that the root of concern is with the inner spiritual state, with conscience rather than crime. Marmaduke in fact passes beyond social sanction for his crime to personal grief and hoped-for purgation. His crime—a gullible and arrogant decision to leave his beloved's father to die—is so intricate in its relationships as to make its legal implications the least interesting of all. And his punishment, separation from humankind, is both self-imposed and, in time, potentially self-terminated. Perhaps at bottom "crime" and "punishment" are red-herring terms. The paramount issue revolves around Marmaduke's recognition of the consequences of his righteousness and his devotion to Idonea: namely, homicidal gullibility. A distinction between punishment and consequences may be of advantage here. Punishment refers to a condition of deprivation or restriction imposed by a self-sustaining authority in view of a fault or infraction which an individual under its jurisdiction perpetrates. Consequences are the effect on an individual whose behavior, whether accepted or beyond the ordinary, discloses to and in that individual dangers and cruelties that gainsay standard presumptions and so prove to be a radical and traumatic revelation of being. The romantic period, whatever sort of social action it purveys, is oriented toward consequences rather than punishment.

Anyone familiar with Byron's *The Prisoner of Chillon* will perceive how the poem converts a punishment situation into an exploration of consequences. But perhaps the point can be more tellingly made if we look at the way retribution-repentance is played down in a variety of romantic documents and the way, correspondingly, the personality and self-recognition of the actor are brought to the fore. The very precincts of repentance prove idle in *The Giaour* or in *Manfred*, where the Abbot is at once commendable and irrelevant. The unspecified but undoubtable transgression shared by Manfred and Astarte has meant for both of them an unbearable recognition, which undoes her at once and him in time (her death sharpens his recognition, and might actually cause it outright). The center of the play is found in the dynamism of transgression-recognition, and all the conventional agents of repentance (the Abbot) or retribution (the chthonian spirits) represent the world that is being outmoded.[39]

A sort of nullification of retribution-repentance may be seen as typical of romanticism; it recurs in works as various as Coleridge's *The Ancient Mariner* and Wordsworth's "The Thorn." In the former the Hermit's ministry proves inadequate, or perhaps inappropriate, to the self-recognition and self-conviction of the Ancient Mariner;[40] in the latter the prurient and vindictive townsfolk are kept at a remove from Martha Ray, whose torment and bewilderment at her moral and material losses as woman and as lover are more sacred than the law. Put another way, the consequences to Martha Ray go deeper than any punishment that might ensue from her wrongdoing. The question of punishment gives way, and consequences, mediated by the narrator, become the unspoken subject of the poem. The silences of the poem—Martha Ray's inarticulate cry, "Oh, misery!", and the narrator's careful professions of ignorance, "I cannot tell,"[41] —are reminiscent of the besetting silence of romanticism when it comes face to face with consequences, in the ultimate moment of recognition and responsibility.

Something of the fascination of romanticism with consequences (almost its readiness to make not just a necessity but a virtue of consequences) can be inferred from the

criticism which the poets level at those who cling to unex-
posed positions and so avoid the risk of consequences. In
effect avoidance entails its own consequences for the likes of
the "youth pined away with desire" and the "fair virgin
shrouded in snow," in Blake's "Ah, Sunflower"; or again for
the central figure in Blake's *The Book of Thel.* Thel's name
derives from the Greek word for "desire" or "will," but her
desire is trammeled by her intuition of what it may entail.
In effect she anticipates that the fruits of desire in action
become the consequences of desire, and she fixates on that
prolepsis. She reads her fate in the condition of worm and
cloud and lily and clod of clay,[42] because that is what she
desires to see; but she misreads or plays down the responses
of her metaphorical stand-ins, because they go counter to her
desire for mortal melancholy. (It is important to observe that
Thel upholds her negative or skeptical desires, against clear
and valid opposition; she has a certain self-will, then, but
ironically cannot exercise it toward a positive achievement.)
At bottom Thel, avoiding the domain of her sisters, is avoiding life;[43] avoiding the illustrative counsel of her natural
counterparts, she is avoiding wisdom as well as an enriched
participation in life.

The irony is that Thel avoids this participation in obedience
to a childish assumption that to avoid living is to avoid dying.
The sinister paradox is that the harder she holds back from
engagement, the faster she approaches dissolution. In an
intensely ambiguous scene, she is afforded the privilege of a
harmless visit to "the couches of the dead" and "her own
grave plot." The fact that "'tis given [her] to enter,/And to
return" by itself suggests at least the immortality of resurrection, and should allay her fear of mortality. But then the
experience of "the dead" cannot but confirm her fear; the
"voice of sorrow" that "breathed from the hollow pit"
(4. plate 6, 10) seems to be her own, and it declares nothing
but confusion and discontent. The ambiguity of the scene

repeats itself in the epithets used of Thel at this juncture in the poem. She is "the daughter of beauty" and "Queen of the vales" (3. pl. 5, 7, 14), with an obvious enlargement of her social and sexual power; but she is also "The Virgin" (4. pl. 6, 20), with a no less obvious contraction of her scope and confirmation of her desire for avoidance.

It turns out that this creature of avoidance has actually gone outside the vales of Har, her usual haunts; certainly she returns to them as the poem ends. But Thel is only indirectly involved in a pattern of transgression and recognition (in truth she refuses to acknowledge and abide by what her interlocutors bring to her attention, and spins from one to another in self-blinded wilfulness). She sneaks out of the vales, in effect, and we see her seeking not a dimension beyond them, like Christabel, but "the secret air"—somehow a denial in spirit of the gesture she makes in actuality. We have to think of her as shut off, shut in, when it proves impossible to see her: "Down by the river of Adona her soft voice *is heard*" (1. pl. 1, 4; italics added). The only threshold she overtly crosses is an illusory one, the threshold of death which is, in the first place, nullified for her, and in the second place essentially indistinguishable from the terms of life she has chosen. The poem, I think, appreciates her powers of intuition and reflection, and understands the nature of her fear. In a sense she is superior to her sisters going through a kind of monotonous perpetuity: "The daughters . . . led round their sunny flocks." But for all its sympathy the poem also demonstrates the narrowness and danger of her fear. At the end Thel ignominiously "fle[es] back" to the vales of Har, not as an enlightened but as a frightened soul, so that she is distinctly inferior to her sisters and inadequate in herself— her reflective virtues have recoiled upon themselves. She flees from the evidence of mortality which after all she carries within. As Horace says, "Coelum non animum mutant, qui . . . currunt." Thel does not really transgress the vales, does not come to any special recognition for better or worse, but she does not enjoy safety or impunity. Rather she demonstrates for romanticism the fact that to seek to avoid consequences beyond is to suffer them at home. Poison breathes from the walls of the fortress we have acquired against the world.

The syndrome of transgression and recognition, consequences and silence presents itself often enough to be thought romantic.[44] Yet it is not a simple syndrome. One of the most striking embodiments of the principle of consequences in romantic literature will be found in Blake's *Visions of the Daughters of Albion*. But the poem stands out for its refusal to stop with the characteristic silence of recognition; instead, it breaks through to speech as it were on the far side of silence, when Oothoon defends herself against the very idea of consequences. Through her, as a result, we must ask whether consequences in the form of silent self-recognition constitute a natural law of the romantic mind, or a cultural norm of the romantic period.

If Thel's "transgression" of the vale-world is secretive and subjective, Oothoon's is forthright and principled. Like Thel she acknowledges a kinship with the natural world, but unlike Thel she understands that the kinship stems from her own capacity to make metaphors: "Art thou a flower!" she apostrophizes the marigold, "art thou a nymph! see thee now a flower; Now a nymph!" (1.6–7). Also unlike Thel, Oothoon is prompt to respond to the living counsel of her natural counterpart *carpe diem* (or *florem*). But the fallacy of identification that Foucault has analyzed[45] does not work so well for Oothoon as it does for the dark-willed Thel. The difference between woman and flower, nature and humanity comes home for Oothoon with all its wrenching finality. The cheerful picking of the self-offered "flower" and "nymph" turns out to forecast not her "exulting swift delight" and yielding to her lover Theotormon, but a terrible deflowering by the arch-rapist Bromion. Instant, harsh, and evidently final are the consequences of her transgressing the vales of Leutha. Oothoon's initial response is one of stunned dismay, distress, bafflement; she is as inarticulate as the betrayed Martha Ray ("her woes appalld [Bromion's] thunders hoarse"; 1.18), and as paralyzed as Christabel ("Oothoon weeps not: she cannot weep! her tears are locked up"; 2.11). We are essentially here in the early phase of the *Visions*, and the action and its upshot—transgression and the endemic silence of recognition—seem accomplished. But the poem has some way to go, and the rest is anything but silence. The overt dramatic action is swift and bitter, and gives way to the deeper, prolonged action of the mind which in Oothoon is shocked into interpretation and philosophy.

Oothoon enunciates, debates, and eventually transcends silence. To begin with, she makes the voice an instrument or metaphor of purity: "I call with holy voice! kings of the sounding air,/Rend away this defiled bosom that I may reflect./The image of Theotormon on my pure transparent breast" (2.15-17). If it is as "kings of the *sounding air*" that the eagles have power to disclose "Her pure breast,"[46] then metonymically the sounding air contributes to disclosure and, contrariwise, silence must lend itself to enshrouding. Silence is intrinsic to the situation of transgression-recognition, but not absolute in it. In a sense the silence represents a kind of captivation by the moment of recognition; certainly with the underlying political freight of the *Visions* Blake suggests a correlation between inarticulateness and imprisonment: "*Enslavd*, the Daughters of Albion *weep*: a trembling lamentation/Upon their mountains; in their valleys. *sighs* toward America" (1.1.2; italics added). Oothoon's access of speech after the consequences of transgression then not only potentially frees her but also extends freedom to the Daughters of Albion who "eccho back" what she says.

Oothoon's breaking of silence is required to free Theotormon as well as herself from the captivation of Bromion's rending "thunder" (it is as though, as form succeeded chaos at creation, enunciation must succeed thunder, or unshaped sound, for the creation of personal integrity and freedom). Theotormon also is arrested by the superstition that Oothoon's rape, more than incidentally resulting from her going beyond (trans-gressing) her vale-world, *answers to it* as a necessary event. The action of the poem is then not only largely verbal, but also forensic. The basic scene is a tableau[47] of fixed feeling and philosophy that Oothoon strives to move into a genuine correspondence with moving life. In this tableau, Bromion stands for oppression, as a figure exhibiting conviction without the least understanding or sensitivity; Theotormon stands for authority, as a figure attached to principles but lacking in affection or confidence; and Oothoon stands between them as a figure of cabined hope, whose understanding and affection are at the mercy of oppression and authority.

All that Oothoon achieves is a variation of the tableau, as prostitutes replace the rapist Bromion at the third corner of the triangle, and Theotormon becomes the advantaged male where she herself had been the victimized female:

Silken nets and traps of adamant will Oothoon spread,
And catch for thee girls of mild silver, or of furious gold;
I'll lie beside thee on a bank & view their wanton play
In lovely copulation bliss on bliss with Theotormon.
                                    [7.23-26]

But Oothoon's effort to achieve change, rather than mere variation, warrants close attention. Though she does not, like Thel, give her name to the poem, she dominates the *Visions* far more than Thel does her *Book*, bringing to it both thought and passion, travail and magnanimity. She gives the title-bearing Daughters a voice. She makes the substance of their Visions. At the outset she knows what she wants, "breasts" and "whole soul," but she hardly knows what a flower is, let alone herself. The grounds for her development are anything but favorable. She experiences the traumatic stress of being raped, and the resulting social stigma (emphasized, ironically, by the culprit Bromion) and spiritual isolation (Theotormon forsakes her, and no one comes to her aid). Nevertheless Oothoon presents one of the finest and most compelling images to be found before Henry James, of a woman coming into her own under pervasive adversity.

It is a sense of anomaly that instigates Oothoon's quarrel with the consequences of her transgressing her vale-world, a sense that it makes no sense for the man who has victimized her and the man for whom she has come to be victimized to hold that victimization against her: she has *done* nothing and meant none of what has befallen her. This sense of anomaly will evolve into a sense of injustice, in the attack on Urizen, and Oothoon herself can be seen to move from a position of inquisitive instinct to one of independent principle and, finding nothing consonant in the world, resigned magnanimity.

Oothoon suffers not only under Bromion's physical coercion, but also tacitly under moral coercion from the system she at first seems blithely unconscious of. We can read back to her having acquired a certain theological lore when she turns against Urizen and his puritanic order:

O Urizen! Creator of men! mistaken Demon of heaven:
Thy joys are tears! thy labour vaine, to form men to thine image.
How can one joy absorb another? are not different joys
Holy, eternal, infinite! and each joy is a Love.

[5.3–6]

Her familiarity with a morality of punishment can actually be discerned right after Bromion's assault on her. In "calling Theotormons Eagles to prey upon her flesh" she becomes a Promethean self-punisher; she is like the Titan not just in being rent by eagles, but in taking on that suffering for an act of enlargement and love.

She is unlike Prometheus, however, in that dynamism of nature which enables her to treat the eagles as an episode, rather than an eternal necessity, in her relationship with Theotormon. Her sense of anomaly suggests the beginning of her freedom from moral and philosophical rigidity, and that freedom is advanced at once by her conversion of the eagles, the emblem of rigidity, from an element in an imposed mythology to an illustration of a self-developed vision. When she puts it to Theotormon that "the Eagle returns / From nightly prey, and lifts its golden beak to the pure east" (2.25–26), she takes the "king of the sounding air" out of mythology and puts it into nature, takes it from Theotormon's scheme of values into her own. Thus what has seemed his instrument helps to establish her underlying purity (preying, for agent and victim, passes with the night), and equally works against his position of simplistic puritanism.

The eagle that "lifts its golden beak to the pure east" is but one of many analogies that tumble forth from Oothoon in her defense of her purity (2.23–27). Her defense quickly modulates into counterattack, against Theotormon who is so lacking in discernment ("to him the night and morn / Are both alike"; (2.37–38), and against authorities and all "They told me" (2.30, 31). Her crisis is causing her to look at herself, at the world, and at her mentors effectively for the first time, and she finds that received wisdom (what "they" told her) amounts to a constrictive falsehood. As with the proof of her purity, she goes to nature to establish "their" perniciousness and error. But her use of nature now goes beyond straight analogy—she is analytical, inferential, challenging with logic:

They told me that I had five senses to inclose me up.

. . . .

With what sense is it that the chicken shuns the ravenous hawk?[48]
With what sense does the tame pigeon measure out the expanse?

. . . .

Ask the wild ass why he refuses burdens: and the meek camel
Why he loves man: is it because of eye ear mouth or skin
Or breathing nostrils?[49] No. for these the wolf and tyger have.

[2.31-3.9]

The rapidity of Oothoon's responses and development stand
out sharply against Bromion's bluster—"thunder" does him
too much credit—and Theotormon's pathos. She enunciates a
new law of personal value that claims enhancement—and not
just recovered purity—after contamination: "Sweetest the
fruit that the worm feeds on" (3.16). Nor is she long taken up
with her own interests and needs, as sophisticated as she
makes them. Rather she pursues the question of value into
society and politics, religion and time. Here she is scarcely
defending herself any longer against the curious conspiracy
of depreciation that Bromion and Theotormon join in against
her. Rather her every word has a dark trenchancy of attack
against the entire system of judgment and authority:

With what sense does the parson claim the labour of the farmer?[50]
What are his nets & gins & traps. & how does he surround him
With cold floods of abstraction, and with forests of solitude,
To build him castles and high spires, where kings & priests may dwell.
Till she who burns with youth, and knows no fixed lot; is bound
In spells of law to one she loathes: and must she drag the chain
Of life, in weary lust! must chilling, murderous thoughts obscure
The clear heaven of her eternal spring?

[5.17-24]

It is but a short step from this to enunciation of a new law of
conduct: "Take thy bliss O Man!/And sweet shall be thy
taste & sweet thy infant joys renew!" (6.2-3).

At first spontaneously, perhaps even a little selfishly, speaking out, Oothoon ends by offering magnanimous, formal
judgments for all humankind. But is speech by itself sufficient
to break the spell of silence that falls around the romantic
complex of transgression-recognition? Perhaps the versatility
and persistence of Oothoon's attack on the order oddly

divided among Bromion, Theotormon, and Urizen should mean a decisive victory for her; actually, these are the versatility and persistence born of desperation and reared on a Sisyphean test. Urizen does not hear, Bromion does not listen, and Theotormon does not understand what Oothoon says. Her *speaking* is invaluable in relation to herself,[51] but as far as her audience is concerned her speech must be judged of dubious worth. To some extent the refrain that is supposed to double up her speech by echoing reduces it to empty sound, or at best the inarticulation of "woes" and "sighs": "The Daughters of Albion hear her woes, & eccho back her sighs." And the fiery immediacy and creativity of her speech are reduced to stubborn monotony (and a genuine desolation) when at the end of the *Visions* it is revealed that she makes that speech once a day: "Thus *every morning* wails Oothoon" (8.11; italics added). Oothoon has gone beyond silence, but not after all beyond consequences.

The *Visions of the Daughters of Albion* remains striking for its championship of sexual liberty and its scalding contempt for "this hypocrite modesty!/This knowing, artful, secret, fearful, cautious, trembling hypocrite" (6.16-17). Within this general stand it becomes a matter of special note that Oothoon treats Theotormon as a victim no less than herself: "Why hast thou [Urizen] taught Theotormon this accursed thing [jealousy]?" (7.13). She in effect forgives him for proving incapable of looking beyond the accident of her rape to the essence of her being. Hers is no simple act of forgiveness, of course. In her readiness to "catch" for him "girls of mild silver, or of furious gold" (7.24), she is rising above Urizenic jealousy to express an extraordinary, giving love; but she is also expressing superiority and a serene contempt: "Oothoon shall view [Theotormon's] dear delight [with provided girls], nor e'er with jealous cloud/Come in the heaven of generous love, nor selfish blightings bring" (7.28-29). In a sense she is making the double standard a double bind for him—the inflexible upholder of Urizenic proprieties will receive "girls" from a woman whose wrongs he does not think to rectify and whose rights he cannot recognize. She is, in his warped view, celibate but not pure; he is licentious but untouched.

And yet the central phenomenon remains Oothoon's forgiving him. It is an important event in the romantic complex of consequences, because it extends and authenticates her *forgiveness of herself*. For what can she have to forgive herself? For her mortality. For being subject to chance and to force. For the fact that her best will can be betrayed into Bromionic hands, and that her choice of freedom from what "they told me" entails such limiting consequences.

Forgiveness here may represent the most vital contribution of the *Visions of the Daughters of Albion* to the romantic format of consequences. It is an unspecific and yet very intimate form of forgiveness, originating in the intrinsic condition of the self, and indicating in one stroke the two extremes of that self—its mortality and its magnanimity. The forgiveness that we remember from the old dispensation has no play; after all, where Oothoon is concerned no sin is committed, no one is sinned against, no deprivation/repentance is exacted. And yet the very lack of theological protocol makes the forgiveness more decisive and complete. Perhaps it anticipates an ideal of modern therapeutic psychology, which so emphasizes self-acceptance and openness to life, as against intimidated obedience to law.

The ideal of self-forgiveness was (and remains) by and large a distant beacon, rarely glimpsed. Blake's preoccupation with total social regeneration keeps him from resorting to it often; the Josephite forgiveness that he builds into *Jerusalem* (3.61) as a transcendent act of human love seems more typical of him. It is left for Shelley to set forth the positive dimensions of self-forgiveness, and he does so in a context where obsession, the ultimate barrier to self-forgiveness, appears at a premium, that is to say, in *Prometheus Unbound*. For the basis of the enormous transformation in the stand Prometheus takes toward Jupiter is the former's letting go of the principle of defiance or *justification of a suspect position*. It should be noted that as long as Prometheus operates within the Jovian power system, everything he does, including benefactions to man, belongs in that framework and is judged accordingly. Fire for man is only a new phenomenon; what is needed to break the Jovian world-set is a new principle. This emerges only when Prometheus relaxes from the sly or savage opposition he has shown Jupiter. In his utter inability to recall his curse against Jupiter, he has cleansed himself not only of attraction but of guilt in relation to it. To forget is to have forgiven. At a stroke Prometheus translates himself from a world of punishment to a world of consequences, and here, uniquely, the consequences are both articulate and affirmative.

In the romantic period in general the sources of guilt vary as never before, including Christabel's charitable impulses and the Ancient Mariner's unreflecting self-expression and Manfred's calculated experiment with Astarte. And guilt itself operates according to a new economy. Still in the Renaissance guilt, or sin, is the occasional negation of a known and definitive good within a framework capable of surviving that negation: as Spenser says, Night has her power, but Jove rules both night and day. But here in the romantic period guilt is a matter of revealing or releasing a new dimension of experience that cannot be expunged. In theological terms, Satan errs when he claims for himself and promises Eve a gain in knowledge springing from transgression; all that amounts to, Milton bluntly states, is the knowledge of good lost and evil gained. But in the romantic dispensation, as Blake and Shelley eloquently attest, it is harder to dispute Satan, even if the gain is only a grim awareness of vulnerability and finitude. In truth, even the latter bugaboos do not survive scrutiny.

The Marriage of Heaven and Hell embodies the argument that we impose our dreads on reality, which emerges in beauty and grace when we view it with open courage. Browning, in *Sordello*, seems almost to provide a gloss for Blake with his comment "what seems a fiend may prove an angel" (3.988).

Here, finally, the ontological component of Satan's guilt comes articulately to the fore. But whereas Milton completely encloses the personal shock of consequences within an inviolable cosmic structure, the romantic poets cannot but enunciate that shock as part of the emerging cosmos of definition, or an emerging definition of cosmos. Imaginative ignorance is no longer a specific moral fault, but a general condition, indeed a general activity of being, with the result that to do anything is to have done more than was bargained for, and to suffer more than the very universe of action could have foreseen. Christabel is innocent, but her innocence provides a purchase for an evil which the elaborate system of protections embodied in the castle cannot prevail against. Evil occupies innocence, as Geraldine occupies Christabel, and no amount of lamentation, indignation, or poetic diligence can remove the resulting distortion/expansion of the area and definition of experience. We are in the orbit of a bleak, naturalistic conception of human liability, with the suggestion that to be finite is to be infinitely liable, and we can hardly avoid the observation that this is taking effect explicitly against the old order of redemption. Geraldine, representing the force of a dis-eased and perverted naturalism, will have her "hour," notwithstanding Christabel's mother or her very name (Christ's beauty).

The mind of the Ancient Mariner offers a graphic illustration of the case. "O shrieve me, shrieve me, holy man!" he cries, as it were for his own sake, and he offers for the sake of mankind a vision of a total community of grace:

O sweeter than the marriage-feast
'Tis sweeter far to me
To walk together to the kirk
With goodly company!—

To walk together to the kirk,
And all together pray,
While each to his great Father bends,
Old men, and babes, and loving friends
And youths and maidens gay!

But this is not to be. This pious wish is the light side of a confession of clinging impiety. He cannot be purged and healed, but remains as Milton would say "obnoxious" to his intolerable memory, his intolerable discovery of his wild nature and of the wild order of the universe.

Not every revision or avoidance of the structure of redemption in romanticism is as overt as we have seen in Byron and Coleridge. Keats's ode "To Autumn," for example, confesses the annihilating power of time even as it tends to annihilate time itself, without departing in the least from a natural frame of reference. The poem exploits language to create the consciousness of a permanent state of passing time. Its final words—"gathering swallows twitter in the skies"—may suggest either early spring or late autumn, and the effect of the present participle "gathering" is to represent both a transitory action and a dynamically invariable state. The swallows that are gathering in fact also stay—ontologically *are*, gathering— in language and consciousness. If we recall, further, that the direction upward is identified with life in the poem—the gnats rise or fall "as the soft wind lives or dies"—then their being in the skies intimates life even though they gather against winter. In effect the destructive powers of time are vividly recognized, at the same time as the independent, even constitutive power of *recognition* is discovered and embodied in such a way as to nullify the felt effects of time. It is the use of language, not as in *Antony and Cleopatra* to transform and overpower circumstances, but to see their self-contradiction ("full-grown lambs" is both imaginatively deft and linguistically "false" and wrenching); spring and autumn—gathering swallows, full-grown lambs—are possible together *without paradise*. Satan's conflict between his identity, which is singular and insistent, and his dependent creaturely state is avoided, and so is his choice between heaven and hell. In effect Keats has broken the hostile force informing the structure of redemption in that it always responds to and exploits a psychology of dread. Satan enunciates this dread and converts it into aggression. Conflict is the metier of his mind, of his world. Possession and loss, mastery and submission, redemption and damnation: these are the governing terms of Satan's experience, but more, they are the implicit values of *thinking* for preromantic England. What Keats almost casually accomplishes in the ode "To Autumn" is the dismissal of the assumptions of antithetical thinking, and the seeing through to that persistent presence of things in altering form which allows for identity without creating rigid institutional states.

This I would be inclined to view as an avoidance of the structure of redemption. A more direct confrontation of that structure presents itself in *The Recluse*, which also maintains the romantic capacity for inclusion that Keats consummately expresses. A certain generic inclusiveness is apparent where Wordsworth redefines the grounds and goals of epic. As he challenges "the abyss" of the human mind, we may hear an echo of *Paradise Lost*, an echo and a tacit dismissal. Wordsworth, having acknowledged Milton's poetic ascent into heaven and descent into hell, seems here to call up *Satan's* mytho-historical plunge into the abyss of space. But he breaks down the opposition between Milton and Satan, and synthesizes the two figures. In fact he outdoes Satan in the personal exultation with which he meets the occasion. But clearly Wordsworth's abyss is removed from the framework of perdition and salvation. Milton's moral-religious agoraphobia (based on opposition) is Wordsworth's spiritual-naturalistic opportunity (the basis of inclusion). No wonder that the images of the "way" at the end of *Paradise Lost* and at the beginning of *The Prelude* are so much at odds with each other. Adam and Eve, "with Providence their guide," take their solitary way in sober buoyancy, and there is a strong sense that their situation is viable only because they have Providence for their guide. Wordsworth is much more on his own: "free / Free as a bird to settle where I will." And he is much more spontaneous and as it were exempt alike from rule and happenstance: ". . . and should the chosen guide / Be nothing better than a wandering cloud, / I cannot miss my way." In Milton the abyss and the way are both predictable and effectual, working within the ordained universe. For Wordsworth both abyss and way are emergent, fecund, tending toward some ultimate vision of universe.

Where punishment responds to behavior, let us remember that consequences respond to being, and Shelley's Prometheus has come into a purified and gracious state of being. As Paradise deteriorates to reflect the fall of Adam and Eve, the Promethean world appreciates to manifest his recovery. With the beginning of act 2 the play is a dynamic pageant of recognition and celebration of a recreated pristine order. Panthea and Ione see the initiation of the new in Asia's sleep, and the three of them together cover the new world with continual surprise; cries of "look" and "listen" herald physical change, and the sustained songs of description throughout deepen perception into understanding and praise.

It is noteworthy that the positive consequences of *Prometheus Unbound* take the form of ingression (as opposed to transgression). The bower may be called the consummate place for Prometheus and Asia. They have lived the life of ultimate transgression, at the farthest reaches of separation from society and convention, and they know it is not a great improvement over stifling social convention. They go back in to a place that is, like Paradise, prepared for them, a place with the added virtue that they are not confined to it. One may ask why the self-forgiveness of Prometheus transforms the world whereas Oothoon's barely reaches far enough beyond her to be nullified by Theotormon. Perhaps it is because only men are allowed the scope to bring about radical change, though of course women, being more victimized and frustrated, as Asia is equally with Oothoon, need change more. Not until we get to Henry James and Virginia Woolf do women find a context and a field for self-determination and material influence over the values of a fictive world.

It may be asked, however, whether the romantic writers had not paved the way for James and Woolf. Even in relation to the question of consequences, as they advance beyond the *physique* of punishment to a preoccupation with the personality of mortal experience, they consistently accord women a central *place*.[52] The fact that a central social *power* is at the same time withheld is consonant with the general tenor of the romantic period as a literature of power, with the emphasis on human value and meaning, rather than a literature of power politics, with the emphasis on formal social relations. Paradoxically, too, women are less bound to repetition and routine, more open to innovation than men, because they are deprived of practical power. That their openness entails great uncertainty, *for the same reason*, becomes a basis of the romantic concern with consequences. Whether they tempt men across safe-but-stultifying boundaries, as in *Lamia* or "La Belle Dame Sans Merci," or whether men tempt them, as in *Manfred* or, implicitly, "A Slumber Did My Spirit Seal" and *Visions of the Daughters of Albion*, the intuition of a new potential—and new risks—is inseparable from the feminine figure. Likewise the projection of a new potential, as in "Kubla Khan," and its achievement, in *Promethues Unbound*, is intrinsically tied up with the feminine figure. Even so, the force and value of that figure is but intimated in terms of the question of consequences. A fuller inquiry into that force and value will complement this study and add an important dimension to our understanding of romanticism.

The Feminine as the Crux of Value

Two great sexes animate the world.
Milton
Mistrust and jealousy animate the sexes.
Anon.

In the division of the sexes we may recognize not merely what Nietzsche calls "a piece of nature,"[1] but also a redundancy. For at root "sex" and "division" come down to the same notion: the former means a cutting or separation (from Latin *seco*) and the latter means a parting asunder or separation (from Latin *dividere*). The redundancy cannot be put in its place by grammatical authority, though. It carries a subtle message, as a mark of multiplication and formalization. If "sex" means separation in fact, "division" means separation in spirit, in principle.

There are those who would see it otherwise, and have as a motto the following: it takes two poles to make a world, and neither in itself is livable. But the spirit of division is not so readily exorcised. It is like dust in the air, everywhere and yet, unless an intense slant beam of light is thrown through it, unnoticed. Then again it is particularized in many of the cultural phenomena that charm their way into our innermost system of expectation, before we even know that this is also a defense system. Let us consider, for example, the widespread tale of the Sleeping Beauty, that of the transformed hag, and that of the frog metamorphosed into a prince by the maiden's kiss. Don't all of these tales, notwithstanding drastic differences on the surface, conduce to a conviction of male primacy?[2] The prince awakens the sleeping beauty who would have remained, without his attention, as good as dead;[3]

besides, her "death" results from handling a spinning-wheel, a traditional female exercise. By innuendo, what is female kills, what is male restores to life.

The story of the transformed hag, perhaps best known in Chaucer's *The Wife of Bath's Tale*,[4] seems like a way of correcting the inequity of the privilege males enjoy vis-à-vis females. But its effects are curiously conservative. The injured woman is first of all imposed by law on the man who has spotted and despoiled her in the fields. This decision is rendered as a form of punishment—no happy omen for the relationship between them here. Then she issues the ultimatum: he can have her (since have her he must) as a hag and faithful, or as a beauty and unfaithful. Because he has neither the standards nor the character to choose, he begs off and tells her to settle the question for him. And, treating this as a concession of freedom and authority to her, she turns mellow and decides to give herself to him as beautiful and faithful. Clearly he has the best of all possible worlds—*droit de seigneur* in the fields, where he first has his way with her, and utter satisfaction in the castle, where again he has his way. Neither punishment nor consequences befall him; those are part of a dismal and unreal interlude before male privilege reasserts itself.

No two stories could appear more at odds than "The Sleeping Beauty" and "The Frog King." In the former the male by a kiss redeems the female from death, in the latter the female by a kiss redeems the male from animality. Are not the tables turned, and is not balance achieved? Hardly so. Once again the princess proves to be "dead" to the realities and responsibilities of the world. She ignores her promise to share her place at table, her glass, her plate, and her bed with the frog who has aided her in recovering her special "golden ball." On the other hand the frog proves kind, wise, just (if insistently so). The princess is obliged by the king her father to keep her word to the frog—male authority collaborating with male

opportunity. When the frog upon being kissed at last[5] emerges
as a prince, we can only infer that it is her imagination, her
reluctance to face reality, that has constituted him in a
grotesque figure.[6] The kiss in this instance does not mean a
conferring of power, but a concession to it. The female serves
as a foil to male power, whether kissing or kissed. A striking
analog of such privileging of the male appears in the exchange
of property that commonly accompanies marriage. When the
bride's family gets material compensation, it is for the loss of
her services, and constitutes a mark of her status as a convenient object. When the bride brings a dowry and the groom's
family gets a material advantage, it is as an inducement for
him to assume responsibility for her. The female is demeaned
in either case, and male primacy sustains itself under opposite
manifestations.

It has even been plausibly argued that the biblical story of
creation embodies a male forensic myth that takes away from
the female two richly authoritative functions: childbirth and
infant nurture.[7] Male primacy on the social level escalates
here to male priority in time, and furthermore the male
determines the female being by the sacrifice of a rib for her
substance. (A comparable maneuver occurs in the initiation
rites of the Sherbro of Sierra Leone, where the male "min"
or spirit is supposed to eat the adolescent youth and after-
wards regurgitate him as a complete adult, with a new name;
thus clearly supplanting the original mother.) When, in Milton's version of the creation myth, Adam calls Eve away from
her own image in the water, we may make an association with
the Sleeping Beauty. Eve is unconsciously taken up with herself, lost to reality, and Adam has to call her to a larger truth
and responsibility. Her failure in relation to reality is rein-
forced by the fact that she is fascinated with her face *in
water*, always symptomatic of the amorphous state of things.

But in the prevailing order of giving precedence to the male
even where the female seems to gain an equity or an edge, one

outstanding case can be found going the other way. This occurs at the end of Aeschylus's *Oresteia* trilogy, where Athena appears to give primacy to the male while in effect working out an independent and original principle of relationship with the female Furies. The latter are of course called the Eumenides (the Gracious Ones), not ironically but proleptically. The subject of this third play, significantly named after them, is as much their conversion as it is the salvation of Orestes; in fact Orestes and his sponsor Apollo by and large get shunted aside. Also, the agent of conversion is a woman, Athena, acting with the kind of influence and authority that, say, the paternal king enjoys in "The Frog King." The negotiation between Athena and the Eumenides is the culmination of the trilogy and should be more carefully assessed within that context than the habit of treating it as symbolic cultural history[8] allows us to do.

Basically, *The Oresteia* presents a series of antagonisms of male against female, with incidental alliances (as of Orestes and Electra) along the way. Then *The Eumenides* opens with the novel male alliance of Orestes and Apollo against the novel female unanimity of the Furies. That male alliance proves ineffectual, though Orestes as a male is supposedly favored by one of the "adversary" sex, Athena. The eventual alliance between Athena and the Furies takes on special importance as resolving an unstable system of antagonisms and alliances throughout the trilogy. In culminating the series, however, it also moves decisively into new relations and values. It is the first female alliance; the first alliance based on persuasion and equity, rather than expediency; and above all the first alliance that involves reconciliation rather than an escalation of hostilities.

The terms of reconciliation can be simply explained: Athena recognizes that one basic right can disagree with another, and that accordingly two rights can make a wrong. Instead of denying and rejecting the Eumenides, she redefines their function and character. She takes away their place—the dark vindictive forequarters of the mind—only to give them another place of equal significance in the broad, deliberative framework of the Agora. In this way, the positive principle of a place for a place both preserves and supplants the negative principle (hitherto upheld by the Furies) of an eye for an eye.

The conversion of the Furies into the Eumenides, based as it is on persuasion and consent, preserves internal continuity of nature while accepting sharp alteration in form. It is a natural conversion, a response to a cogent self-revelatory process, with little of the emotional shock or physiological glamor that we find in, say, a metamorphic fairy tale like "The Frog King." In all but one respect. For one distinctly physiological "miracle" accompanies the change of values in the Eumenides: the erstwhile Furies become young again, and radiate, if they do not quite embody, loveliness.[9] Their conversion, then, would seem to fall into the same category as the tale of the transformed hag. The points of analogy are clear enough; but *The Eumenides* here, as in so many other respects, departs from the typical pattern and the typical effect.

For one thing, the Eumenides are not ugly or beautiful to grieve or gratify any male. The degree of pulchritude they show depends on the degree of stern fury (*Erinyes*) or of gracious persistence (*Eumenides*) with which culture and principle require them to protect the cause of justice in a society. They are not really, like the typical transformed hag, capable of bargaining with fidelity—their fidelity is not personal and conditional, but abstract and absolute. Furious or gracious they hold to the same cause. Their recovery of youth and beauty symbolizes the falling away of fear, resentment, desperation, rage, and pain at the wrongs they feel they suffer as females and upholders of justice, and symbolizes at the same time an access of confidence, appreciation, and joyful anticipation of their enhanced position in the Athenian order. Their appearance corresponds to *their own* condition of spirit, and not to the demands of another, especially not of a male. They have greater integrity and significance in and of themselves than is customary in the transformed-hag pattern, and this status is enhanced by the substitution of a female for a male authority figure as well as the adoption of negotiation in place of ultimatum where their transformation occurs.

The fact is that in the alliance between Athena and the Eumenides two major revisions of social order occur: mere authority is repudiated (Athena wins them over, she does not triumph over them); and power begins to distribute itself rather than imposing itself on others (Athena gives up some of her putative prerogative to them). It is tempting to conclude that a male way is given over in all this, with a female way supervening. Historically, of course, the Athenian social system continued to be run by males (*plus ça changeait, plus c'était la même chose*). But Aeschylus both structurally and conceptually locates all hope for betterment in a redefinition of female status and function. The same cannot be said for Orestes (let alone Agamemnon); he hesitates before doing in Clytemnestra, and recognizes the ambiguity of his position, without coming to a higher point of reconciliation and redefinition. It is the Eumenides who, as their renaming suggests, come to new ground, and it is through the female goddess Athena that they do so.[10]

The mosaic image of the female in *The Oresteia*—Iphigenia and Cassandra as victims, Electra and Clytemnestra as avengers, and Athena as creative understanding leading the Eumenides beyond victimization and vengeance to positive dignity and gracious power—proves more dynamic, fuller, richer than that of the male. This, however, leads to the irony that worse men make better women, the irony that has plagued society and personality in any generation not too smug to perceive it. To be better is to be taken advantage of by the worse. The onus reverts to the male, to his willingness and ability to pursue his own human betterment, to pursue not the female but the feminine that completes him and enriches social life.

It will come as no surprise that Greek literature repeatedly shows the male, especially the male in authority, in fear of any such improvement. Aeschylus himself shows it as a material factor in *The Oresteia*, when Agamemnon expressed dread of being softened, womanized by Clytemnestra. But of course the situation is fraught with irony and even malice. Neither husband nor wife has a positive conception of the feminine; they work in terms of the privilege of male or female roles. Agamemnon sees only a loss or defeat in accepting the Oriental[11] splendors Clytemnestra lays before him. And he is right, within the narrow values of operation here, to think so. Clytemnestra offers him honors which she herself considers excessive, hubristic, as the final way of showing that, as much as she intends to kill him, he deserves to die. The only roles available are male might-and-toughness, and female subjection-and-softness. They can be switched— the Greeks would say perverted—but not amplified or redefined. In the nature of human psychology, the party with the advantage in such a system keeps, and indeed canonizes, it. There is no reason for surprise that Agamemnon holds back from Clytemnestra's offer. The female role will not enlarge but undo him.

The same resistance manifests itself in Sophocles' *Antigone*, in the person of Creon. Finding his orders defied by Antigone, he steps them up in force and rigidity. But if Agamemnon represents the danger of unqualified softness, Creon discovers that of unqualified force. But this comes too late. Antigone and Haemon, the lovers whose union should have insured the future of the kingdom and the race, are dead, and Creon left with a barren new wisdom and equally barren old power. The play may afford a glimpse of the grounds for acceding to the female, but these remain practical rather than philosophical grounds, and lead to a nostalgic, perhaps even elegiac, emptiness.

Exemplary consequences of the grimmest sort arise from male intransigence in Euripides' *The Bacchae*. The picture of Pentheus swinging from the fir-tree is an ultimate in humiliation, and his dismemberment by the Maenads—an Orpheus who sings the wrong song—an ultimate in desolation. Even better than Aeschylus and Sophocles, Euripides brings out the inner dread around which male rigidity forms a bulwark. Pentheus has fears of the females who surrounded him throughout his growing years, but most he fears the female in himself. It is intimately close and at the same time entirely obscure. In a sense he is trying to destroy his obsession with the female, not the female as such (since he scarcely knows that part of human nature). His basic ambivalence emerges when he adopts female dress to spy on the female activity in the woods; prurience and moralistic rigor present themselves as two sides of one coin. But he has, so to speak, no valid currency, being a fake woman and a failed man. Thus Pentheus is exposed *to* the Bacchantes as neither fish nor fowl, and their tearing him apart renders in physical terms the breakdown of his narrow rigid structure of behavior and understanding.

I would stress that the death of Pentheus has the Bacchantes, including his blindly ecstatic mother, for its *instrument*, but that its *cause* is Pentheus's inability to accommodate or withstand reality. Dionysus makes this manifest; he does not impose it on Pentheus. *The Bacchae* on one level organizes itself as a deadly war of the sexes held in check by the framework of the city but violently released beyond its bounds. Pentheus as male is programmed to keep the female (in and around himself) down, but the female is programmed, if a moment of unreflecting expression arises, to undo her oppressor. As in *The Oresteia*, son ends up pitted against mother.

The question then remains whether Dionysus is a model of reconciliation and transcendence of the narrow law of opposition? Is he the equivalent of Athena in *The Bacchae*? If we follow the symbolism of the body, and recall that Dionysus was born from Zeus's thigh, the omens will not seem favorable.

It seems to me that Dionysus brings to humankind a sense of its own ineligibility for any kind of transcendence that keeps. Pentheus, in a word, knows only a self-destructive crossing of boundaries and elevation, and his mother Agave only a murderous ecstasy. In addition Dionysus serves to show that reconciliation of male and female occurs only in a god, and at that under the most volatile conditions. Dionysus really is an alternating extremist, now too indulgent, now too primitive, a sensualist and sadist in quick succession, more Oriental than a Phrygian woman, and then more Greek than a Theban king.[12]

In sum, a cultivated resistance and dissonance spoils any progress toward a new vision, a new way of the sexes in Greek literature.[13] There are intimations of a need for a new vision, but this is not pursued on any significant scale in Western culture until the romantic revolution. The change is not clean and abrupt, but some things that we might take for anticipations, for example, *The Wife of Bath's Tale*, prove dubious at best, and others, including the Paston Letters, two or three poems by Anne Finch, Countess of Winchilsea, and, most notably, Pope's sentimental poems and Richardson's sentimental novels, somehow confirm the status quo under the guise of deploring or opposing it.[14] It will be useful to compare Anne Finch with Pope (and a certain pungency may be added to the comparison if we recall that she is still more noted as his friend than as a poet in her own right).

The tendency has been for criticism to treat Anne Finch, if at all, as having "a subtle power in rendering natural impressions, a quiet delicacy."[15] But one may discern in her work something more akin to what Thoreau calls "quiet despera-tion," and a degree of quiet rage. This is apparent in her "Nocturnal Reverie," a poem praised—on other grounds—by Wordsworth in his "Essay, Supplementary to the Preface (1815)," where she longs for the "free soul" and the "short-lived jubilee the creatures keep,/Which but endures whilst tyrant man does sleep." Her desire for freedom and her distaste for constraints and oppression emerge even more sharply in her poem "To the Nightingale." Under the guise of dealing with nature and poetry—"rendering natural impres-sions [with] a quiet delicacy"—Anne Finch manages to sound very like Byron, in the "Dedication" to *Don Juan*, taking on the forces of denial and constriction.

The poem plays between a hopeful future ("Free as thine [the nightingale's] shall be my song") and a harsh present ("And still the unhappy poet's breast,/Like thine, when best he sings, is placed against a thorn"). But that future cannot realize itself ("Twill not be!"), and the summary of the way of things is cast in a perpetual present that pertains not only to the poet's pain but to a principle of punitiveness:

Thus we poets that have speech,
Unlike what thy forests teach,
If a fluent vein be shown
That's transcendent to our own,
Criticize, reform, or preach,
Or censure what we cannot reach.

The observation of nature is hardly subtle, here; it is forthright, and is made to show that the freedom, receptivity, praise sub-sisting beyond civilization are not at all maintained within it.[16] The achievement of human culture and traditions revolves into an art of censorship and depreciation, trenchantly described by Wordsworth in the same essay where he praises Anne Finch:

To be mistaught is worse than to be untaught; and no perverseness equals that which is supported by system, no errors are so difficult to root out as those which the understanding has pledged its credit to uphold. In this Class are contained censors, who, if they be pleased with what is good, are pleased with it only by imperfect glimpses, and upon false principles; . . . who, if they stumble upon a sound rule, are fettered by misapplying it, or by straining it too far. . . . In it are found critics too petulant to be passive to a genuine poet, and too feeble to grapple with him; men, who take upon them to report of the course which *he* holds whom they are utterly unable to accompany,—confounded if he turn quick upon the wing, dismayed if he soar steadily "into the region."

The final image of the bird soaring is reminiscent of Anne Finch's phrase "transcendent to our own," just as Wordsworth's censors and critics resemble her poets who do not practice poetry but "Criticize, reform, or preach,/Or censure what [they] cannot reach." It cannot be wholly unjust to hear in this outcry, besides a political undernote, a personal one, the outcry of a woman denied the place of the nightingale ('Twill not be) and denied a place among the freest, most original poets, though believing that "Poets, wild as" the nightingale have been "born,/Pleasing best when unconfined,/When to please is least designed." To appreciate her situation we need only recall the remark of Anne Finch's contemporary, Dorothy Osborne, concerning a woman who would want to be taken seriously as a writer: "Sure the poore woman is a little distracted, she could never bee soe rediculous else as to venture at writeing book's and in verse too, if I should not sleep this fortnight I should not come to that."[17] For a woman to "turn quick upon the wing" or "soar steadily 'into the region'" seems unnatural even to a woman; it is a startling irony that science is only now, two centuries later, beginning to recognize a species of derangement resulting from a drastic lack of sleep; but Dorothy Osborne turned her brilliant observation into an ironic weapon to cut down another woman's creativity. Here stands the perfection of captivity, when the captive immures herself, and the jailer need not even go to the expense of a guard to keep her in *his* place.

Alexander Pope in "Eloisa to Abelard" gives evidence that men also associated with women that desire for freedom which Anne Finch expresses (and which perhaps John Taylor's runaway wife may as a courtesy be credited with). More than this, Pope gives substance to Dr. Johnson's abstract dictum "Nature has given women so much power that the law has very wisely given them little." Clearly Johnson is recognizing a "power" that inheres in women because they are women, and begrudging them that power rather than in any way seeking to share in it, or benefit from it. Pope will enable us to see that something besides curmudgeonly malice motivated him,[18] in that his time had not the means or the conception of the means of correcting a practical situation so sanctioned by custom as to seem natural. The principle at work may be summarized as *the inhibition of the feminine*, a limitation of its power and scope in direct proportion to awareness of its potential power and scope. For the feminine, then, power remained less a matter of *potestas* than of *potentia*.

Pope himself seems to have been attracted to Eloisa's letters as "a picture of the struggles of grace and nature, virtue and passion" (see the "Argument" of "Eloisa to Abelard"). The poem rather presents itself as a struggle between what Anne Finch sensitizes us to call feminine poetry and masculine criticism, between feminine desire for freedom and masculine adjustment to institutional safeguards.[19] Pope of course gives Eloisa, the poem's voice, freedom of speech, but nothing like freedom of expression. In an exile of the spirit, she is like Shakespeare's Mowbray "doubly portcullis'd" in a convent ("Relentless walls!" l. 16) and in her heart ("Hide it, my heart," 11). Yet she remains the only figure in the universe of the poem with a feeling for the "forest" ("Why *rove* my thoughts *beyond* this last retreat?"; italics added). The forest, as its etymology (*foris* = what is beyond) and its historic associations (Sherwood Forest) show, represents unknown dimensions of being. It corresponds to possibilities and capacities not only of the world but also of the self in the world. The fusion of the two is finely caught in Eloisa's phrase "rebel nature" (26), which refers equally to the sublunary world, as opposed to Heaven, and to her own inner regimen, as opposed to ecclesiastical/theological rules. She is a rebel without an objective or an instrument.

The poem, her address, is conducted as a sort of philosophical hysteria. Eloisa comes out with two ideals, one for the state of human life itself, the other for the state of the relationship between herself and Abelard; both are so far from anything feasible in her world that they resound with a crazy pathos. First, she envisions a "happy state! when souls each other draw,/When love is liberty, and nature, law" (91–92). This is lovely, but hopeless. It involves a self-contradiction within her own terms, since "rebel nature" and "nature [as] law" will not consort with one another. Then, in a more openly tumultuous way, she cries to an unwitting Abelard:

Come thou, my father, brother, husband, friend!
And let thy sister, daughter move
And all those tender names in one, thy love!
                    [152–54]

The very existence of titles in a litany suggests the improbability of that ultimate reconciliation of being, "all those . . . names in one." Eloisa's outcry has about it a sort of female incontinence or hysteria, but it also has in it a deep and original feminine vision of an integrated, synergistic pattern of human relationship, in which a saving subordination would come into play and make harsh exclusions unnecessary, and in which a whole, self-reconciled person would hold at bay the spirit of division and self-sacrifice.

And yet division, dualism, self-reversal crop up everywhere in her utterance, as though her own directions could not be pursued but only bounced back off obstacles and objections again and again. There is one point, however, when she breaks through for a moment, and it is significantly in relation to a "forest" scene in nature:

The darksome pines that o'er yon rocks reclined
Wave high, and murmur to the hollow wind,
The wandering streams that shine between the hills,
The grots that echo to the tinkling rills,
The dying gales that pant upon the trees,
The lakes that quiver to the curling breeze;
No more these scenes my meditation aid,
Or lull to rest the visionary maid.

[155-62]

It is true that the phenomena of "meditation" and "vision" associate the forest with the religious calling, but the overriding fact is that Eloisa goes out of the convent precincts for something lacking or impossible within them. The forest scenes "lull" her to a "rest" that presumably the convent does not afford, and as "visionary maid" she seems rather personally carried away than religiously so. An impulse akin to what takes Christabel or Oothoon beyond orthodox precincts is at work here in Eloisa. But even this respite of individuality is converted by the power of orthodoxy. The forest of freedom becomes a site of pre-gothic oppression, and healing "rest" turns to "a dead repose":

But o'er the twilight groves and dusky caves,
Long-sounding aisles, and intermingled graves,
Black Melancholy sits, and round her throws
A deathlike silence, and a dead repose:
Her gloomy presence saddens all the scene,
Shades every flower, and darkens every green,
Deepens the murmur of the falling floods,
And breathes a browner horror on the woods.

[163-70]

Eloisa does not *realize* freedom in the forest; at no point does she reach a stage of clear, purposive pursuit of that goal. The important thing is that she evinces an impulse

toward it, gropes toward it, when there is no encouragement
and no receptivity to build on. The poem never becomes
polemical, but Pope does present her with a sort of helpless
sympathy. If she is understated as a personality and a
philosopher, it is not at bottom his fault. Her venture into
new dimensions—at crucial times we find her resorting to the
word *yon*—has to be purblind, because her world has not
developed a suitable angle of vision. But she unmistakably
anticipates, before the convent swallows her up again, a new
way of relating to nature, and a new way of being feminine,
as a "visionary maid." The difference between her and
Oothoon is that she cannot break the spell of hysteria and
find a strong articulation of her vision and values. But she
differs from the Eumenides, in a favorable way, in that she
does break the rigidity of established rules on her own, and
she also tries to impart to Abelard, still adored but no longer
simply dominant, some of the promise of what she has
stumbled upon. Eloisa represents the first tentative, fore-
shortened activity of the feminine against entrenched institutions (the convent) and authoritarian personalities (Abelard).
The teacher may hereafter begin to be taught, the master to
be meek.

Authority, institution, sameness: these are the terms that
arise in connection with the masculine when it is established
as a norm. The feminine then is obliged to represent obedience,
tameness, mimicry;[20] as Anne Finch and, albeit obliquely,
Pope demonstrate, there is occasion for more, but neither
ground nor environment for that "more" to find itself in.
One crucial flaw in any impulse to change appears in what
may be called the Eumenides syndrome—the fact that the
injured party must bear the brunt of change (in the sense that
the Eumenides, though growing, give up more than Orestes),
thus tacitly reinforcing a status of weakness.[21] Clearly a
process of interchange is requisite, and within that a disposition to change on the masculine part. This is precisely what

the romantic period comes up with, a sense of the natural but untapped power of the feminine which, because it had so little social or political expression, was doing less than it should for the masculine and for the human.

How this comes about is ultimately obscure, and may be radically beyond analysis, but one can learn to take it in according to a principle of familiarity: it is the sort of thing that romanticism has a capacity, and even a penchant, for. This of course relates to the revolutionary impulse in romanticism, but it would be well to recognize that the revolutionary impulse does not operate scot free. It affords the pleasure of brushing things aside for those who are inclined that way, but those things recoil and others crop up; the element of exposure and eruption at least matches the glad excitement of the case. But romantic literature evinces a rare promptness in *accommodating the new* and incorporating it into an enlarging, evolutionary scheme of values.[22] Such promptness results from the fact that the new is not left in traumatic isolation, "in limbo," but is recognized "under the positive conditions of a complex group of relations."[23]

Nowhere is the romantic promptness and candor in coming to terms with the feminine more neatly conveyed than in Wordsworth's "Nutting."[24] The fact that this poem was "struck out" of *The Prelude* "as not being wanted there"[25] has caused an aura of the expendable to cling to it, and has partially hidden its richness and originality.[26] "Nutting" is too full and finished to have fitted into a poem as patient and elaborative as *The Prelude*. We must be careful to take in a neutral spirit Wordsworth's remark about not wanting it, as also his comment that the poem "arose out of the remembrance of feelings I had often had when a boy, and particularly in the extensive woods that still stretch from the side of Esthwaite Lake towards Graythwaite."[27] What feelings are meant, and about what? We really know when (boyhood) and where (in the woods), and must refer to the poem for more.

Let me suggest that the feelings are about nature as feminine, and about the analogies and substitutions by which nature and the feminine are encountered, and about the capsule development of a boy's relation to the feminine in various guises; and let me further suggest that the feelings range from clownish resentment through deliciously savored revenge to an almost sacred blending of protection (which cancels revenge) and aspiration (which cancels resentment).

The poem is framed in judgment ("It seems .../One of those heavenly days that cannot die") and logical invocation ("then ... move .../In gentleness of heart; with gentle hand/Touch—for there is a spirit in the woods"). The central action, immediate and gripping as it is, never breaks free of a reflective energy and a sense that knowledge arises as a refined form of action, that action exists as a rough groping for the rectitude of knowledge. The action can be broken down into three stages: withdrawal from the jurisdiction of the "frugal Dame"; consummation of the act of ravaging the hazel bower; and the aftermath of exultation, qualified by a flash of "pain" (as something inward) and of "the intruding sky" (as something outward). The simultaneity of inner and outer in this third stage is the tacit goal of the poem, which begins with an emphatically outward orientation and moves, in the middle stage, the ravage, to a succession of outer and inner. The "pain" and the "sky" are versions of one another, an emotional sense of having done harm matched with a symbolic perception of a realm that watches over culprit and victim; as Coleridge says, "the blue sky bends over all."

There is a subtler integration of "opposites" that we need also to recognize here. The sky that "intrudes" into what the boy wants to think of as a secluded, private scene [28] represents authority, and has a masculine character in itself. But it refers back to the frugal Dame, the feminine authority from whose attention ("intrusions" in short) the boy has gone off into the uncharted forest. Thus authority in these two guises constitutes a second frame within the frame of reflection and judgment already referred to. The hazel-grove activity nestles, as a nucleus and a radiant point, within the two pairs of frames. The poem lends itself to schematization as follows:

[Reflection [Authority [Hazel-bower] Authority] Reflection]

Thus we can see what the boy, with his circuitously calculated foray into the woods, could not have seen, namely, that the bower and its ravage are not the goal of the poem,[29] but a pivot whereby it can reach its true goal *and origin*, in rectified understanding and action.[30]

Toward what is his action directed, and of what is his understanding rectified? Of the feminine, in a word. And through the feminine, of himself and a deeper order of things than his momentary plans and impulses can approach. What I am calling the feminine here identifies itself through two features. The first is the invariable presence of a female figure, occurring obviously as actual women in the frugal Dame and the dearest Maiden, then as a metaphor, a metaphysicial evaluation of the hazel-bower on the boy's part, where he calls the woods "a virgin scene." The idiom of a rape that the writer retrospectively adopts to convey the boy's behavior extends this definition of gender, and some portions of the description (e.g., "with my cheek on one of those green stones that, fleeced with moss . . .") have a distinctly Freudian smack.[31] The second feature that warrants the term "feminine" is the treatment of the female figures, not merely as practical actors or participants, but as typical, symbolic, revelatory ones. The female figures express themselves naturally, even, in the case of the hazel-bower, naturalistically, but out of that also arises a formal awareness in the boy that they express what *female figures as such express*, a value, a law, and a way.

This is best understood if we focus on the process informing that law and way, which emerge in relationship, in conflict

really, with what is ignorant alike of law and way, and
casually hostile to them. The boy seems to laugh it off,
dressing like a clown ("a Figure quaint"), but there is evidence
that he regards the frugal Dame as exercising a restrictive and
repressive force. There arises a real discontinuity between her
jurisdiction and the forest, into which he retreats, in essence,
for his freedom. He tacitly counterbalances her restraints
upon him by tearing up his clothes more and more (being as
wanton as she is frugal), and by casting himself as a figure of
impropriety and excess ("Motley accoutrement, of power to
smile/At thorns, and brakes, and brambles,—and, in truth,/
More ragged than need was!"). The law here seems severe, the
way narrow, and the boy compensates by playing the clown,
going in "motley"—even his clothes "smile."

He is, we must infer, biding his time. Certainly a kind of
volcanic calculation is expressing itself as he moves on the
hazel-bower. Imperceptibly, and yet decisively, he ceases to
be a clown, ceases to be a small boy at the mercy of the
mature woman. In a way reminiscent of Blake's "The Mental
Traveller" he assumes a pre-manhood power which he turns
on the female figure corresponding to his present state, as his
boyishness was symmetrical with the state of the frugal dame.
For modern taste Wordsworth's displacement of the act of
rape unto the hazel-bower may be unduly cagy, but there is
very little loss of precision or power, and some clear
advantages to the metaphor,[32] which avoids trauma and
fixation, thus allowing the *growth* which is basic to the poem
to continue, and which, even more importantly, allows for a
more richly subtle definition of gender boundaries than
literalness could conceivably have done.

For we need to deal with the fact that the hazel-bower is
not entirely or simply feminine, any more than the rapacious
youth is entirely or simply masculine. When the youth acts,
the bower is feminine as far as the single-mindedness of his
act allows; it is "typically" passive, that is to say defenseless

before superior force. But it has a *power* to make up for its lack of *force*, and we can see that in the very first encounter, where the description runs: "the hazels *rose/Tall and erect*, with tempting clusters hung,/A virgin scene!" (italics added). The youth's imagination, for its own uses, sums up the scene as "virgin," which in context pertains to the feminine character. But what he *sees*, not what he concludes, is of a different character. The hazels have a definite posture of their own, and one with a tacit masculine strength ("rose Tall and erect"). The bower represents a whole nature, including masculine and feminine, but the youth forces it into one dimension, distorting its quality and his perception. The two aspects of the bower are not, let it be said, equal; the feminine is more prominent, and is emphasized to the last. But a sort of sub-hermaphroditic condition manifests itself in the bower. Perhaps it does so in the youth as well; when he is called a "Figure quaint," we may hear a distinct echo of the Chaucerian and Marvellian use of *quaint* (modern *cunt*) and see a hidden feminine dimension there.

As youth and bower confront us, the feminine element in him and its masculine element represent sidelong possibilities, not active capacities. But the attempt to deny or eliminate them as capacities proves paradoxically the basis of establishing them as such. In the very act of taking revenge for earlier weakness by driving home the weakness of another, the youth puts himself in intimate contact with weakness and so increases his exposure and its hold over him. He approaches it as an object. But such an approach is based on an illusion, as Rousseau recognizes in *La Nouvelle Héloïse*:

Nature seems to desire to hide from the eyes of men its real attractions, of which they are too little aware and which they disfigure when they are within reach. . . . Those who love nature and cannot go seek it so far away are reduced to doing it violence, to forcing it in some manner to come dwell with them, and all this cannot be effected without a little illusion. [Pt. IV, letter xi]

The rapacious boy expects to act solely according to his own will, but the bower has its own "quiet being," which comes home to him willy-nilly. That is to say, one must know that one is hurting another, in rape, and yet not let this knowledge spoil one's satisfaction in having *one's own way*.[33] This proves virtually impossible to do, especially in a universe where one desires to enter into the new; one may jump into the water ad lib, but one is strictly liable to get wet. Thus the youth, *in order* to exult in his own wilfulness and force, must exult over the bower's patience and surrender ("patiently gave up / Their quiet being"), which means that he must recognize the bower's attributes in themselves, and grant the integrity of that "quiet being." Having such a being, the bower exists beyond his purpose, just as his own being extends beyond his purpose. He has raised himself up emotionally and psychologically with a particular object in view, but once having done so he cannot but see whatever is there. His selfish "exultation" and his sympathetic "pain" become simultaneous and continuous with each other. He has damaged the virgin scene, only to find that he has damaged that very thing within himself which would appreciate it enough to make him want to have his way with it. The self amplifies into the not-self, but also concedes something to it. Hence the only truth of gender must be a paradox, that for the masculine to defeat the feminine is for it to fall prey to itself, distempered and automatically locked into its own doom.

The achievement of reconciliation in "Nutting" is couched in much milder terms than the scene of antagonism, and tends to pass unnoticed. The speaker reaches a new pitch of assurance, manhood seeming abruptly to succeed youth as youth has succeeded boyhood. His counterpart at this stage, the "dearest Maiden," has what appears to be a dependent status, lacking in experience and direction. But I would see a complex blending of excellence and humility in both persons.

For example, the man enunciates the philosophy that the woman intuitively lives by. Both, like Thel and the Daughters of Mne. Seraphim, come up ahead and behind, better and worse in relation to each other; philosophy is clearer than intuition, intuition purer than philosophy. They are strengthened by each other, he in the gentleness she embodies, she in the conviction that is his.

If inhibition of the feminine marks Dr. Johnson, Wordsworth gives evidence of the incorporation of the feminine. A complementary wholeness which at least can be pursued (the poem significantly concludes with logic and a subjunctive, not an indicative, mood) arises as the norm of "Nutting." Of paramount importance is the willingness, or rather the capacity, of the masculine figure to take new ground, though this means conceding old ground. In this light we can see how far things have come from the likes of Agamemnon, Pentheus, and Creon; indeed, we should recognize that the bower-rape scene could as easily have ended with the youth raising *force* to a principle, and rejecting the softening influence of his victim's quiet being as another feminine ruse. But another world is crystallizing, and is gaining acknowledgement and adherents. We can profitably listen to Schiller enunciate what is virtually a gloss on "Nutting":

The need to please subjects the all-conquering male to the gentle tribunal of taste; lust he can steal, but love must come as a gift. For this loftier prize he can only contend by virtue of form, never by virtue of matter. From being a force impinging upon feeling, he must become a form confronting the mind; he must be willing to concede freedom, because it is freedom he wishes to please. And even as beauty resolves the conflict between opposing natures in this simplest and clearest paradigm, the eternal antagonism of the sexes, so too does it resolve it—or at least aims at resolving it—in the complex whole of society, endeavouring to reconcile the gentle with the violent in the moral world after the pattern of the free union it there contrives between the strength of man and the gentleness of woman. Now weakness becomes sacred, and unbridled strength dishonourable; the injustice of nature is rectified by the magnanimity of the chivalric code.[34]

Yet it might be thought that the element of redefinition and reconciliation in "Nutting" works as a neat trick in the mind of the youth and man who finds female figures to serve the role of pushover or convenient foil. Genuine feminine power, the argument might run, would check him more than the maiden's gentleness does. He has conveniently gone out of the register of the frugal Dame, who really saw to it that he measured up, and with his dearest Maiden he could even be said to have brought off, surreptitiously, the rite of the transformed hag. In reality, rather than wish-fulfillment, he would have had to face her in all her severity, and would have had his comeuppance.

One inconspicuous detail does suggest, though, that he does go home again; in fact he makes a binding principle of the very strictness he had resented in the old woman. We may recall that "frugality" and "dearness" (old form, "dearth") are bound up with each other, and connect the "frugal Dame" and the "dearest Maiden" in a basic way. The Dame of course represents the domestic order, the Maiden a spiritual one, but both call for a response to what is rare, hard to find and maintain. In rising to a harmonious relationship with the Maiden, the boy comes to a rectified relationship with the Dame, as the two are stages of one another.[35] Neither the boy nor the Dame is truly removed from the poem. Only the sort of relationship that subsisted between them is removed. The boy has grown from clown to philosopher, the domestic has become the spiritual, and in keeping with the poem's primary (but far from exclusive) concern with reflection and the spirit, it is at the level of spirit that the underlying love and reverence between boy and Dame are brought out, and even the underlying appreciation and and fascination between the youth and the hazel-bower.

Of the three sexual pairs in relationship in "Nutting," two must be termed unequal and mechanical, being marked by ignorance, automatic advantage, and rigid patterning, and only one would seem to deserve characterization as reciprocal and human. The three break down as follows:

1. *Boy-frugal Dame*: here the Dame knows nothing of the boy's inner hungers, which he must gratify in secret—she dominates him effortlessly, and he slyly retaliates by picking on the hazel-bower, where also he can act out the hunger he dares not show the Dame; nothing within the situation makes for change, or responds to it, though change is desirable.

2. *Youth-hazel bower*: the "virgin scene" is even more at the youth's mercy than the boy had been at the Dame's—no law applies here in the "forest," except the law of opportunity and force, and the hazel-bower does not even have the boy's privilege of turning to some surrogate relationship, but must stand or fall with what the youth can give; something in the situation demands change, for which there is no compass, except to the extent that the youth's being surprised by sympathy might suggest a dimension beyond what is given.

3. *Man-dearest Maiden*: communication, and not just interaction, begins; speech goes beyond the Dame's giving orders to the boy, and rises to a level of reverent persuasion, while silence is no longer the mark of a bower's helplessness, but becomes the manifestation of at-homeness in the woods and in the self, in the person of the gentle Maiden, and this indeed is *how the man responds to it.*

The new position toward the hypaethral woods, with which the poem ends, is new only to the masculine figure. It is habitual in the feminine figure. This involves a real distinction between masculine and feminine, but nothing like an opposition. No attribute, no activity is exclusive, no capacity or power unavailable to one or the other. Clearly the Dame dominates the boy in her way, just as he dominates the bower in his way (there is no comprehensive domination, no one is entirely *dominus* to another). Even within one stage of the poem we can see that the youth overpowers the hazels with force and *is overpowered* himself by the bower's gentleness. By the same token the Maiden's reverence for the woods controls the possibility of desecration. She may do it spontaneously, where the youth has to learn by painful experience, but both *naturally* relinquish their power to wreak havoc in favor of a spirit of reverence. The poem does not make the point explicitly, but the "spirit in the woods" is also in the human spirit.

The main point as to sex boils down to this: there is no fixed position on either part, but only a disposition, a statistical probability that the masculine will face one way and the feminine the other (as two sides of a sphere that has been split, or *sexed*, will seem to face opposite ways, though actually both look toward reunification). Probability can in no way predict or dictate to personality, and cannot be used as a sexual yardstick in individual cases. The habit of oppositional thinking, as we have seen, leads us to canonize single moments and lose sight of complex patterns, even constellations of experience and nature. But if, instead of being imposed upon by a masculine *versus* a feminine *nature*, we leave ourselves free to consider a feminine *and* a masculine disposition, we can readily follow the romantics in their high original investigation of how those dispositions relate to each other.

Basically, they question the necessity and, to some extent, the legitimacy of roles set in human behavior. This is easy to take in on the sociopolitical plane; the French Revolution has accustomed us to the idea of overthrowing hereditary privilege. But in the sphere of personal behavior, of tacit presumptions in everyday dealings, we are not really ready to approve, or to understand. The French Revolution, with its macrocosmic scale, has come to obscure the deepest level of the romantic revolution, which is projected at the microcosm, the individual person and personality that must form the macrocosm for it to exist. The individual revolution was supposed to add up to the total revolution, before time ran out. And so we concentrate on the failed macrocosm, and miss the trees for the forest.

Even today this is so. With all the clamor for equal rights, affirmative action, and other slogans, there persists a sense that the solution can only be institutional, macrocosmic, and tacitly then a sense that the individual—who is supposed to profit, after all—is helpless and useless. But if help for the individual is hard to come by, other ways of dealing with him—or her—are not lacking. We are pathologically quick to turn on anyone who causes us to imagine that equal rights and affirmative action do not ride topmost on their totem pole of values. Such a person decorously eats a date and throws the pit aside, only to find a genie on his back, half-blind from the accidental pit and calculated rage.

A small story from my classroom will indicate how closely the spirit of oppositional thinking and of microcosmic opposition of the sexes clings to us. It was a seminar of some sixteen students, and well balanced in the mixture of males and females. Everyone was asked to participate in a simple experiment, or exercise. I would put on the blackboard a list of traits that history has identified as masculine, and I would ask them to fill in a list of feminine traits. When their list was complete I would compare it to mine, which was written down in my notebook and could be consulted for verification, if deemed necessary. My original list, with the feminine undeclared, read as shown on the next page.

Only very slowly did the students begin to respond. They seemed uncomfortable with themselves, with the idea, with me. The only comment was that the list was rather positive, and might have been better balanced. But they agreed that we should train attention on the feminine, rather than dwelling further on the masculine. Still, few suggestions came out. "Perhaps," one young man ventured, "'pretty' could be put up beside 'beauty.'" And another student, a young

Masculine	*Feminine*
Wisdom	
Strength	
Beauty	
Endurance	
Courage	
Creativity	
Dignity	
Authority	
Justice	

woman, offered "intuition" as a feminine trait matching masculine "wisdom." It looked like a fairly meager yield, and I exhorted the class to be more forthcoming; surely the men had more definite ideas about women, and the women about themselves. This is how the blackboard looked after several minutes of squinting, sighing, leaning back in chairs, shaking heads, looking up at the ceiling or out of windows:

Masculine	*Feminine*
Wisdom	Intuition
Strength	
Beauty	Prettiness
Endurance	
Courage	
Creativity	
Dignity	
Authority	
Justice	

I expressed the hope that they were not being inhibited by me. When nothing further materialized, I offered to produce my own list of feminine traits. Eyes brightened up all around, either because the pressure was off them for the nonce, or because they wished to see how I would handle myself in

those perilous waters. And so I turned again to the blackboard, which soon looked like this:

Masculine	Feminine	Feminine
Wisdom	Intuition	Wisdom
Strength		Strength
Beauty	Prettiness	Beauty
Endurance		Endurance
Courage		Courage
Creativity		Creativity
Dignity		Dignity
Authority		Authority
Justice		Justice
(Intuition)[36]		(Intuition)

Everyone really brightened up now. We were in accord. No
one could account for the failure to fill out the feminine
column at once, in just that way, or explain why it had been
thought that "opposite" qualities should be found. I could
have taken heart from the fact that the feminine column was
slow to fill in, along the lines of "intuition" and "prettiness,"
but it bothered me more that something like that was held as
a norm.

Obviously I was not contending, with those identical
columns, that feminine and masculine are the same, only that
they have the same qualities. Each expresses these qualities in
a distinctive way or mode, but it's also true that each
expresses itself along a spectrum that bears into the other's
statistically probable area. Many women are stronger than
some men, many men finer than some women, but it is only
a rigid and narrow imagination that fails to recognize (a) the
propriety of these facts and (b) the aggregate masculinity of
those men and the aggregate femininity of those women.

The problem comes from applying simple role-standards
where complex principles ought to be invoked. If we say, as

we do in the usual antithetical way, that men are "aggressive" and women "passive," we are really prescribing roles rather than describing qualities or establishing principles. It would be otherwise if we sought to identify *dispositions* and came up with comparative rather than antithetical terms. After all, the supposedly "aggressive" man and the supposedly "passive" woman have the same end in view, namely, the satisfaction of desire. Let us go to the trunk from which the branches move to give grace and scope to the tree. Let us, for instance, say that the masculine disposition is acquisitive, the feminine cumulative, and we will see two modes of the same activity, taking possession (sexually or materially); also, we will see that the acquisitive disposition may in a given situation freely choose or else pragmatically adopt the cumulative mode, and vice versa, without violation or impropriety. Old folk used to say, when I was a child, "A whistling woman and a crowing hen are an abomination unto the Lord," but the analogy is vicious and repressive. The hen *cannot* crow; the woman can whistle, and might add something to domestic harmony if not the history of music if she didn't have dogmatic folklore sealing her lips.

The deadly quality of what might be called an unprincipled relationship between the sexes (a relationship of fact and matter where role-bound males and females self-protectively and self-seekingly interact with each other) is graphically presented by William Blake in "The Mental Traveller." An atmosphere of outrage at the entire scene pervades the poem, but there is also an uncontrollable fascination that the speaker freely imparts; we are meant to sit forward and prick up our ears when he announces that he, in his travels, "heard & saw such dreadful things/As cold Earth wanderers never knew" (3-4). These dreadful things consist in all possible permutations, and perversions, of male-female relationships. The social restraint inculcated by Wordsworth's frugal Dame becomes savage repression in the case of Blake's Woman Old:

Her fingers number every Nerve,
Just as a miser counts his gold;
She lives upon his [the Boy Babe's] shrieks & cries.

In like manner Blake, when his "bleeding youth" binds down
the "Virgin bright," seems to be articulating and illuminating
what is only implicit in "Nutting," the maimed condition
("bleeding") of the youth who turns with rampant force
upon the "virgin scene," and the outright temporal and
causal link that connects the boy and old woman as a pair
with the youth and the maiden:

Till he becomes a bleeding youth,
And she becomes a Virgin bright;
Then he rends up his Manacles[37]
And binds her down for his delight.

But no redefinition of understanding and value, such as
marks the conclusion of "Nutting," occurs in "The Mental
Traveller." Rather the youth advances into age and prosperity
(sts. 7–10), the maiden dwindles into depths of helplessness
(st. 11) until the laws of symmetry and entropy produce the
inevitable reversal, and hostilities are resumed on a new footing, because the "female Babe," however helpless, is at a
beginning, and the man as an "aged Shadow" is, for all his
array of might, at an end. The hostile cycle Blake depicts here
will go on forever, and this is usually taken as its most
burdensome feature, like Atlas under the everlasting circle of
the world. But mere everlastingness would lead to tedium
and, by that token, relief. Blake allows us to see a correlation
between everlastingness and infinite variation in the evil of
sexual hostility, and therein arises its "dread."

The forms and motivations of sexual hostility multiply
rapidly in the poem: a liaison between a maiden and a male
for the purpose of wresting power from a previously dominant
male (st. 13); an outcast male playing on a maiden's sympathy
to recover a position in the world and a sense of productivity

(sts. 14-15); the old male finding religious symbols (honey, bread, and wine) in the sensuality of his passion for a young female, and both of them pursuing a baptismal pilgrimage (on the desert wild) that they can neither believe in nor cope with (sts. 18-19). Moreover, sexual hostility reaches into and co-opts every field of endeavor. It becomes part of the agricultural enterprise (sts. 7-8), and we are left uncertain whether the woman is made into the man's surrogate garden or whether the garden is turned into an ersatz woman. It is involved in the mining enterprise (sts. 8-9), and again the commercial and the personal-symbolic valences of the case twine together inseparably. It seems to lead to philanthropy (sts. 10-11), with the bitter paradox that the benefactor gives with triumph and the beneficiaries receive with hatred. That emotional and moral confusion is ingrained in the situation we can recognize when the "arts of Love" (st. 20) modulate effortlessly into "arts of Love & Hate." All arts are one, all feelings are one, and the necessities of art and feeling drive the world, without rudder or gyroscope, through perpetually turbid seas.

The ultimate irony, the ultimate bafflement, occurs when the poem returns to the opening situation, the Woman Old "binding" the Boy Babe, and reveals it as a misguided act of courage, rather than systematic cruelty.[38] For the Babe, potentially the Savior who could break the spell of sexual hostility and pandemic dis-ease, is regarded as a threat ("They cry 'the babe! the babe is born!'/And flee away on Every side"; st. 24). He is of course in a real sense a threat, to the law of familiarity, to the value of inertia, to whatever does not need to be disturbed by new demands, new prospects. The imagery of stanzas 3-4 suggests that the Babe is Christ or Prometheus, and the reluctance of the world to be helped by them cannot but recall the response of the poor to the philanthropist in stanzas 10-11. It becomes difficult, then, for the reader to be too smug about the rejection of Christ, since he has already empathized with the rejection of a proffered good. And it is difficult not to admire the resolution of the Woman Old who "can touch" the threatening Babe and bind him down, when young men flee. The poem poses us a quandary, which it asks us to deplore and entertain.

The root problem of sexual interaction in "The Mental Traveller" is that no figure, male or female, attains the complexity of a nature, as all are bound to the insistent simplicity of a role. We give a charmed assent to Shakespeare's declaration that "all the world's a stage." Is this not, though, a specious charm? To "play a part" one must *encompass* a role, and not be identical with it. One's part in life is a part of life. One in a measure writes and directs that part, and revises and redirects it, rather than finding it pre-scribed on barren sheets. But roles exhaust the possibilities of relationship in "The Mental Traveller." Everything and everyone follows the simple logic of ferocity, which takes the form of consumption or of confinement of one another. In this universe an accommodation of the new is unheard of; the new, even as Christ, is itself consumed or confined. Still the poem, without generating the kind of alternative that Wordsworth rises to, in "Nutting," affords room for reflection and dissatisfaction. It carries an undertow of elegy ("dreadful things"), and also, in its final expression of simultaneous truth and disbelief, a tinge of satire: "And all is done as I have told." Wordsworth, as a dramatic male figure, incorporates a feminine, a whole-making value in "Nutting." In "The Mental Traveller" Blake adopts a general posture from which he can lament the absence of masculine *and* feminine values where males and females intensely and eternally act out constrictive roles. It is striking, within scant decades of Dr. Johnson's nonchalant dictum on the use of "the law" to inhibit woman's "power," to see Wordsworth finding an unexpected wisdom and grace in the incorporation of that power, and to see Blake elaborating the deadly effects of inhibiting or perverting that power. Not just a new receptivity but a new activity of surprised recognition and groping toward a new economy of gender relations comes into prominence. It would still be possible for no less a reformer than Cobbett to say that Bentham had made a mockery of the idea of universal suffrage by proposing to include women,[39] but the drive toward what Horace L. Friess calls "variety and fulness of life"[40] emphatically included its feminine dimension. But Blake and Wordsworth, even as they signal a tendency of their age, also evince a tension over it, and in themselves effectively set up the grounds of a cultural debate. For the question of the feminine was an overt one. It was hotly taken up, in terms of sociopolitical assumptions, cultural philosophical postulates, and metaphysical imperatives, by writers as various as Friedrich Schlegel, Jean-Jacques Rousseau, Mary Wollstonecraft, and Arthur Schopenhauer.

Schopenhauer comes out as something close to a perfect model of the unconscious conflict, in this period of half-conscious transition, between cultural norms and natural ideals, between history and prophecy. His governing mood was opposition. He led a self-embattled life in his own time. He emerged as a renowned philosopher while spending a minimum of time and affection on standard academic philosophy. The year he was to have taught at the University of Berlin he happened to schedule his lectures at the same time as Hegel's, and confronted an empty classroom. He withdrew into private life, domiciled in a boarding-house, and having as his chief companion one uncelebrated dog. Schopenhauer's sense of a better and a truer way was no doubt enhanced by his experience; equally, though, his sense of spite was aggravated. Thus, he opposed "orthodox" philosophy with an acute and dynamic analysis of the tacit complementarity of the sexes, and opposed the aspirations and indeed the rights of the feminine with an all but scurrilous survey.

The latter occurs in the essay "Of Women." One could imagine that it is an ironic *jeu d'esprit*, but the irony nowhere becomes palpable; the language is too fluent and too consistent for the tongue-in-check. It shows Schopenhauer at the mercy of his time and, perhaps, of his loneliness.

The fundamental fault of the female character is that it has *no sense of justice* [shades of Athena!]. This is mainly due to the fact ... that women are defective in the powers of reasoning and deliberation; but it is also traceable to the position which Nature has assigned to them as the weaker sex.

It is only the man whose intellect is clouded by his sexual impulses that could give the name of *the fair sex* to that undersized, narrow-shouldered, broad-hipped, and short-legged race.... There would be more warrant for describing women as the unaesthetic sex. Neither for music, nor for poetry, nor for fine art, have they really and truly any sense or susceptibility.... The most distinguished intellects among the whole sex have never managed to produce a single achievement in the fine arts that is really great, genuine, and original; or given to the world any work of permanent value in any sphere.

When Nature made two divisions of the human race, she did not draw the line exactly through the middle. These divisions are polar and opposed to each other, it is true; but the difference between them is not qualitative merely, it is also quantitative.

Just in proportion as the honors and privileges which the laws accord to women, exceed the amount which nature gives, is there a diminution in the number of women who really participate in these privileges, and all the remainder are deprived of their natural rights by just so much as is given to the others over and above their share.[41]

Beside these outbursts, Dr. Johnson's comments to Taylor resemble the height of hospitality. But Schopenhauer's position here represents only the irritable part of what he was capable of (besides, we can leave him and Dr. Johnson, both apparent defenders of the principle of inhibiting the feminine, to fight out the question whether the law gives women "little" power to counteract nature's largesse, or "honors and privileges" in excess of nature). More is to be gained by focusing on Schopenhauer's sly concession that all women have "natural rights." He gives this notion short shrift in "Of Women,"[42] but it is the notion that rises toward philosophy and abstract authority, where everything else he says images local preferences and temporal organizations. It is in fact the notion that Schopenhauer develops when he speaks on his own original authority, in "The Metaphysics of the Love of the Sexes."[43]

In this document Schopenhauer still has an axe to grind, but it is Diallo's axe.[44] He seeks the advantage of philosophical truth and originality, rather than social position: "I have no predecessors," he asserts, "either to make use of or to refute. The subject of love of the sexes has pressed itself upon me *objectively*, and has entered of its own accord into the connection of my *consideration of the world*" (p. 339, italics added).

In effect, Schopenhauer takes the magic mask off romantic love to reveal the face of the future; he points to a complex evolutionary impulse in which the individual to come employs the couple joined in passion as a birth instrument, while they choose each other for the possibility of perfection they mutually represent (pp. 343, 344). In Schopenhauer's view each person born—male or female—does or could reproduce this passion, whose ideal accordingly remains remote, and perhaps unrealizable. Even so, the importance of the passion and the importance it gives the participants are in no way diminished. Male and female, or, better—to bring out the representative sexual natures—masculine and feminine actors are equal and necessary to each other. They enter both freely and inevitably, both distinctively and typically into each other's dream of perfection. They are each other's dream of perfection, each other's escape from sex-as-division into the new unity of the offspring, and each other's escape from individuality-as-separation into the union of love. As Schopenhauer says, "the eagerness and vehemence" of passion will be "the more powerful ... the more the loved individual is exclusively suited, by virtue of all his or her parts and qualities, to satisfy the desire of the lover and the need established by his or her individuality."

By contrast with the fleering cock-loftiness that marks the essay "Of Women," Schopenhauer in "The Metaphysics of the Love of the Sexes" earnestly sets forth the *shared* enterprise of being human, with all the reciprocal needs and strength and, often, illusions that this entails. If anything, he gives an edge to the feminine over the masculine. It is the feminine here that supplies "the intellect" (in the teeth of his denying women "powers of reasoning and deliberation" in "Of Women"); the masculine supplies "the will, or character," a relatively cruder, less lucid attribute (p. 344).[45] Correspondingly, also, the feminine "has one instinct more than man; and the ganglion system is also more developed in the woman as a class" (p. 351).

"The Metaphysics of the Love of the Sexes" makes a major breakthrough in thinking on the nature and function of genders. It is radically concerned with the species and the future, on the one hand, and with the individual and the present, on the other. It is simultaneously reverent toward the complex articulation of the evolutionary impulse and ironic toward its illusionary effects. It seeks a poise and comprehension of view that sets it off from the tendentious description in "Of Women," where immediate social interests predominate. But one is struck by the fact that even in the latter essay women as a class get the credit for being interested in "individuals" while yet maintaining responsibility for the "species." It is as though Schopenhauer could not altogether sacrifice his philosophical intuitions to his polemical occasions; he set out to score points off women, but reached out to make a point concerning the feminine.[46]

Schopenhauer significantly advances the understanding and the impact of the feminine in at least three ways. He recognizes the natural *rights* of women (which, needless to say, are much more radical and permanent than civil rights, while yet including them implicitly), and so rests any question pertaining to any woman upon the power and value residing indissolubly in the category she embodies, in the feminine principle. He recognizes the intrinsic equality and reciprocity of the sexes, thereby disarming the inhibitory force under which the feminine was used to suffer (even at his own hands). And he recognizes the great latitude of expression available to the sexes, a fact which he sees as beneficial to the species, and which we can see as benefiting the individual by loosening the stranglehold of stereotypic roles. His comments on sexual range are well worth noting:

All sex is one-sided. This one-sidedness is more distinctly expressed in one individual than in another; therefore in every individual it can be better supplemented and neutralized by one than by another individual of the opposite sex, for each one requires a one-sidedness which is the opposite of his own to complete the type of humanity in the new individual that is to be produced, the constitution of which is always the goal towards which all tends. Physiologists know that manhood and womanhood admit of innumerable degrees, through which the former sinks to the repulsive gynander and hypospadaeus, and the latter rises to the graceful androgyne; from both sides complete hermaphroditism can be reached, at which point stand those individuals who, holding the exact mean between the two sexes, can be attributed to neither, and consequently are unfit to propagate the species. [p. 357]

One may feel that a personal animus enters into the phrase "repulsive gynander" (Schopenhauer is again harsh toward homosexuality elsewhere in the study); and one may feel that the mixture of traits commonly associated with the masculine or the feminine *disposition* will usually prove more untidy than a phrase like "the exact mean" allows for. But even if one wants to insist that males may in some respects go beyond the exact mean toward the feminine without harm or loss, and females without harm or loss go equally toward the masculine, it is necessary to signalize the scope and freedom of individual behavior within the categories of gender that Schopenhauer formulates. His is not a static but a driving and versatile metaphysics of the sexes. He recognizes without canonizing distinctions, and leaves neither party to the sexual "confrontation" an advantage that is not also a liability, so that "collaboration"—spontaneous, intricate, uncertain— would be the sole hope for individual or species.

If Schopenhauer, as the pièce-de-résistance "Of Women" baldly shows, failed to extend his vision beyond the ad lib domain of passion, how much less could the time- and role-bound male of his era mutate into its world, or the time- and role-bound female expect and abet this. The law of familiarity is in human beings the counterpart to instinct in the other animals, and leads to a holding of positions and patterns that are not only uncomfortable but unprofitable, and with a strange contentment. But such contentment springs from a fear of the unknown, and implies a settled choice of the lesser of two evils. As Shakespeare says, we had "rather bear those ills we have than fly to others that we know not of." And Byron sees even deeper, in "The Prisoner of Chillon," where he comments that "a long communion" makes us "what we are." The Prisoner chooses the security afforded by his knowledge of his prison, over the risk involved in an ignorant entrance into the supposed freedom of the world.

To give way to the feminine entailed more than a revolution in custom and conduct, then; it entailed a revolution in principle and spirit. Difficulties within and resistance without: these make up the standard terrain in which the revolution was pursued. Not surprisingly, paradox abounds. It is a matter of necessity, not paradox, for males to participate in developing the feminine, but Schopenhauer's way of doing so was indirect ("The Metaphysics of the Love of the Sexes") or sidelong and accidental ("Of Women"). On the other hand, when Mary Wollstonecraft comes out with *A Vindication of the Rights of Woman*, she both forwards the feminine position and unmistakably falls into the privileged male value-system she sets out to combat. In fact, so strong is her adherence to the male shibboleth of "reason" that, with her marriage to William Godwin in mind, we could plausibly sum up her career in this motto: if you cannot become a man, at least acquire one.

Plausibly, but not fairly. There is unusual courage and skill, as well as pathos, in Mary Wollstonecraft's decision to challenge male authority on its own ground. In effect she is obliged to overcome the superstition that women lack powers of reasoning and deliberation, before she can establish a position concerning inalienable feminine powers. Perhaps the second volume of *A Vindication of the Rights of Woman*—projected but evidently never embarked on—would have filled the gap. As it stands, the *Vindication* is so taken up with the conventional male frame of reference that it can hardly see beyond it to an alternative.[47] Mary Wollstonecraft's ideal woman, and her ideal society, can best be identified by a post-Enlightenment stamp. In the relation between the sexes "intellect will always govern," she declares, and again, "the perfection of our nature and capability of happiness, must be estimated by the degree of reason, virtue, and knowledge, that distinguish the individual, and direct the laws which bind society." Where today we might stress language, Mary Wollstonecraft sees reason as the human factor: "In what does man's pre-eminence over the brute creation consist? . . . In reason."[48]

The universal inheritance of reason is the leitmotif of the *Vindication*, which tacitly sets itself against "hereditary" privilege; in effect Wollstonecraft is taking a second run at Edmund Burke, whose *Reflections on the Revolution in France* and championship of privilege and "prescription" she had already assailed in *A Vindication of the Rights of Men*. She makes the opposing of reason to prescription an explicit and formal part of her second, more famous work; the nature of man and the good of society, she says, require that "the strong hold of prescription—be forced by reason," in that the use of "prescription as an argument to justify the depriving men (or women) of their natural rights, is one of the absurd sophisms that daily insult common sense" (*A Vindication of the Rights of Woman*, pp. 12-13, et passim).

Given her emphasis on the homogenization—or hominization—of women, it would seem odd that she has enjoyed such honors for her voice in the libertarian tradition on the feminine side (though the Victorian suffragettes were not fond of her). Two observations seem apropos. First, Wollstonecraft's comments on the pernicious effects of abuses and inequities throughout the social order—in the army, in education, in literature, in religion, in child-rearing, in romantic love—these comments have a cogency of their own, and tend to shore up the central argument (or at least obscure its limitations). Second, and more important, is the undercurrent of intense feeling everywhere in this document of "reason." To obey and praise reason is a social obligation of her world; to resent indignity and despise injustice is a natural necessity that fires into her highest and brightest moments. Her thinking ceases to be constrained by clinical and analytical forms, bursting into new dimensions and new conceptual turns. Here, in one or two flashes, what is held back when she identifies nature with reason alone presses forward—her personality, her feminine acuteness of perception and feeling (attributes in which Dorothy Wordsworth instructed her brother William, to his incalculable benefit). And it results, ironically, in an increase in weight and drive for her basic argument,[49] as the metaphor concentrates and vivifies mere explanation:

But the fear of innovation, in this country, extends to everything—This is only a covert fear, the apprehensive timidity of indolent slugs, who guard, by sliming it over, the snug place, which they consider in the light of an hereditary estate; and eat, drink, and enjoy themselves, instead of fulfilling the duties, excepting a few empty forms, for which it was endowed. These are the people who most strenuously insist on the will of the founder being observed, crying out against all reformation, as if it were a violation of justice. [p. 159]

"The fear of innovation," "crying out against all reformation": these are phrases that suggest a scope and depth beyond that careful adherence to "reason" as received from and judged by men. But a positive version of something more is not forthcoming. The revulsion we feel against slugs repeats itself once, when instead of promising that women can and will be reasonable, Wollstonecraft invites us to feel, and not distantly analyze, what the lot of a woman comes down to:

I have always found horses, animals I am attached to, very tractable when treated with humanity and steadiness, so that I doubt whether the violent methods taken to break them, do not essentially injure them. . . . Be just then, O ye men of understanding! and mark not more severely what women do amiss, than the vicious tricks of the horse or the ass for whom ye provide provender—and allow her the privileges of ignorance, to whom ye deny the rights of reason, or ye will be worse than Egyptian taskmasters. [pp. 189–90, 194] [50]

When all is said and done about "reason," the basic object of *A Vindication of the Rights of Woman* is probably to urge that no man be, or be allowed to be, a slug, and equally that no woman become, or be made to become, a horse or ass. Its primary energy comes from a deep but inarticulate revulsion against oblique brutality and brutalization. Its positive proposal of a straightforward adherence to reason oversimplifies reason and history (for men have never done much in that line) and also oversimplifies nature and the interests and powers of women. In the pursuit of the value of the feminine, it would seem equally profitless for all men to go out hacking down hazel bowers as for all women to go about conforming to current formulations of reason. Clearly Wordsworth and Wollstonecraft, as they both point to something on the horizon, also betray the fact that the individual impulse lacks a *generally* applicable and authoritative form. The creative moment for the feminine falls short of conversion into a cultural principle or convention.

This is the principle that Rousseau, in *La Nouvelle Héloïse*, and Schlegel, in *Lucinde*, seek to embody in a manner at once dramatic and systematic. It should be noted at the outset that Schopenhauer invokes Rousseau as an authority in his diatribe "Of Women," and that Wollstonecraft devotes long pages and many incidental references to denouncing and rebutting the said Rousseau in her *Vindication* of Woman. In effect Rousseau appears in the same Janusian guise as Schopenhauer. In *Emile* he gives the woman the name of wisdom (Sophia) but the character of shrewdness and calculation. He out-Miltons Milton in the notion that woman is made for man and should systematically adapt her interests and desires to his. There is nothing of Athena in Rousseau's Sophia. Chapter 5, devoted to the ideal woman and marriage for the hero, Emile, might easily stand as a handbook for male egoism.[51] But this work, coming hard in the tracks of *La Nouvelle Héloïse*, obviously involves a sudden turnabout and even a relapse into gender stereotyping, as though the cultural and spiritual adventure of *La Nouvelle Héloïse* had cost him more than he could bear and left him warily seeking what Wollstonecraft calls a "snug place."

It is certain at any rate that Rousseau defies and transcends social prescriptions for gender in *La Nouvelle Héloïse*. The fact that this work centers upon the female character in a new hypostasis (the full title is *Julie, ou La Nouvelle Héloïse*) gives a fair indication of its bent, whereas the reactionary view of women appears in a work heavily biased toward the male and toward a temper at once subjective and doctrinaire (the full title is *Emile, ou L'Education*). It is imaginable that Sophia in *Emile* is Rousseau's wishful, indeed wilful, reconstitution of the character of Madame Sophie d'Houdetot, for whom he had harbored an unrequited passion in the years before composing this work—Sophia yields in spirit and principle, *because* Sophie had not.

In a sense Rousseau's treatment of Julie constitutes a more honest and more magnanimous response to the justice and wisdom (philo-sophia) of a woman's refusal. In youth and in the flesh, Julie succumbs, once, but she does not yield. What makes her the *new* Héloïse is the fact that she steadily assumes centrality and authority in her world, rather than being its pampered pawn. If St. Preux tutors her, she educates him. She becomes the vital center of a renovated order emphasizing the play of community over the rigors of institutions, and thus requiring of the individual constant integration and measure rather than flights into egotistic partiality. This distinction between community and institution goes to the heart of the tension between feminine and masculine modes of interaction in society. It is important to realize that the all-for-love syndrome with its headlong romantic passion represents as *much of an institution* as the bonds of marriage and family it sets up against. In like manner the pattern of male bonding[52] represents an institutional alternative to marriage and family on the one hand, and to mutual absorption between a male and a female on the other. With this in mind we can readily see that Julie promotes, more or less consciously, a breakdown of the self-perpetuating mechanisms and formulae that institutions come to exist on. The business of an institution is to preserve itself, and it uses its mechanisms and its members alike to that end. But the business of a community is to preserve (and serve) its members, and it applies itself to that end. If we keep in mind that we are talking about *dispositions*, not compulsions of nature, then we may say the masculine associates itself with the institutional, the feminine with the communal mode. Agamemnon's treatment of Iphigenia and of Cassandra *and of Achilles* would hold up the masculine standard; the interest is not in the persons but in the procedures sanctified by the institution—in this case, war. Athena's treatment of the Eumenides and, even more important, their treatment of her would illustrate the feminine turn, which equally avoids sacrificing principle and personality, because it finds a way to meld the sanctity of procedures with the sanctity of personal commitments.[53]

The basis of Julie's success in opposing institutions is her creation of, first, a sense of community and, ultimately, the roots of a new community. She does not resort to persuasion like Athena, but by the power of her *ethos* moves those who have formal authority over her, but who happen not to be in complete accord with one another, to a new, conciliated position. Her conversion of St. Preux from the possessiveness of a once-only-and-would-be-again lover to the selflessness of a lifelong follower is only the hinge of a door swinging wide on a new world. As she banks (physically and monetarily) St. Preux's ardor, so she checks the typical sneering jocularity of Lord Bomston and his male-bonded cronies. In this, she exorcises two "opposite" but interdependent "institutions," the spirit of what we now call *machismo* and the myth of virginity.

Both exorcisms occur in the same moment, when Lord Bomston, instead of pursuing the engaged duel with St. Preux, comes to apologize to him for failing to grasp Julie's character and the true nature of the bond between her and St. Preux. By institutional definition this would be an act of grovelling, as between Bomston and St. Preux, or inanity, as it affects Bomston and Julie. But the text faces such an interpretation down, as Bomston reaffirms his prowess and courage *against* any one who would challenge the propriety of his conversion. Julie's having once given herself to St. Preux becomes thus neither secret nor shameful—all that the old dispensation allowed. Rather, intactness and defloration cease to have automatic valences. Virginity loses its status as a synecdoche for virtue, and the total ambience of the act of love protects the personality from the narrow barbs of institutional thinking.

The abortive duel and the reconciliation of Bomston and St. Preux may be seen as a forecast of various other reconciliations in the text: that of St. Preux and Julie's husband, Wolmar, would be salient, but one may cite also the reconciliation of St. Preux and Julie's father, the Baron D'Etange, because it tends to suggest a harmony of diverse social classes and not just diverse personal interests. These reconciliations clearly reflect the integrity (as distinct from the conventionality) of the Julie-St. Preux relationship. It is clear that Byron, say, would have made merry over the scene of their lovemaking; Rousseau does not. He indicates that it is at once natural and out of keeping with the rhythm and aim of Julie's mind. It is contemplated again, but not repeated, because it belongs to itself and not with a full complex of human response. To pursue lovemaking for itself is to institutionalize it, but for Julie and St. Preux to find a living place for it within the community proves impossible. For a second moment circumstances conspire to make it seem that they can meet their obligations to the community and their desire for each other, but the neutral blank is quickly filled in with the needs of Fanchon Anet, who will lose her betrothed forever if Julie enjoys St. Preux for a night. All is out of proportion here. The night is subordinated to the lifetime, the institution of personal passion to the community of compassion and succor. Julie makes the decision, but it is significant that St. Preux carries out the errand of mercy— here begins that training in magnanimity that will make him not just an academic but a spiritual tutor for Julie's children.

While *Emile* deals artificially and formally with education, it is the *Nouvelle Héloïse* that gives the subject substance and breath. Much has been made of the fact that Julie never effaced her love and passion for St. Preux, but in a sense was compelled to confess it on her dying day. As if this derided or degraded her more temperate devotion to her parents, her husband, her children, her servants, her friends, and for all practical purposes to St. Preux himself. But an active and sustained and luminous choice underlies her containment of passion. Her passion is not destroyed but more generously distributed and applied from a larger perspective (in psychotherapeutic jargon, sublimated). She chooses in effect whether to experience a better copulation or to create a better community. Each is a mode of the same energy for giving and growing. Thus one should be relieved rather than distressed to discover that, to the end, Julie preserved the explosive option for her energy. Without it under control, her devotion to everyone from her parents to St. Preux might have been stagnant and cold. "People stifle great passions," she herself declares; "rarely do they purify them." But she proves an exception to her own dictum.

And yet one must recognize the autumnal, indeed the renunciatory, spirit with which the work concludes. Julie almost seems to renounce life ("I am dying content"), and certainly commends her children to her friend Madame D'Orbe in such a way as to suggest a cheerful renunciation. In addition, Claire D'Orbe renounces St. Preux. There is, of course, a view to the future, where Claire will be a surrogate mother and St. Preux a consummate tutor to the Wolmar children. But there is little feeling for the future, even in the children, and little of that vivacious feeling for the autumn that inspires Julie's quotation from Petrarch: *Frutto senile in su 'l giovenil fiore* (the aged fruit culminates the young flower). It is as though the uniqueness claimed for Julie, for different reasons, by St. Preux, Bomston, Wolmar, and Claire D'Orbe cannot be retained, but only regretted. More than this, it is as though that uniqueness has exhausted itself in the very effort to realize itself.

That uniqueness, it is fair to propose, has taken the form of an enlargement of the feminine, in the sense that it has free expression and considerable scope. Obviously the masculine is not hereby curtailed. It has already emerged, in discussion

of Lord Bomston and the institution of duelling, that the
masculine focus is reoriented and itself enlarged. Julie grows
up in a world divided and systematically at odds with itself,
class against class, sex against sex. She describes her parents
and characterizes her world: "My mother is weak and without
authority, I know the inflexible severity of my father." She
works, really lives, the spirit of reconciliation between blind
and averted extremes. She reconciles tenderness and virtue,
wisdom and charm; she seems to reconcile her parents; and
she assembles not only "incompatible impulses" but dis-
sociated powers "in one heart." In a frenzy Pope's Eloisa
projects a fantasy involving the total integration of functions
and values in one person: "Come, thou, my father, brother,
husband, friend." In an equal frenzy but with a bit more
hope, St. Preux apostrophizes Julie: "Oh my charming
mistress, oh my wife, my sister, my sweet friend!" But Julie
can be all these things best in succession. In the long run it is
as important that she *is reconciled* as that she reconciles. For
her feminine power would be expressed implicitly *under
subjection* if she could only enjoy it by its effect on and
service to others. Long before Virginia Woolf hypostatized
the term, Julie D'Etange had a room of her own, and as a
"symbol . . . of the soul of the one who had chosen it"
(Bk. IV. 12). It is a personal Elysium, of this world, without
the institutional "patriots and heroes" of Roman mythology,
without a Rhadamanthus, and indeed without any male
presence not admitted by her grace.

There is a point in *La Nouvelle Héloïse*, in the Elysium
series, where Wolmar sets forth the foundation of Julie's
power. The passage goes beyond a mere description of her
practices. It gives authority to her way, which is uncommon,
and in effect sets that way as a matter of principle above what
it takes the place of. It seems appropriate, then, to think of it
not just as a woman's way, but as the feminine way.
Here is Wolmar's explanation of the "miracle" of Elysium,

where plants and birds are both free and part of a system of culture, a *locus communis*:

Patience and time have performed this miracle. These are the expedients which rich people scarcely think of in their pleasures.[54] Always in a hurry to enjoy themselves, *force and money* are the only means they know. [Bk. IV. 11; italics added]

The distinction between patience and time as feminine resources, and force and money as masculine ones, is of course modal, not absolute. Indeed, it is worth repeating that the terms "masculine" and "feminine" register a likelihood, and cannot either predict or dictate the response of individuals. Patience and time have the same objective as force and money, and either means could conceivably be interchanged with or developed into the other. "Money," it may be well to observe, does not at first glance image character or gender as directly as the other terms; it rather seems to reflect social mores and the control of wealth by men. But the issue goes beyond ownership or control. It is the use of money as an instant, artificial expression of the self that Rousseau would have us recognize. "Money" is institutional, a metonymy for the masculine disposition. With the difference between "patience" and "money" Rousseau effectively dramatizes the principle of "accumulation" and "acquisition" discussed earlier.

The identity of *act* that joins the sexes and the divergence in *mode* that *statistically* distinguishes them can be more amply set forth in the following schema:

		masculine	*feminine*
(1)	*functions*	provide	sustain
		protect	defend
(2)	*relationship*	regulation	guidance
		criticism	sympathy

	masculine	*feminine*
(3) *traits*	force	balance
	aggression	responsiveness
	explosiveness	perseverance
(4) *defect*	sterility	barrenness
(5) *physique*	shoulders	hips
	androgens	estrogens
	semen	ovum [55]
(6) *method*	penetration	envelopment
(7) *objective*	efficiency	effectiveness
(8) *personality*	acquisitive	accumulative
(9) *politics*	institution	community

Like sex itself, these represent *twin* occurrences within one
stereoscopic ground of existence. It is only a polyphemus
vision that gives it all to one side, or tries to take it all for one
side. But only a painstaking vigilance can ward off such a
development. An appeal that stems from a particular moment
or conjunction of circumstances will canonize itself as a convention, and thus usurp the rightful place of another appeal
in another ambience. Thus explosiveness with a six-gun comes
to seem, throughout pioneer life and on into the present, not
just the height of street survival but the height of heroism and
humanity, and prowess at the piano or poetry a bit elitist or
effete (that term which means one has no leg to stand on).
Humankind, as Joseph Royce has observed, suffers from an
"inability to tolerate ambiguity," and its sexing is nothing if
not ambiguous. And what the enlargement of the feminine
did in the nineteenth century was effectively to restore and
legitimize ambiguity. Freud's early-twentieth-century cry,
"What does a woman want?" almost seems to sound an
exasperated demand for an end to that ambiguity. The answer
is of course that a woman wants *to be*, as an equally active,

equally independent, equally valued party in the relationship with the masculine.

Friedrich Schlegel's *Lucinde* not only confronts but creates ambiguity, and embodies as richly as any document to date the real distress as well as the real achievement and generosity of the feminine in the human equation. Once again the stress falls on masculine perception, because that must be reclaimed from rote responses if a free creative relationship is to come about. At all points relationship is the key to a philosophy of gender in the nineteenth century; only once, in Tennyson's *The Princess*, is there an experiment in isolation, and it is striking that when the women sequester themselves the prince takes on a feminine guise to bring about a rapprochement, as though in its absence the male must impersonate the feminine. The attention to the masculine must not distract us from the fact that it is the feminine leading into new life and new value. Conventional forms of belief and behavior range from denial to neglect to rejection of this possibility. But in the abstract contemplation, admission and consent are equally eligible responses. We have seen the development from the inhibition (Johnson) to the incorporation (Wordsworth) of the feminine, and may turn to Schlegel's *Lucinde* and its primary incarnation.[56]

Lucinde's name, as Peter Firchow suggests, contains both light (lux) and divine powers of childbirth (Lucina).[57] But Schlegel develops these resonances in singular ways. Lucinde represents the principle of *bringing to* light and birth, not their simple presence. Julius, Lucinde's lover, is completely surprised by her pregnancy, and is as much transformed by it as she.[58] Childbirth is not her commanding function but an entrance into new dimensions of personality for them both, as well as new dimensions in their relationship. Furthermore, Lucinde's life is threatened by illness, so that she almost does not get to carry out her "Lucina" role. The whole question of childbirth in the novel has more important reverberations

at the symbolic than at the practical level. From the outset
it is clear that his meeting Lucinde is the midwife of Julius's
stifled and jaded spirit, and at the end the child-to-be-born
bears his hopes of a new world: "Now I love the earth, and
the rosy dawn of a new spring raises its radiant head over my
immortal existence" (p. 107). As the Christ child confounded
the Elders in the temple, as the boy Cupid overmastered the
sagest adult with his arrows, as the infant Hercules destroyed
the deadly snakes, so this child symbolizes the infinite
possibilities that must contend against the "shades of the
prison-house." Julius all but makes this explicit: "It's right
that I should be adorned with the symbol of young innocence,
since now I dwell in nature's paradise" (p. 107).

The very form of *Lucinde* insists on infinite possibility. The
novel is incomplete and its parts utterly subject to "chance"
and a "right to confusion," ranging from letters to dithyrambs
to character sketches to allegories to idylls, and shifting
casually from first- to third-person narration and back. It is
in effect a fragment made up of fragments, a system of freewheeling moments whose natural integrity and momentum
rather than order make it get somewhere. The story of "little
Wilhelmine," placed at the beginning in casual symmetry with
the childbirth at the end, combines youth and freedom as an
emblem of infinite possibility (pp. 50 f.), and affords Schlegel
an opportunity to present his own work as analogous: "And
if this brief story of my life seems too wild, remember it's
only a child and tolerate its innocent playfulness with
motherly forbearance, and let it caress you." The child as a
signal of infinite freedom and possibility helps to bring out
another feature of the feminine, namely, its power of
rejuvenation (we may recall that the Furies not only become
the Eumenides, but they become young again as Athena
generates her new values in *The Oresteia*). Julius is conscious
of the association of the feminine and rejuvenation, rediscover-
ing "his youth in the arms of Lucinde." He applies the term

"female" to the "fault that custom and caprice" maintain, but uses the term "feminine" for the attributes and actions that spring from Lucinde's unaffected nature (p. 47). For Julius, rejuvenation occurs as much by moving across to the feminine as by moving back into childlikeness. The former movement is really at the heart of the novel, not unilaterally, but as an interpresence and interpenetration of genders:

One above all shapes and situations is wittiest and most beautiful: when we exchange roles and in childish high spirits compete to see who can mimic the other more convincingly, whether you are better at imitating the protective intensity of the man, or I the appealing devotion of the woman. . . . I see here a wonderful, deeply meaningful allegory of the development of man and woman to full and complete humanity. There is much in it—and what is in it certainly doesn't rise up as quickly as I do when I am overcome by you. [p. 49]

Here is philosophy through eroticism, and it is well to note the radical equality created by the sexual pun (rise up). For the phallus, that hidden prominence behind most claims of male superiority, gets its power from its defeat: "rise up . . . as . . . I am overcome by you." Each triumphs, or is defeated, making the posture and the phraseology of battle meaningless.[59] Penetration *means* envelopment, entails both victory and defeat, or neither.

For all its sensuous intensity, there continues through *Lucinde* a symbolic, even a platonic, streak.[60] The body must be the source and locus of ultimate spiritual appreciation. There is a veritable platonic progression from "sensitivity of the flesh" to "the summit of life" in the early pages of the novel:

One could divide all young men into those who have what Diderot call° the sensitivity of the flesh, and those who don't. A rare gift! Many talented and perceptive painters strive in vain for it all their lives, and many virtuosi of masculinity end their careers without ever having had the faintest idea of it. One doesn't gain it in the ordinary way. A libertine may know how to undress a girl with a kind of good taste. But only love teaches the youth the higher art of voluptuousness by which alone masculine strength is transformed into beauty. It is an electrictiy of feeling and yet at the same time a still, secret listening inside, and a certain clear transparency outside, as in those luminous places in painting that a sensitive eye feels so distinctly. It is a wonderful mixture and harmony of all the senses: thus, there are in music, too, completely artless, pure, and profound tones that the ear doesn't seem just to hear but actually to drink, when feeling thirsts for love. But beyond this, the sensitivity of the flesh can't be defined. To do so would be unnecessary in any case. It is enough to say that it is the first grade young men attain in the art of love while it is an innate gift with women, by whose grace and favor alone men can discover and acquire it. One must not speak of love to those unlucky ones who don't know this gift; for by nature man feels a need for love, but has no notion what it is like. The second level in the art of love already has something mystical about it and might easily appear to be irrational like every ideal. A man who can't completely fulfill and satisfy the inner longing of his beloved doesn't really know how to be what he really is and ought to be. He's actually impotent and can't contract a valid marriage. To be sure, even the highest finite greatness disappears in the face of the infinite, and consequently even with the best intentions the problem can't be resolved by brute force. But whoever has imagination can also communicate imagination, and where imagination is, lovers will go hungry in order to be extravagant. Their way leads inward, their goal is intensive infinity, inseparability without number and measure; and actually they need never want because their magic can replace everything. But no more of these secrets! Any young man who possesses it no longer loves only like a man, but at the same time like a woman too. In him humanity has reached perfection, and he has climbed the summit of life. For it is a fact that men are by nature only hot or cold: they have to be educated first to warmth. But women are by nature sensually and spiritually warm, and have a feeling for warmth of every sort. . . . Let me confess it: I don't love you only, I love womanhood itself. And I don't merely love it, I worship it; because I worship humanity, and because the flower is the apex of the plant, the apex of its natural beauty and form. [pp. 58–60, 61]

There is a grim underside to this aspiration and universality. It is lightly intimated when Lucinde becomes irritated with Julius for the *"galanterie* and *coquetterie"* he shares with

Amalie. It is presented in the abstract, in a severer light, when Julius describes the "two large classes" of women. The first "respect and honor the senses, nature, themselves, and masculinity," but the second have

lost this real inner innocence, and so purchase every pleasure with remorse, even to the point of being bitterly insensitive to their inner disapproval. This is of course what happens to so many women. First, they shy away from men, then they're sacrificed to unworthy men whom they soon hate or deceive until they despise themselves and their womanly destiny. They consider their own limited experience to be the experience of all women and think of everything else as ludicrous. That narrow circle of vulgarity and meanness in which they always move becomes their whole world and it doesn't occur to them that there might be other worlds. For women like this, men aren't human beings, but just men, a species unto themselves who are dangerous but unfortunately indispensable for avoiding boredom. They then become simply types themselves; one like the other, without originality and without love. [pp. 60-61]

But it emerges that such female "types" are not solely choosers of their state. Julius himself, driven to be "sensual" by "spiritual despair" (p. 78), all but makes a "victim" of an intrinsically chaste young girl, "gentle Louise" (p. 80); and by a harsh and ill-judged selfishness becomes the "ruin" of Lisette, a prostitute who presents a singular combination of efficiency and spontaneity, detachment and devotion (pp. 83-88). Julius indeed moves with helpless arrogance from woman to woman (pp. 78-97), not knowing who he is or what he wants ("his whole existence was a mass of unrelated fragments"). This is the background to his discovery of Lucinde, and of himself through her. Instead of being predatory and possessive, he now finds in himself "a feeling of universal tenderness," and instead of forcing himself into artificial and erratic relationships, he finds that he is "almost always just as ready to take part in some childlike sport as in the most sacred solemnity" (p. 103). He has become both spontaneous and versatile, as if he has caught from Lucinde the gift of overcoming formal oppositions and finding the essential unity of things. In connection with the reconciliation of opposites it may be noted that the word *harmony* occurs as a motif through the work, and Julius is described as finding "full harmony only in Lucinde's soul" (p. 103).

One might suspect, though, that Schlegel has relapsed into gender prejudices concerning passivity and dominance when he has "the germs of everything magnificent and everything holy" in Lucinde's soul awaiting "only the sunlight of [Julius's] spirit in order to unfold themselves into the most beautiful religion" (p. 103). After all, he is the one whose soul has unfolded most graphically. The question resolves itself, though raised to such a pitch of platonic imagery, in the same way as the bedroom tumble discussed before. There is a *reciprocity* in their relationship, a reciprocity which a momentary or a partial focus will miss. He "rises up" (the idiom is consonant with the "sunlight" at issue here) because he has been "overcome." Similarly, she is natural and indeed she also is *his* sun:

Sweetly reposing the childlike spirit slumbers and the kiss of the *loving goddess* stirs only happy dreams in him. . . . He smiles and seems to open his lips, but does not awaken and does not know what is happening to him. Only after the stimulus of the outer world, multiplied and intensified by an inner echo, has penetrated into every corner of his being, does he open his eyes, *rejoicing at the sun*, and remembering the magic world he saw in the glimmering light of the pale moon. [p. 105; italics added]

If the way they "mimic" each other here admits of distinction, that distinction is in mode rather than function and effect. Julius is a "god" to Lucinde's "priestess," only to recognize her "goodness and godlikeness" with a kind of priestly adoration (pp. 112, 114). The basic thrust of the novel is toward holiness, but away from canonization of moments or gestures or even achievements, to the extent that this would imply constant repetition and thus inhibit discovery and enlargement. "Only in the search itself," Schlegel says, "does the human mind find the secret that it seeks." As he goes on, he sets up a distinction between masculine and feminine that purports to hold good invariably, and yet the two image, or rather "mimic," each other and lose all value apart:

But what, then is the definer or the defined itself? For the man it is the anonymous. And what is the anonymous for the woman? The indefinite. The indefinite is more mysterious, but the definite has greater magical power. The charming confusion of the indefinite is more romantic, but the noble refinement of the definite is more like genius. The beauty of the indefinite is perishable, like the life of flowers and the eternal youth of human feelings; the energy of the definite is fleeting like a genuine thunderstorm and genuine inspiration.

Who can measure and who can compare two things that are infinitely valuable, when both are joined by the real definition that is destined to fill all lacunae and be the mediator between the individual man and woman and eternal mankind? [pp. 119–20]

The genius of *Lucinde* resides in its power of continuity, manifested first at the formal level, where each section or fragment becomes a new perspective and force bearing on Julius's development of a conscientious freedom, and his development into a "harmonized" human being. At deeper levels we find continuity also between the masculine and the feminine, between seriousness and play, between the sensual and the spiritual. In many respects the besetting problem for the feminine in the nineteenth century is one of continuity. In *Madame Bovary*, for example, the heroine cannot bridge the gap between memory and presence, between her convent upbringing and her indoctrination to a romance mentality through reading; nor can she bridge the gap between her romantic fantasies and those harsh phenomena of Tostes and Yonville and Rouen which so dominate her experience as to give Flaubert the name of realist. Her mind is geared to roles, to flat and repetitious negotiations that make her prey to the shallow oiliness of Rodolphe Boulanger and alternately prey on Leon Dupuis. She knows and adopts male manner-isms and male apparel (scandalizing a town, by the way, by appearing in long pants), but this is to mistake the froth for the force of a river. Baudelaire in his critique calls attention to Emma Bovary's "masculine" traits and sees her as a "man of action."[61] But that is the problem—either she affects the man, or she is possessed by romantic fantasies (she wanted to "die," but she also wanted to "live in Paris"). She thereby lives on a rack between intolerant extremes. It is not surpris-ing that the word *suddenly* dominates her life, with its register of rank uplifting occurrences, or that she keeps waiting for "extraordinary events." Her days, in reality, are constant enough, but there is no continuity or coherence in her apprehension of them. She has, in a metaphysical rather than a moral sense, no integrity. Her suicide concentrates that loss of a "sense of selfhood" which marks her entire experi-ence. She comes before us as the feminine manqué, too simply and truly passive and dependent, a succession of roles in search of a character.

Between the rigidity (or institutionalization) of roles and the playful abstraction of nature, it has continued to be a trial for women to draw on the power of the feminine, and there-fore also for men. By now the explanatory or argumentative approach to the feminine, with an eye to institutional politics, has very much the upper hand. This affords pragmatic satis-factions, not the least of which is the venting of resentments and, in a curious revision of Mary Wollstonecraft, the vindica-tion of the wrongs of woman. But these are satisfactions that add to what one has, and not what one is. As reflective and sophisticated a champion of women's rights as John Stuart Mill, in his essay *The Subjection of Women*, seems to pre-occupy himself with roles rather than relationships, with static and discontinuous shibboleths of value. Yet a powerful cor-rective to this tradition arises within its very confines.

In *A Room of One's Own* Virginia Woolf goes through the

gamut of victimization and indignation, argumentation and repudiation of male privilege and presumption, consolidation and nurture of female prospects and resources. But the very lucidity and thoroughness and candor of her attack lead her beyond its explicit forensic purpose. What commences as a gospel-cum-handbook for women in particular (with mock alarm and seriousness she asks her audience to assure her that no man lurks behind a curtain) ends up as a spontaneous vision of man and woman joining, casually but symbolically à la Schlegel, to embody a stronger humanity.

This comes at a point where, in fact, she is preoccupied with the need for "the development by the average woman of a prose style completely expressive of her mind." Beyond this gender bias, she has thoughts of an intrinsic isolation in human experience: "The fascination of the London street is that no two people are ever alike; each seems bound on some private affair of his own." But, in a lull of action on the street, in a lull of intention in her mind, a pedestrian epiphany occurs:

At this moment, as so often happens in London, there was a complete lull and suspension of traffic. Nothing came down the street; nobody passed. A single leaf detached itself from the plane tree at the end of the street, and in that pause and suspension fell. Somehow it was like a signal falling, a signal pointing to a force in things which one had overlooked. It seemed to point to a river, which flowed past, invisibly, round the corner, down the street, and took people and eddied them along, as the stream at Oxbridge had taken the undergraduate in his boat and the dead leaves. Now it was bringing from one side of the street to the other diagonally a girl in patent leather boots, and then a young man in a maroon overcoat; it was also bringing a taxi-cab; and it brought all three together at a point directly beneath my window; where the taxi stopped; and the girl and the young man stopped; and they got into the taxi; and then the cab glided off as if it were swept on by the current elsewhere.

The sight was ordinary enough; what was strange was the rhythmical order with which my imagination had invested it; and the fact that the ordinary sight of two people getting into a cab had the power to

communicate something of their own seeming satisfaction. The sight of
two people coming down the street and meeting at the corner seems to
ease the mind of some strain, I thought, watching the taxi turn and make
off. Perhaps to think, as I had been thinking these two days, of one sex
as distinct from the other is an effort. It interferes with the unity of the
mind. Now that effort had ceased and that unity had been restored by
seeing two people come together and get into a taxi-cab. . . . Clearly
the mind is always altering its focus, and bringing the world into different perspectives. But some of these states of mind seem, even if
adopted spontaneously, to be less comfortable than others. In order to
keep oneself continuing in them one is unconsciously holding something
back, and gradually the repression becomes an effort. But there may
be some state of mind in which one could continue without effort
because nothing is required to be held back. And this perhaps, I thought,
coming in from the window, is one of them. For certainly when I saw
the couple get into the taxi-cab the mind felt as if, after being divided,
it had come together again in a natural fusion. The obvious reason
would be that it is natural for the sexes to co-operate. One has a profound, if irrational, instinct in favour of the theory that the union of
man and woman makes for the greatest satisfaction, the most complete
happiness. But the sight of the two people getting into the taxi and the
satisfaction it gave me made me also ask whether there are two sexes in
the mind corresponding to the two sexes in the body, and whether they
also require to be united in order to get complete satisfaction and
happiness. And I went on amateurishly to sketch a plan of the soul so
that in each of us two powers preside, one male, one female; and in the
man's brain, the man predominates over the woman, and in the woman's
brain, the woman predominates over the man. The normal and comfortable state of being is that when the two live in harmony together,
spiritually cooperating. If one is a man, still the woman part of the
brain must have effect; and a woman also must have intercourse with
the man in her. [pp. 100-02]

There is in this a quiet stroke of genius that it would be well
to highlight. Virginia Woolf is not only dealing with gender
complementarity (which it would be absurdly suicidal to
oppose), but also with radical reconciliation of opposed views,
or in short with the apprehension that the only legitimate
orthodoxy is paradox. In particular we may note that "effort"
is both valuable/necessary and harmful/artificial. A second

paradox emerges later, in a veritable epithalamium, where Woolf recognizes that the fear of death produces marriage, rather than marriage producing an attraction to life:

it is fatal for any one who writes to think of their sex. It is fatal to be a man or woman pure and simple; one must be woman-manly or man-womanly. It is fatal for a woman to lay the least stress on any grievance; to plead even with justice any cause; in any way to speak consciously as a woman. And fatal is no figure of speech; for anything written with that conscious bias is doomed to death. It ceases to be fertilised. Brilliant and effective, powerful and masterly, as it may appear for a day or two, it must wither at nightfall; it cannot grow in the minds of others. Some collaboration has to take place in the mind between the woman and the man before the act of creation can be accomplished. Some marriage of opposites has to be consummated. The whole of the mind must lie wide open if we are to get the sense that the writer is communicating his experience with perfect fullness. There must be freedom and there must be peace. Not a wheel must grate, not a light glimmer. The curtains must be close drawn. The writer, I thought, once his experience is over, must lie back and let his mind celebrate its nuptials in darkness. He must not look or question what is being done. Rather, he must pluck the petals from a rose or watch the swans float calmly down the river. And I saw again the current which took the boat and the undergraduate and the dead leaves; and the taxi took the man and the woman, I thought, seeing them come together across the street, and the current swept them away, I thought, hearing far off the roar of London's traffic, into that tremendous stream. [pp. 108-09]

Woolf's "marriage of opposites" contains a curious reflection of and complement to Schlegel's consummation scene in *Lucinde*. The latter speaks of Julius rising up when overcome, but Woolf has a writer, referred to by the masculine pronoun, "lying back" when triumphant. "His" here seems but an idiomatic courtesy—the full force of meaning is human, hermaphroditic. Mode and emphasis vary from gender to gender, even moment to moment. But nature is not divided, except in the convenience of analysis, and *except as a way of manifesting the integral richness* of whatever analysis takes up. That richness finally cannot be represented straightforwardly.

It presses toward paradox, and renders itself in metaphor. After all the intense study and deliberation of *A Room of One's Own*, one can hardly fail to be struck by the articulate inclusiveness of the dramatized image, in contrast with the partiality of explicit arguments by Wollstonecraft or Mill or Woolf herself. It will be necessary to look at a broader and perhaps more typical range of argument in the romantic period, but here a summary comment on the feminine must take precedence.

The pursuit of the feminine in the nineteenth century—before the depersonalization of the industrial revolution and the collectivization of imperial advances rendered men, as well as women, subjects and instruments of amorphous institutions—blazed a way toward freedom and wholeness. It promised a way out of rigid partitions and oppositions, an *enlargement* of the feminine and, through the feminine, of the masculine complement of our humanity. It involved a way of recognizing that there is something better than being right and pure, namely, being true and fully recognized. It is a way of reconciliation, and not a separate way save in the sense that it requires one to leave the paths of exclusion. It makes much of grace, because that is the term most effectively combining power and ease, strength and delicacy. It provides for Wolmar and Julius to marry non-virgins, but it holds no brief for prostitution (which is the obverse of institutional virginity, a dictation of roles and a desecration of personality.)

Above all, whether we encounter an inhibition or an incorporation or an incarnation of the feminine, an underlay of debate appears: will the institutional forum hold, or be broken, will the new bones love, or petrify? If the feminine occurs often in connection with forests, with what is beyond the bound world, it is only to convert enclosures into bowers. If it finds convents anathema, it is not that it opposes holiness, but that it dreads constriction. It depends everywhere on the courage in women to accommodate the new, and in men the courage to be led thereto. It subsists on relationships, and demands an attitude at once rigorously devout and playfully experimental. For the feminine cannot be canonized once and for all in time, or truly represented without the inextricable paradox the Greeks conveyed with their triune goddess, Selene-Artemis-Hecate, in whom chaste aloofness, bloody athleticism, and spectral victimization occur as aspects of one another. Ideally we would wish to know it as nature, or comprehensive presence, and conduct, or intrinsic purpose, and value, or absolute effect. But these are in process, *in spe*. At present we have myths, or would-be-comprehensive statements, and gestures, or potentially representative manifestations, and impressions, or intimations of value. Perhaps the feminine is a power as impalpable, as ubiquitous, as irresistible as the wind. It is a power that every woman fears she does not command, and every man that she does. Its greatness as a power resides in its willingness, demonstrated by Athena as well as by Oothoon, to distribute rather than codify itself. Its force is patience, and time its money. But its atmosphere is implicit denial and debate. Even in the nineteenth century, which recognized it without alarm and pursued it without ulterior motives, it existed in such an atmosphere. Perhaps only the fact that the nineteenth century, and most especially the romantic period, constituted itself on an internalized principle of argument made room for the brief and brilliant recognition and realization of the feminine that we have just held up for scrutiny.

4
The Mode of Argument
in Wordsworth's Poetry

Romanticism is the only major movement that has given its basic impulses and aspirations a plenary indulgence, and at the same time a stern critique.

Anon.

T. S. Eliot, I. A. Richards, Irving Babbitt, T. E. Hulme, F. L. Lucas, Cleanth Brooks: these are among the names that gave personality and weight to the anti-romantic "movement" predominating in Anglo-American literary circles from the 1920s to the 1950s. All brought fame, learning, eloquence, and philosophy into play, in an effort to expose the speciousness and unfitness they saw in romanticism. Under various guises these critics leveled charges of unleavened melancholy, untempered vision, unwarranted self-assertiveness, unreflecting enthusiasm, unauthorized sentiment, and unmeasured phrasing. Perhaps their root objection was to the presence of intensity without range and complexity, or again to the canonization of a flat perspective and flat posture in romanticism.

By the mid-1970s, of course, it had come about that romanticism was being held up as the staging ground of modernism, and the prevailing self-satisfaction of "the modern" had brought romanticism into a latitude of unprecedented favor. One oddity, however, emerges. The champions of romanticism could seem to have saved its name by bringing about not a new grasp on its constitution, but a new appreciation of the very features its opponents had disparaged. R. A. Foakes writes a favorable study entitled *The Romantic Assertion*; Frank Kermode pays homage to the romantic phenomenon of "necessary isolation or estrangement of men who can perceive" the "Image as a radiant truth out of space

and time," and asks us to celebrate *The Romantic Image*;
Stephen Spender, somewhat uneasily perhaps, acknowledges
the "miracle-producing resources of the individual imagination," in *The Struggle of the Modern*; and Robert Langbaum,
in *The Poetry of Experience*, upholds "the doctrine of
experience—the doctrine that the imaginative apprehension
gained through immediate experience is primary and certain,
whereas the analytic reflection that follows is secondary and
problematical." Through all these works there appears to run
a disposition to canonize unleavened melancholy, untempered
vision.

But in fact these critics bring out what the anti-romantics
clearly missed, the fact that the romantics candidly acknowledged, confronted, and perhaps actually created an uncertain
and "problematical" situation. A "flat" position is at best
precarious in such a context. It becomes necessary then to
look with patience and care at what Morse Peckham in
Romanticism and Behavior calls the failure of romantic
"explanation," and to seek to identify the peculiar terms of
"the poet's struggle," as George Bornstein terms it in *Transformations of Romanticism in Yeats, Eliot, and Stevens*. For
in fact the idea of the "primary and certain" moment in
romanticism may be misleading; there is rather a slowly
emerging mosaic or even pointillist field of moments, too clear
to be denied, too unsettled to result in dogma.

Even when they were not always personally embattled, like
Byron and Blake, or agitated like Rousseau, or unmoored like
DeQuincey and Keats, the romantics were quite aware that
they stood on argumentative ground. For all his quasi-
Platonic insistence that imagination, unconstrained by nature
and actuality, alone yields knowledge of the reality of man,
Blake never blinks the necessity of relating reality to actuality,
and he makes his "forms" as much "dramatic" as "visionary."
His vision is not given but willed, not achieved but intrinsi-
cally striven for; his "strife" may be "mental," but it is

ubiquitous, and there is reason to conclude that as Blake's man is infinite so must be his "strife" in the interest of full realization. In turn Wordsworth virtually enunciates the necessity of argument as a *sine qua non* of romanticism: "every author, as far as he is great and at the same time *original*, has . . . the task of *creating* the taste by which he is to be enjoyed."

Perhaps a jaded observer could see in Wordsworth's position the prototype of twentieth-century promotional hype, and the travesty of the modern "taste-makers." The situation is of course more modest, and more complex. Just as Shelley signalizes a condition of deep challenge and unease when he admits that his legislator-poet goes "unacknowledged," so Wordsworth poses for his poet a lack of acknowledgment and acceptance, along with the challenge of enabling, or maybe persuading, the audience to see the pleasure and justice of positive appreciation. The position is thus dynamic and shows a far from simple psychological torque for the audience, as for the poet. The situation seems far less simple than Stephen Spender implies when he says that "every reader [of romantic poetry] is free to imagine himself to some extent . . . taking over [the poet's] feelings and behaviour . . ." (*The Struggle of the Modern*, p. 136). Some empathy of participation may naturally occur, and is a compliment to the writer; but it is no favor to Byron, say, to "take over" the Giaour's feelings without seeing that the poem is more intricate and ironic than its protagonist, without coming to grips with the formal and conceptual framework that contests all mere dogma and passion by putting values and sympathies athwart one another. It is well to recall that *Prometheus Unbound*, after proceeding through perhaps the fiercest antagonism and the most copious mind-training that romanticism conjures up, does not really come to a redeemed, secure world, but only to a redeemed, secure perspective on the world of tyranny, grief, and hate. The work ends with Demogorgon's summons to the jubilant assembly, gathered around Prometheus and Asia, to feel the pressure of Jovian tyranny seeking to reestablish itself, and to accept the pressure, within their jubilation, of suffering for the sustenance of good.

In fact Shelley, though he has been made something of a scapegoat for the supposed sins of romanticism, exhibits the typical romantic alertness to the need for a defense of its poetry, for arguing and substantiating its images and its dreams. He is still sometimes thought of as the blatherer *par excellence,* spewing images hither and yon, and indulging himself in unseemly displays of metaphor and sentimentality ("I fall upon the thorns of life! I bleed!").[1] Taken out of context this verse may well induce a touch of hilarity; but then, in harsh isolation, King Lear's "Pray, sir, undo this button" could seem foppish, and even "Why hast thou forsaken me?" somewhat maudlin. Within the "Ode to the West Wind" Shelley's phrasing can be shown to work, and tellingly. The speaker has let himself get carried away with his desire for identification with the power and elevation of the West Wind. His attempt to loft away may be laughable, but the line describing the consequence (his downfall) is not. It is filled with a fearful realization of his subjection, his vulnerability, his mortality. In context it serves as a transition to a more sensible, humble posture, where he does not make demands on the West Wind and claim parity with it, but is content if it will use him as its instrument ("Let me be thy lyre," versus "Be thou me" earlier).

In general, dramatic and logical propriety in Shelley's use of language is surprisingly consistent, and effective. At times the language seems to smear, and the reader concludes that Shelley lacks control of syntax, images, thought. The cause may, however, lie elsewhere. Shelley's thoughts and attitudes are certainly not of the garden variety, and often they move with such rapidity and complexity that we are left wandering in a maze which he has occasioned, not created, for us. As

Susan Hawk Brisman remarks, "in Shelley's poetry the possibility of closure almost always coincides with an access of self-consciousness concerning voice, but precisely how Shelley achieves or loses conviction and whether the poems record the process are matters but partially explored."[2] The opening lines of "Mont Blanc" may well stand as illustration.

The everlasting universe of things
Flows through the mind, and rolls its rapid waves,
Now dark—now glittering—now reflecting gloom—
Now lending splendour, where from secret springs
The source of human thought its tribute brings
Of waters,—with a sound but half its own,
Such as a feeble brook will oft assume
In the wildwoods, among the mountains lone,
Where waterfalls around it leap for ever,
Where woods and winds contend, and a vast river
Over its rocks ceaselessly bursts and raves.

A couple of simple impressions come home immediately to any responsive reader: Shelley is talking about big things, and he is talking with a high degree of declarative assurance. Then the intricacy of the subject matter, its momentary changes (now . . . now . . .) within the stability of the initial clauses (ll. 1–2), can hardly be missed. The question will naturally arise whether the empirical impulse to change or the basic philosophical postulate controls the poem. But close attention reveals that the lines pose far more complex problems. A radical difference develops between the declared truth (the universe of things flows through the mind) and the way in which that truth manifests itself and is apprehended. The truth is not of fact but of relationship, and that relationship not linear but reciprocal and emergent. Accordingly the entire opening section of "Mont Blanc" should be taken as the setting up of a *problem inherent in* what may seem an axiomatic relationship between universe and mind. The involvement, really the involution, that takes set in the lines after the opening declaration is but an image of the uncertainty and intricacy the subject entails. Shelley should win points for precision where he is blamed for obscurity.

What sort of relationship is he asking us to apprehend? One of intrinsic paradox. We must visualize a situation in which the universe of things is as a river flowing through the mind, but the mind is at the same time an independent stream flowing into the river ("the source of human thought its tribute brings/Of waters"). Besides, the mind could be conceived of as part of the universe flowing through it. If we construe the mind in a divine-platonic way, then it could encompass all things, but at the expense of its tributary function. It does not take great ingenuity to see that the mind and the universe are mixed up with one another, in grammar and syntax as well as actuality. In line 2, is it the "rapid waves" of the mind or of the universe that are rolled? To which of the two, mind or universe, does the succeeding play of epithets ("now dark— now glittering . . .") refer? Shelley is conveying a definite and yet inextricable relationship, competing autonomies that tend to exhaust attention, defy explanation, and pass for the entirety of things.

The thrust of the poem is away from the very credulity that the opening section *seems* to rest upon. The declarative presumption of absoluteness in that section is immediately checked in the second verse paragraph, where Shelley shows that it amounts to no more than a metaphor of the way the Ravine of Arve impresses him. And he affords us ready intimations of a *tertium quid*, "a remoter world" marked by "some unknown omnipotence." The poem, when at last it reaches that world (section v), stands in defiance of "the universe of things" and of "the mind" alike. All available or workable or bearable terms of mind and universe break down, so that neither subsists there though both are paradoxically invoked. It is a world where there is no effective difference between night ("the calm darkness") and day ("the lone glare")—the same truth holds, to wit, that it is timeless. We are privileged, given the poem's imaginative reach, to see the things of that world which "none beholds," and these things turn out to be riddled with contradiction, riddles of nature and of thought: "flakes" that "burn"; "star-beams" darting through snow-flakes; "winds" that "contend/Silently"; lightning without thunder ("voiceless"); and lightning that "like vapour broods/Over the snow" (which makes the snow into a fruitful egg).

In the end, "Mont Blanc" is a poem about incomprehensibility, and about the ways in which it is preferable to "vacancy" (144). The poem conveys *and enacts* the intricacies of the path to understanding. It moves, significantly, from initial flat declaration (1-2) to metaphor (12) to speculation ("Some say," 49) to a struggle for interpretation (80-83), to a final interrogation (141-44; "And what were thou . . .?"). The language of the poem is everywhere intense, and so is its rhythm, with the effect that the reader is moved in ways that are not always open to quick explanation. Perhaps this could lead to a sense of incantatory possession, but then it is possible to demonstrate that Shelley is proceeding responsibly, lucidly, even analytically. Far from rushing pell-mell to conclusions, he is exploring relationships and is content, when that fits the case, to end with a question.

The movement Shelley presents in the "Hymn to Intellectual Beauty" from declaration to interrogation—a refusal to force issues—appears notably again in Keats's "Ode to a Nightingale," and seems typical of romanticism. Where the romantic poem moves, as in the "Ode on a Grecian Urn," from interrogation to declaration, the declaration is not just carefully circumscribed, but emerges from a desire for understanding and answers well worthy of being called inquisitive. Intensity of emotion, crisis, extreme confrontation do occur endemically in romanticism, but they warrant and inspire acute attention and judgment, not careless (or carefree) verbiage. It bears repeating that "the romantics' plunge into the 'abyss' of the human mind was neither desolate nor headlong, but a finely calibrated, even analytical adventure." Within the work of one poet we will find great variety and cogency in bringing analysis to adventure. Let us take William Wordsworth in illustration.

In his lecture "On the Living Poets" Hazlitt proffers a couple of seminal, if cryptic, insights into a problem arising within the very structure of romanticism and affecting both the content and the formulation of its poetry. He observes (1) that romantic poetry in principle deals with what is at once "natural and new," and (2) that the romantic poet "sees nothing but himself and the universe."[3] On the surface these could be taken as positively fruitful and just remarks; but in actuality they come from Hazlitt with a challenging air of complaint. As Lascelles Abercrombie says, Hazlitt "meant it maliciously."[4]

It may be well to recall that, in his essay "Mr. Wordsworth" in *The Spirit of the Age*, Hazlitt speaks admiringly of this same Wordsworth, whose "genius is a pure emanation of the Spirit of the Age"; he who had seen fit to query has come to praise:

As the lark ascends from its low bed on fluttering wing, and salutes the morning skies; so Mr. Wordsworth's unpretending Muse, in russet guise, scales the summits of reflection, while it makes the round earth its footstool, and its home! Possibly a good deal of this may be regarded as the effect of disappointed views and an inverted ambition. Prevented by native pride and indolence from climbing the ascent of learning or greatness, taught by political opinions to say to the vain pomp and glory of the world, "I hate ye," seeing the path of classical and artificial poetry blocked up by the cumbrous ornaments of style and turgid *commonplaces*, so that nothing more could be achieved in that direction but by the most ridiculous bombast or the tamest servility; he has turned back partly from the bias of his mind, partly from a judicious policy.[5]

The idea of the morning "lark" choosing his song essentially as the arch-practitioner of the artificial style had done, with a view to the "one way left of excelling," has a pungency all its own; this by the way. The main point of the essay, at least in connection with Wordsworth's early "productions," is to show the poet who "has given a new view or aspect of nature" (p. 89), thus implicitly reconciling the natural and the new. But the charm and authority of Hazlitt's change of disposition do not quite yield a critical solution to the problem he originally posed. A new principle, rather than an altered disposition, would be in order here.

The source of Hazlitt's complaint is not far to seek; both his statements, separately and together, suggest problematical polarities and obscurities which, one is led to infer, the poetry can neither expel nor explain. The oxymoronic joining of the natural and the new sets up a quizzical perspective, with the state of something general, permanent, and necessary falling in danger of being confused with or usurped by the busy vividness of something lately seen, accidental, and unproved. In like manner the self and the universe, though presented as coordinate, verge on becoming identities in an implicitly solipsistic scheme, where the universe is too huge and indefinite to bear any independent relation to the self. One can, without straining, sense in the poet's tendency to see nothing but himself and the universe an imminent threat of seeing himself *as* the universe, or, like Oswald in *The Borderers*, compulsively reproducing himself there. Two problems then develop with real moment for practical romanticism: how to convey the propriety and in fact the agelessness of what to consciousness appears like mere innovation, and how to set forth the complementary oneness of "personality and infinity."[6]

Certainly, though, these problems did not beset the poets without their full consciousness. The Preface to *Lyrical Ballads* plainly recognizes them, as does the "Essay Supplementary to the Preface" of 1815 with its exposition of the "true difficulty" inherent in the poet's need to "call forth and communicate *power*" or, alternatively, to "call forth and bestow power." The problematical relation with the reader repeatedly attracts Coleridge's attention in the *Biographia Literaria*, and Byron's (if on different grounds) in his letters and journals as well as in *Don Juan*. There is room for arguing that in the Major Prophecies Blake pays scant courtesy to the reader in the way of honoring the difficulties of the literature of power.[7] But Blake himself bears witness to the diversified portfolio of rhetorical resources which the romantic poet can boast. The style of the *Songs of Innocence and Experience* is markedly dramatic, that of *Auguries of Innocence* declamatory or assertive, that of *To Tirzah* abstract and analytical; and none of these quite sorts with the compacted style of the Major Prophecies.

In short, the romantic poets give little warrant for supposing they did not seek to impose order, as any work of art must do, not only on their subject matter but also on the mind of the reader. This is, of course, the period which saw Coleridge enunciate the principle of "poetic faith," and Macaulay, in his *Life of Dryden*, aver that "poetry requires not an examining but a believing frame of mind." But such remarks intend to free poetry of the ultimate requirements of expository rigor, not to license it for arbitrary propositions. It is obvious, too, that the latter gets no countenance from any of the poets in question.

The issue, as it boils down, becomes not whether but how any romantic poet copes with the true difficulty of communicating power. It possesses a peculiar interest in the case of Wordsworth, because he gives the appearance of bluntly ignoring in practice the problem he so sensitively defines in principle, and arriving at that sort of *dixit* in communicating which succeeds through a predisposition or cowed submission in the reader. We call him a poet of statement and—amply supported by his reading style, which counted so much on "an animated and impassioned recitation"—sum up his work as the poetry of assertion.[8] But at least as late as 1838, in the "Valedictory Sonnet" to the volume published that year, Wordsworth announces another ideal. He wants Truth and Fancy to agree, and would win "a passage" to the reader's heart by "simple Nature *trained by careful Art*" (italics mine).[9] This is hardly the sexagenarian Yeats avowing the ageless energy of his heart and imagination, but it does confess a continuing artistic conscience and aspiration. We may deny that Wordsworth wins us (especially with the late poetry), but we still need to consider the nature of the attempts he made. On this ground something valuable stands to be learned about the cast of his poetry, and indeed the cast of his mind, in that the former continually reflects scruples about the accuracy or clarity of what is being said, and further a lively sense of the problem of meeting potential doubts and objections from a neutral, or perhaps antagonistic, mind. Between the claims of accuracy and the claims of persuasion, Wordsworth gets into his poetry something worthy of being considered a mode of argument.[10]

This will not resemble good neoclassical practice any more than the summary prefacing "Descriptive Sketches" or "An Evening Walk" resembles the argument of book 4 of the *Dunciad*—indeed, what Wordsworth calls the argument of *The Prelude* (1.643, 14.277) is really its subject matter or "theme," and not a thing of rhetorical disposition. But a variety of features, ranging from the habitual use of litotes to the use of Coleridge in *The Prelude*, sufficiently attests to the point that "the poetic imagination cannot hope to shake itself free from scepticism. . . . It is impossible to claim that the imagination can give us what can be known for truth, or what may, in all strictness, be called knowledge."[11]

The skepticism of Wordsworth as poet is salient in *The Prelude*. Wordsworth reveals a more than conventional anxiety

over his worthiness and fitness for his task—an anxiety over
himself as subject, as artist, and as seeker of an unprecedented Muse with the paradoxical trick of "vexing its own
creation" (1.38). In relation to Coleridge, as of his first major
appearance at the end of book 1 (612 ff.), this anxiety takes
a specifically argumentative turn. Coleridge, when the lines
are scrutinized, simply is made to burst out of the role of
auditor and dedicatee, and to assume the functions of a
devil's advocate (whose understanding can be assumed but
still must be cultivated), of a father confessor or, perhaps,
sounding board, and of a lightning-rod for skepticism, in a
complex utterance of self-deprecation and vindication on
Wordsworth's part.

The self-deprecation is easy enough to see:

> I began
> My story early—not misled, I trust,
> By an infirmity of love for days
> Disowned by memory—ere the breath of spring
> Planting my snowdrops among winter snows:
> Nor will it seem to thee, O Friend! so prompt
> In sympathy, that I have lengthened out
> With fond and feeble tongue a tedious tale.
>   [612–19]

In short, both good sense, which would overcome doting
nostalgia (613–15), and good taste, which should renounce "a
tedious tale," stand to challenge the present undertaking. But
the lines actually have built into them a correction of attitude
which protects Wordsworth from their seemingly fatal weight
and aim. Two rhetorical features may be glanced at here: the
litotes of "not misled" and the image of the snowdrops. Both
tend to reverse the negative bearing of the lines. Substantially
the rest of the poem is to answer the question whether Wordsworth is misled, but here the effect is to open the issue and
relieve its pressure, as a safety-valve might do. The negative
possibility, "misled," is explicit, but gets blocked and negated

itself by the assurance (partially qualified by "I trust") that he is "not." The poem thus admits, as it denies, the negative possibility; it incorporates potential resistance and rejection in a controlled, innocuous form. This is the rhetorical work of the litotes, to staunch the flow of objections, if not to establish validity.

The image of the snowdrops, linked to the question of being misled, supports the litotes by giving a positive dimension to the state of which a negative version has been denied. It brings up the earliest flower of spring in, and out of, the apparently inhospitable context of snow, and develops substance and familiarity for the faith which, in the litotes, must seem abstract, or even cryptic.

It is important to see that Coleridge, who now enters as one "prompt/In sympathy" with Wordsworth, takes a part in a process of deliberation and confirmation that is already underway. The process does not depend on him and his sympathy. He extends it into a new area.[12] Beyond the concretization brought about by the snowdrop image, he allows for the incarnation and personalizing of the problematical relation between Wordsworth and his material. Clearly he provides a likely audience for an ample statement by Wordsworth, in assessing his stage of progress, of his hope and object in the poem (620-25)—that the hope is of psychological and philosophical stability, and the object honorable toil, can but work in Wordsworth's favor. Furthermore, in his role as recipient of the poem, Coleridge comes to stand for and function as *the reader*, the fit audience, and thereby curtails and controls the play of skepticism around the working of *The Prelude*.

This is not to suggest any sort of sinister or artificial maneuvering on Wordsworth's part. Rather, there comes to the surface here a deep pressure of inquietude to which the poem, or the poet, responds in keeping with characteristic rhetorical resources (litotes, imagery, as agents of affirmation);

also here we see emerging the nature of an implied contract
with the audience (Coleridge as a conscious, independently
sympathetic participant in the issues and causes of the poem).
In a sense the poet not only creates the taste by which he is
to be relished, as Wordsworth maintained, but also, as Milton
resignedly saw, he *presupposes* a fit audience. Alessandro
Manzoni, the Italian romantic, enunciates this latter view as
a law, which Lascelles Abercrombie renders thus: "Every
composition offers in itself . . . the elements" by which it
should be judged.[13] Modern aesthetics subscribes to this view,
of course, without allowing Erasmus Darwin or Stephen
Duck, or Richard Blackmore or Barry Proctor, to step over a
high threshold of regard; that is to say, the principle of judgment in the poem is neutral as to value. For present purposes,
it needs to be observed that, with Coleridge, Wordsworth
effectively sketches in some of the necessary features of the
poem's audience and, hence, some of the factors involved in
judging the poem itself.

The resurgent force of doubt in Wordsworth's mind
becomes apparent as each difficulty met yields to another
seen. The problem thus far has had to do with the past: the
dwelling on bygone days, and staying with a poem upon
them. The shift of attention to the future, as stated hope,
produces a candid fear for the future:

> Yet should these hopes
> Prove vain and thus should neither I be taught
> To understand myself, nor thou to know
> With better knowledge how the heart was framed
> Of him thou lovest. . . .
>
> [625–29]

What follows, in the implied "no" to the possible incurring
of "harsh judgments," at one and the same time checks the
negative impetus and positively capitalizes on Coleridge's
favorable position in the poem. For if doubt presses up from
a considerable depth in the poem, its ultimate depth is

occupied by the affirmation that gains strength from the very act of sustaining doubt and rendering it harmless; here is Wordsworth's "power growing under weight" (8.555). We can recognize in these lines (629–35) a complex rhetorical recapitulation: the submerged litotes of "[no] harsh judgments" transfers to another mind the double negative of Wordsworth's "not misled," paralleling the way the basic activity shifts from Wordsworth's telling his tale to Coleridge's evaluating it; the protective depreciation of memory's function seen in "an infirmity of love for days/Disowned by memory" reappears in "Those recollected hours that have the charm/Of visionary things"; and above all, the suasive use of an image comes back, not as the all-but-wintry snowdrop, but as the scene of infancy in full sun (616 and 634–35). A subtle mastery over skepticism is effected through the latter image, which in context deserves patient attention.

The effect of the sunlight image is both slow in building up and dramatically abrupt when it comes at the end of an accretive sentence:

> ... need I dread from thee
> Harsh judgments, if the *song* be loth to quit
> Those recollected hours that have the charm
> Of visionary things, those lovely forms
> And sweet sensations that throw back our life,
> And almost make remotest infancy
> A visible scene, on which the sun is shining?
> [629–35; italics added]

An indulgence toward self-avowed nostalgia is as much as the opening lines invite; the evocative power of "visionary things" can hardly come into play with the notion of "charm" calling up fancy and romance, instead of transcendence. But this statement, seeming to continue on parallel ground (those . . . , those), smoothly carries itself upward into universal philosophy. While the grammatical construction equates "those recollected hours" with "those lovely forms," the equation entails a major revaluation of our understanding of the first term. Lovely forms, of course, have the strongest roots in the platonic system, but they show a radical mutation, being contained in the past and in actual experience, as are the "beauteous forms" of "Tintern Abbey" (and as against the pre-existence posited in the Intimations Ode). With this instance of concrete idealism, it becomes apparent that Wordsworth remembers, not out of an infirmity of love or owing to any charm, but because what he remembers as belonging to him belongs also in a timeless and perfect domain, and leads him there. How surely it leads him, and *us* (for "our life" in 633 suggests a common experience), can be gathered from the final lines: "And almost make remotest infancy / A visible scene, on which the sun is shining."

It is a metaphor, but so close to its subject as to seem literal: a visible scene, including everything short of remotest infancy. The rational uncertainties of the situation stand resolved, and assurance is made doubly sure by the shining sun, which affords the best light for what we see. The sun also subtly dispels the mist of spiritual uncertainty in the passage, insofar as the phrase "on which the sun is shining" not only bespeaks clarity but betokens blessedness. Hence, for the immediate purposes of the poem, Wordsworth's mind is "revived" and he enters a "genial mood," his spirit filled with vitality and fruitfulness. The spirit of the entire complex of lines is delicately reflected in one of the last details we see, Wordsworth's "certain hopes." The qualifier, "certain," at first may seem tentative in tone, with the sense of something not explicitly fixed and named; but it reverberates powerfully with the other sense of "certain," something beyond doubt or the possibility of failure. The fusion of these two senses confirms, but also grows out of, the temper of poised argument Wordsworth is expressing.

As a whole, the passage checks the course of the poem only to release it with increased impetus and definition. The "end" of the poem is in a sense as mysterious as its beginning, and yet its knowledge of where it might go, and whence—the gist of the lines under analysis—has undeniable authority. From the way the poem's "hopes" and roots become explicit in a context of argument, oblique but precise, one is encouraged to see such argument as material, even intrinsic, to the work.

Perhaps *The Prelude* does not become in any handy sense "a rigorous inquisition" (1.148), but early and late it gives evidence of an informal argumentative impulse and skill. The use of litotes, with its argument-bracing effect, can be abundantly illustrated.[14] In like manner, a current of images continually advances the poem's propositions. These images may be given a brief examination, to bring out a kind of dynamic, self-revising analysis that goes with romantic absorption, and to provide necessary qualification of Kermode's sense of the romantic Image as a mystical light "out of space and time."

Helen Darbishire has spoken of the apt directness and simplicity of Wordsworth's images, with particular stress on their naturalistic aesthetic appeal. They also do distinctive intellectual work, especially in relation to Wordsworth's conception of organically developing time. This conception, recognizable at once in the planting of snowdrops, emerges twice again in the opening books. Wordsworth speaks of himself as "gathering . . ./Through every hair-breadth in that field of light,/New pleasure like a bee among the flowers" (1.578-80); and he asks who can know when "His habits were first sown, even as a seed" (2.207). Without going into questions of activity-passivity or spontaneity-inscrutability in the two images, we can see that they create a lively awareness of a rich productivity resulting from the accumulation of the minutest elements (the bee) or from the irresistible articulation of a single small thing (the seed). Both the inherent power and the ultimate wholeness of Wordsworth's experiences take on a substantiating concreteness from the images.

Furthermore, the long process of the poem's development (that is, the correlation between the character of Wordsworth's experience and the formation of the work) is given tacit reception in the reader's mind. The reader is conditioned to watch and to allow for the slow, partitive way of the poem.

Progressively through *The Prelude* the references to beginnings and ends, to sources, birth, infancy, dawn, and spring, cluster to reinforce the bee and seed images. How they do so would warrant a separate study; here, a couple of special reminiscences of these images will help to show the intricate connections of the poem. The allusion to "Divine Comates" (11.443–48) adds a life-giving and redemptive function to the richness of the bee image. Where before the image had enabled Wordsworth to look forward with clarity and comprehension, now it enables him to look back with assurance, out of a time of crisis. As regards the seed image, reinforcement comes from a piece of literal description:

> Thus long I mused,
> Nor e'er lost sight of what I mused upon,
> Save when, amid the stately grove of oaks,
> Now here, now there, an acorn, from its cup
> Dislodged, through sere leaves rustled.
> [1.80–84]

Here the setting so happily fits the context—Wordsworth is meditating "some work/Of glory"—that a symbolic resonance comes straightway to mind. It is nature now, spontaneously, and not Wordsworth, deliberately, saying that the seed of something great is there; the "startling" acorn (85) intimates the stately oak. A like effect occurs when Wordsworth describes himself as "harassed with the toil of verse" and getting little done, when "at once/Some lovely image in the song rose up/Full-formed, like Venus rising from the sea" (4.110–14).

The foregoing discussion represents major, but not exclusive, ways in which *The Prelude* explicitly certifies the mind of Wordsworth and works on the reader's. The poem displays a continuing pressure toward accuracy, as in the revision of "peace" to "ease and undisturbed delight" (1.24–27), a continual "tentative note"[15] and yet a strong sense of necessary logical cause; a tendentious organization, as in the juxtaposition of the Bartholomew and Helvellyn fairs, with the description bringing home an unmistakable pro-rural thesis, or in the contrasted opening lines of books 3 and 4 which show the same bias; and above all a confidence-winning candor (e.g., 4.612 ff., 5.293 ff. and 510 ff., 14.321 ff. and 336).

Inevitably, this helps to determine the light in which we see the poem; it is not a thing of argument, with a systematic assemblage of topics disposed in keeping with proper rhetorical principles, but neither is it a thing ignorant or innocent of argument. Rather, it incorporates argument in its own lyrical-epical system, to confess and contend with its inherent difficulties of understanding and statement, to meet and answer the difficulties conceivable in the reader's situation.

The use of image-as-argument is fairly widespread in Wordsworth. It attains virtually independent philosophical authority in the "Ode: Intimations of Immortality." The poem has dealt with the depredations of time and personal despair in the subjective framework of the speaker (sts. 1–4), and has turned to what might seem collective grounds of consolation (sts. 5–7), but these ominously fail. The problem now rests not only upon the ungenerous processes of time, but upon a kind of eagerly unwitting self-denial in the individual human being ("The little actor cons another part; . . . As if his whole vocation/Were endless imitation"). Through the "little actor" a singular personality reenters the poem, and the speaker, now as it were in a posture of objective learning and reflecting, apostrophizes that personality (st. 8). The apostrophe begins in celestial idioms ("Mighty Prophet! Seer blest!"),

but as it were duplicating the time-warp the speaker has
experienced, it turns into a savage prophecy of desolation:

Full soon thy Soul shall have her earthly freight,
And custom lie upon thee with a weight,
Heavy as frost, and deep almost as life!

This is a wintry cul-de-sac in the poem. The speaker cannot
get himself free, and the instruments (generality, blessed
racial memory) he turns to for succor deposit him right back
in a state of despair. Rather than the general good availing
him assistance, his personal distress is universalized. The image
of the Soul not only overburdened (freight, weight), but overburdened by a deathliness that seems to sink to the bottom
reaches of life, frankly depicts his present condition and his
conviction of its imminence for anyone and everyone.

By virtue of the image, though, the debate of the poem
between fond memories and conceptions of the self, on the
one hand, and drastic grief for the prevailing lot of humankind on the other, is carried on not only in the soul but in the
earth. In a sense it ceases to be a vocal debate and becomes
an implicit one, intrinsic to the nature of things. At that level,
"deep almost as life," the image imperceptibly discovers the
restorations, as opposed to the depredations, of time. It
elaborates itself in silence, and emerges again in the vitally
modified form of stanza 9:

O joy! that in our embers
Is something that doth live,
That nature yet remembers
What was so fugitive!

It is clear that Wordsworth is not just professing joy
licentiously, but expressing it as newly rediscovered. And it
is clear that the process of the imagery has served as the
instrument of rediscovery. The image makes the argument for
joy. In its second stage (st. 9), it expands the first-stage focus

on frost and the winter outdoors (st. 8), to include a hitherto
unseen house and hearth, in which a fire has seemingly
died. But just as the fire has not wholly died—the embers
remain to generate a fresh blaze—nature under the frost has
not wholly died; the frost is deep *almost* as life, but nature
retains possession of (remembers) what had seemed so swiftly
lost. Thus the inner human order and the outer natural order
fuse and advance with each other. The imagery unfolds new
and saving dimensions of experience, and also implies a new
conception of time. The phrase "what was so fugitive" first
describes how quickly youth and rapture pass away, but it
carries also the secondary sense that what *was* fugitive *is*
no longer so, because of an enhanced understanding. Friedrich
Schlegel expresses the same conception in *Lucinde*: "The fire
of love is absolutely inextinguishable, and even in the deepest
heap of ashes there are still some sparks aglow."[16]

To come, by means of images, to an understanding that is
not available to discourse or analysis is far from uncommon in
romanticism. The image becomes a device for exploring
epistemological and moral and cultural quandaries, and though
we find fault with a "soft-focus" quality in romantic imagery,
its moony as opposed to solar character, it has a precision all
its own.[17] Modern students of perception are aware that the
sun brings out some things and some features of things to
perfection, while certain other things and features come out
best under the moon. The romantic poets knew this,
intuitively, and acted accordingly. They argued against mere
daylight certainties, for the legitimacy and the vitality of
"dreams," as Byron put it, "that day's broad light cannot
remove."

That "soft-focus" romantic images capture, and are intended
to capture, elusive features of reality may, again, be indicated
in the work of the supposed arch-culprit, Shelley. The opening stanza of the "Hymn to Intellectual Beauty" seems simply

to strew around images that barely have enough substance to
qualify as such:

As summer winds that creep from flower to flower,—
Like moonbeams that behind some piny mountain shower,
    It visits with inconstant glance
    Each human heart and countenance;
Like hues and harmonies of evening,—
    Like clouds in starlight widely spread,—
    Like memory of music fled,—
    Like aught that for its grace may be
Dear, and yet dearer for its mystery.

One can readily say that the images are apt to "mystery" and
still not help Shelley's case. The question is whether the
"mystery" is apt to life. Does the poem merely presume on
our understanding of "intellectual [platonic] beauty," or
does it engage us directly, movingly in a serious human
encounter? With the first lines, "The awful shadow of some
unseen Power/Floats though unseen among us," the "Hymn"
establishes a setting that combines the claustrophobic and the
eerie, a setting that any candid adult will at least ruefully
admit is well known: something, or someone, is somewhere
in the room with "us," and we don't know where to turn.
This primordial sense of a spiritual or psychic presence
becomes the foundation of the poem. Shelley builds upon it
a personal and dramatic response to intellectual beauty (by
contrast with Spenser's more formal, catechistic one), and he
extends the reach of his engagement by suggesting also a
pentecostal descent ("Floats though unseen among us,—
visiting . . .").

The images, in this context, anchor us to a sense of reality—
this is no case of self-indulgent neurasthenia. Even more
important, though, the images anchor the visitant—the intel-
lectual/pentecostal presence—in reality. They argue that our
failure to apprehend it directly and securely has nothing to do

with its existence, but only with our perspective and our powers. As they multiply, two effects occur: a demonstration of the broad scale on which we fail to take in what is indisputably there, and a demonstration of the eager search we might make to confirm its likelihood. The passage amounts to an empirical argument against the cruder forms of empiricism. And its images serve as a pivot and a bond between the empirical and the intellectual, between what we know and what we are capable of knowing.

To show the strain of argument in the romantic poets is to bring out a crucial feature of their relationship to the world, to their audience, and to their own minds. But one of the consequences of a well-placed argument is precisely the undoing of argument, the establishment of conviction. Wordsworth of course has been charged with being too comfortably convinced by himself, especially in his later poetry. In fact, a certain sententious and moralistic strain ominously marks Wordsworth's earliest poems, like the "Lines Left upon a Seat in a Yew-tree" or "Descriptive Sketches." But here again an undervoice of Wordsworthian position-taking and position-making can be readily discerned. The very opening of "Lines Left upon a Seat in a Yew-tree" bespeaks confrontation and hoped-for resolution of a difficulty: "Nay, Traveller! rest." The speaker is trying to overcome the aversion of the "stranger"—the silent partner in a tacit dialogue—to a desolate place. The poem is not really focused on the "favoured Being" who became a misanthropic solitary, though it dwells on him so. His story serves as an illustrative anecdote in a course of instruction which, given the context of the stranger's resistance and ignorance, becomes an act of implied argument. Working on an amplifying and incorporating definition of humanity, the poem seeks to show and sympathize with humanity existing "far from all human dwelling." The "what if" constructions of the opening lines explicitly counter the stranger's prejudices, just as the "if" that introduces the second verse paragraph, the second stage of the poem's movement, engages him to promote the poem's terms or confess himself corrupt.

Even the final lines of the poem, which seem most blatantly sermonistic, contain an argumentative thrust, in the phrases "true knowledge" and "true dignity." Milton uses this locution to good effect in *Paradise Lost* to invoke and combat "false" examples, and Wordsworth may be given credit for doing as much. "Lines Left upon a Seat in a Yew-tree" may ultimately ask for direct assent or for conversion, but first it seeks a thinking-through of the propositions it makes concerning the definition of humanity. Not that its argument is orderly and analytical; the dramatic situation makes for an emotional heightening from the outset, and what is argumentative works in complement with this emotion, purposely seeking to attach it to particular, if unfamiliar, objects.

A brief quotation from "Descriptive Sketches," also a solemn and didactic piece, will serve to show the engagement of the reader's mind in argumentative terms:

Think not the peasant aloft has gazed
And heard with heart unmoved, with soul unraised:
Nor is his spirit less enrapt, nor less
Alive to independent happiness,
Then, when he lies, out-stretched, at even-tide
Upon the fragrant mountain's purple side:
For as the pleasures of his simple day
Beyond his native valley seldom stray,
Nought round its darling precincts can he find
But brings some past enjoyment to his mind;
While Hope, reclining upon Pleasure's urn,
Binds her wild wreaths, and whispers his return.
                          [421–32]

These lines casually incorporate the overcoming of denial ("not . . . unmoved") and the recognition of logic ("for") which more obviously argumentative poems of the early years, such as "Expostulation and Reply" and "The Tables

Turned," more formally exploit. Perhaps "Tintern Abbey," the auspicial poem of the first volume, best indicates how naturally Wordsworth's work curves into an area of confronting negative possibilities and actively, logically, confirming its dominant positions.[18] The mode of progression in the poem— with "therefore" and "for," "thus," "but," "and so," "if," and "nor . . . if" continually before our eyes—is as much logical as chronological. John Jones calls these "words of modest function," but they are vital at last; as Jones himself acknowledges, the poem develops "a logical, knitted quality."[19]

Recognizing the presence and the peculiar ways of argument in Wordsworth's poetry leads to valuable modifications of our sense of him as assertive, and of our conviction that in his work truth "is its own testimony" and "a direct revelation of reality."[20] But more than this is involved. "She Dwelt Among the Untrodden Ways," as soon as we recognize that the middle stanza is using the images of violet and star[21] to provide information to ignorant men and thus *to redefine their common standards of value*, moves upon us with striking breadth and power, and ceases to look like an interpretation "of human experience . . . too personal to be sympathetically received or readily shared by most readers."[22] Rather, it puts personal experience over against common assumptions and, with the image serving as a counter of understanding and a pivot, implicitly argues the superiority of personal to common judgment in terms of lucidly observant knowledge and sensitive appreciation. Indeed, the relation exactly images the relation of the subject of judgment (Lucy) to the implied others in the poem; as the images suggest, she is unique; they, merely members of the multitude. The poem, then, is arguing a typical point of view, to wit, that uniqueness is precious, but it advances unrecognized cases. Or again, without implying a philosophical treatise, we may recognize the logical undervoice of the Intimations Ode becoming exquisitely audible in the final couplet of stanza 7: "As if his whole vocation/Were endless imitation." The sacredness of "vocation" is pitted against the superficiality (theatrical? poetic?) of "imitation," and the logical force of the locution, "as if," comes in behind the already overpowering "vocation." The poem, as G. Wilson Knight declares, catches Wordsworth in an ecstasy,[23] but it is a peculiarly reflective and critical one; and that reflection gives the strongest claims of the poem, if not sanction, a more respectful hearing than Coleridge set the pattern for.

Without gainsaying a degree of "assertion" in Wordsworth's later writing, I would like to focus on the continued presence of what he himself calls "obstinate questionings." Perhaps the resiliency and patience that yield so handsome a recovery in the "Ode: Intimations of Immortality" have diminished; perhaps there is more of a voluble demand for grounds of stability and certitude. But there is no suppression of questions. A poem like "Evening Voluntaries (VI)" will show the posture of Wordsworth's matured mind and also tellingly reflect on a famous position he had reached in the early poem "I Wandered Lonely as a Cloud."

"Evening Voluntaries VI" ("Soft as a Cloud") is not well known, and it will be profitable to give it in full:

Soft as a cloud is yon blue Ridge—the Mere
Seems firm as solid crystal, breathless, clear,
And motionless; and, to the gazer's eye,
Deeper than ocean in the immensity
Of its vague mountains and unreal sky!
But, from the process in that still retreat,
Turn to minuter changes at our feet;
Observe how dewy Twilight has withdrawn
The crowd of daisies from the shaven lawn,
And has restored to view its tender green,
That, while the sun rode high, was lost beneath their dazzling sheen.
—An emblem this of what the sober Hour
Can do for minds disposed to feel its power!

Thus oft, when we in vain have wished away
The petty pleasures of the garish day,
Meek eve shuts up the whole usurping host
(Unbashful dwarfs each glittering at his post)
And leaves the disencumbered spirit free
To reassume a staid simplicity.

'Tis well—but what are helps of time and place,
When wisdom stands in need of nature's grace;
Why do good thoughts, invoked or not, descend,
Like Angels from their bowers, our virtues to befriend;
If yet To-morrow, unbelied, may say,
"I come to open out, for fresh display,
The elastic vanities of yesterday"?

The very movement of the poem, from firm assertion to distressed questioning, indicates a breakdown of certitudes. If
Wordsworth seems prompt to find homilies or "emblems" in
experience, he is just as prompt to acknowledge their limitations. Even the opening assertion may be regarded as carrying
the seeds of instability—the order of nature is unclamorously
inverted, with the ridge having the properties of a cloud, and
the "mere" or pool having those of "solid cyrstal." Wordsworth, evidently pressing for something more manageable,
calls the large picture "vague" and "unreal," and turns to
what he can control and observe, at his "feet." But this only
brings into immediate reach the problem of perception and
value that besets him in the poem. The sun, it turns out,
covers as much as it reveals, and twilight discloses as much as
it covers up. Here is a dramatic rendering of the image of
radical epistemological misgiving in the romantic period;
Wordsworth makes an argument against the authority of the
sun, which he calls "garish," and against the "whole usurping
host" of what stands out in the sun. By contrast he finds
"grace" and angelic support of "virtues" in what the twilight
reveals, the "tender green" of a lawn whose "shaven" state
might almost imply a deliberate endeavor to keep it down.
Utter promise resides in that tender green, but also utter

precariousness. And Wordsworth cannot give the lie to the usurpative sun and daisies. They come back, "unbelied," undiminished, to bring his standards and biases into question. He can see in them deformity ("Unbashful dwarfs") and uselessness ("elastic vanities"), but this is from the position of one who has to cry out emphatically to drown the voice of his own fears. He enjoys the triumph of an acute perception, and because of that suffers an acute philosophical distress. "Soft as a Cloud," composed in 1834, may be said to strain for resolution and conviction, but it is straining from out of the toils of an insoluble argument.

One cannot but be struck with the ways in which "Soft as a Cloud" reminisces and revises Wordsworth's "I Wandered Lonely as a Cloud," which dates from three decades earlier. The *mise-en-scene* is alike in both poems, with hills and water framing the focal objects, daisies and daffodils. But in "I Wandered" Wordsworth settles for the brilliant display of the daffodils, and finds in them an abiding "wealth," whereas he is put off by the "dazzling sheen" and specious display of the daisies in "Soft as a Cloud," seeming impelled to look further and deeper than whatever leaps to view. It would perhaps be tendentious to propose that Wordsworth, rather than growing more rigid and dogmatic as he grows older, evinces a deeper capacity for reflection and questioning, or that he learns to review the impressionistic fervor of "I Wandered Lonely as a Cloud." In truth, this poem has an argumentative tinge of its own. He claims no more for the daffodils than ultimate *reflective* experience warrants, for that is what is conveyed by the verse "they flash upon that inward eye. . . ." At the moment of possession, he is simply jubilant, and expects nothing beyond: "but little thought/What wealth the show to me had brought." The capacity for learning, the ability to be fruitfully surprised underlies at once the immediate appreciation of the daffodils, and their eventual elevation into a symbol of reconciliation between past and present, external and internal, solitude and multitude:

They flash upon that inward eye
Which is the bliss of solitude;
And then my heart with pleasure fills
And dances with the daffodils.

A similar candor in response to the world and to his own apprehensions underlies the mode of argument in Wordsworth's poetry.

What the strain of argument manifests in the poetry is a vigorous combination of immediacy and comprehensiveness of view, of definiteness and openness of mind. These features, more than incidentally perhaps, reappear in the more impressive of the later poems: "To a Skylark," "The Wishing-Gate," parts of "On the Power of Sound," assorted sonnets, and of course *The Prelude*. Contrariwise, a poem such as *The Excursion*, though Wordsworth adopted "something of a dramatic form," fails in taking its own statements, and its immediate and effective audience, too much for granted. It is Wordsworth talking to himself, not to Coleridge or someone else definite and substantial.[24] As Geoffrey Hartman says, "we do not wish to ask what the heart understands, or how, etc. . . . But the poet has put it into an argumentative context, so that we are forced to ask questions about 'relations,' . . . and so, finally, to disparage."[25]

But even failures of argument, as in the "Sonnets on the Punishment of Death" or in the strange moment when Wordsworth praises "penniless poverty" for sparing him the contamination of luxury (*Prelude*, 2.78-84), indicate something like a settled habit of argument, early formed and long continued. "Nutting" itself—the poem we see as a record of swarming, rapacious passion—proves cool, inquisitive in writing, with its scrupulous pursuit of accuracy in description and analysis ("or," "perhaps," "unless"); in fact it fosters a sense of detachment and generality through the use of phrases like "such suppression . . ./As joy delights in," "a temper known to those who . . . ," "that sweet mood when pleasure loves to pay/Tribute to ease. . . . " As David Ferry says,

"Wordsworth in all of this is assuming in all of us a practiced libertinism like his own."[26]

It bears stressing that the situation of the romantic poet entails primary problems of definition and value, and that these problems are alive in the poet's own mind as well as in the construction of his relation to his audience. An exacting but pervasive sense of the need for redefinitions appears in the treatment of key conceptual terms (such as dream, pleasure, imagination) and of key literary conventions (such as the ballad, the pastoral, and the epic). It is a situation which presupposes and summons argument. The mode of argument adopted by Wordsworth helps to convey while it also copes with the situation. In fine, it need not be because he was "betrayed by the ineradicable weakness of civilized men" that Wordsworth was inclined "to explain, to rationalize."[27] Nor need his doing so prove a disability. It is at best part of a vital dialogue with himself and his audience.

That dialogue becomes even more direct and intricate in Byron, who in a sense accumulates a position rather than taking and testing one in the Wordsworthian manner. Not only does Byron challenge the reader's every assumption and himself gravitate toward skepticism,[28] but he canonizes imperfection and incompleteness, ostensibly giving each moment its own license, and making Schlegel's haphazard approach to *Lucinde* appear by comparison all but calculated. The problem of containment which we have seen as crucial in the discussion of elegy, prophecy and satire seems to get out of hand in a poem like *Don Juan*. One episode vies with another for tonal and philosophical authority. One mood challenges another, one crystallization of character yields dissolutely to another. And yet *Don Juan* contains a kind of purpose, a form of preference if not determination. This is apparent in two ways: in the way Byron shows the *consequences* of having no preference, and in the way he builds, in the underlying structure of the episodes, a system of repetition and refinement that binds the poem together and leaves it stable, if irresolute.

Byron's *Don Juan:*
The Obsession and Self-Discipline
of Spontaneity

It is the weight of memory that gives depth to new impressions; this can be an oppressive weight, but it is also the weight that may enable us, as we crash helplessly through the mazes of our experience, to break through into clear moments and wider resolutions.

Author unknown

The play of argument in romantic poetry may be seen to work not only to the internal advantage of a given work, but also against alternative positions and presuppositions. It has a securing effect for the speaker, and has also the character of a duty to discern, in the welter of values and experience that we now commonly associate with romanticism, tenable relations and underlying cues. It is important to remember that the romantics, if not bound to a given order, were bent on ordering what was given. This is equally the burden of Coleridge's manifesto on imagination and of Blake's *Jerusalem* (where a veritable babel of argument among all the figures in the work is finally resolved into a common sense by the poet and the concept of forgiveness). A certain pressure toward formalization is perhaps endemic in the human mind, and Blake expresses it for the romantics: "I must create a System or be enslav'd by another Mans."

The resolute individualism of that protestation mollifies its own underlying rigidity; to whom, after all, will Los's "system" apply? But the romantic period affords plainer, less personal, less emotionally charged formulations of system. In musing "On the Principles of Method" in *The Friend*, Coleridge favors the enunciation of laws of understanding as a means of "controlling" events and phenomena; and Hegel, alike in his *Philosophy of History* and his remarks on stoicism in *The*

Phenomenology of Mind, suggests a grand indifference to action and effect, a clean transcendence of personality: an encompassing and ineluctable system of time (*The Philosophy*), or an individual's system of "self-consciousness" in time *(Phenomenology),* defeats the local experience of flux and indirection. Coleridge and Hegel evince a desire to predict the eventualities of the world, and to enjoy the omnipotent freedom of foreknowledge. Blake, on the contrary, seeks but to escape some other person's prediction; his "system" is *to be formulated,* as a sort of perpetually indefinite defensive maneuver.

It would not do to deny to Hegel and Coleridge at their most systematic the romantic cachet. But it would be well to recognize that in practice, in performance, Blake's position falls much closer to the norm, which indeed proves somewhat less insistent than Blake's and more inclined to defend by evasion and undermining than by equal and opposite action. The project of "creating a system" would be in this light premature, and perhaps a tinge presumptuous. Rather a candid quest for fullness of recognition would occur, and systems or constellations or consonances might, or might not, eventuate. Everything may be expected, but nothing summoned, and especially (*pace* Hegel and Coleridge) not the future. The attempt to summon the past in Goethe's *Faust* and Byron's *Manfred* and Shelley's *Prometheus Unbound* had yielded only illusion and pain. The assurance of willed repetition is denied. The inevitability of Faust's cry, "Stay, thou art so fair," has its counterpart in the inevitability of change. The quest for fullness of recognition may be associated with the form of the epic, and we may turn now to Byron's use of that form as another act of inclusion.

The Giaour, at just over 1300 short lines, and *Don Juan,* at something over 16 long cantos, have one crucial structural feature in common: both are fragments. Once this is said, it becomes necessary to ask if they are, as fragments, similar in kind (the question of quality need not even arise). Does fragmentariness express the same boisterous self-aggrandizement in *Don Juan* as in *The Giaour*, the same difficulty with aesthetic and philosophical ordering, the same misgivings about the adequacy of what has been written and the same compensatory faith that bigger is truer, as well as better?

It would be plausible to say that Byron left *The Giaour* unfinished, whereas death left *Don Juan* unfinished. Of course Byron amused himself with the contemplation of 100 cantos of *Don Juan*, a number so magnificent as to leave scant time for Byron's daily business of war and love, which after all pursued him ardently as he them. On the face of it the poem may have been not only unfinished in fact, but in Byron's own conception of it unfinishable, inasmuch as he meant to discourse in it "De rebus cunctis et quibusdam aliis": on everything, and more besides. Such a conclusion, though, comes too easy. It is only justice to urge that Byron not be censured for eking out with fond and wilful tongue a potentially tedious tale. He certainly knew how to abandon an unprofitable venture, leaving the pretentious Polidori to complete *The Vampire*. And as for his going on with *Don Juan* to no known end, we have perhaps been remiss in not recognizing the warrant Byron obtained from his time.

The unfinishable poem stands as a signal romantic contribution to the form and vital entelechy of poetry itself; it expresses a resistance to predictability in poetry, which grows in new modes, and has many fulfillments. The root problem with the long poem in romanticism lay not in the collapse of sustaining philosophical structures,[1] but in the fact that the long poem could not, in reality or in mortality, be made long enough. Which is to say, it could not be infinite.

A link between the fragmentary and the infinite attests itself in various ways in the romantic period. The sense of incompleteness as an emblem of infinity may be derived from Keats's "On Seeing the Elgin Marbles," which seems to make the combination of art's perfection and time's depredation—a fragment in short—the "shadow of a magnitude." But in fact romantic philosophy is explicit about the symbolic value of fragmentariness. Novalis espouses it as our only means of approaching infinitude, and Friedrich Schlegel, in his uncompromisingly named *Fragments*, comes out against the principle of formal conclusion to thought on the grounds that the vital fermentation of intellectual process can only be rendered inert by artificial checks.

This is, however, not a way of committing thought, or action, or for that matter literature, to randomness. With a subtle echo of Shakespeare's "There's method in his madness," Coleridge in "Essay IV" of *The Friend* ("On the Principles of Method") sums up the combination of the casual and the purposive in the "cultivated" use of fragments:

> The true cause of the impression [the man of superior mind makes] on us . . . is the unpremeditated and evidently habitual *arrangement* of his words, grounded on the habit of foreseeing, in each integral part, or (more plainly) in every sentence, the whole that he then intends to communicate. However irregular and desultory his talk, there is *method* in the fragments.[2]

Coleridge emphasizes that "continuous transition" is basic to "method," and at the same time warns that its *abuse* "may degenerate into the grotesque or the fantastical." In a sense, then, method becomes the effect of poising mind and matter between a wild versatility and a rigid unresponsive form. Coleridge as much as demonstrates this by requiring a "preconception" for the proper pursuit of method while yet assigning it to a spontaneous development of the ordering (as opposed to merely orderly) intelligence.

Other romantic writers, too, exhibit an aversion to arbitrary surprise or disconnection, on the one hand, and to an empty rigidity or overrepetition, on the other. The latter we readily recognize from Blake's denunciation of Urizen, whose forte is the mathematics of petrifaction. Less attention has been paid to Blake's own resistance to the opposite extreme of too much spontaneity and disconnection. But it is there, and important, for between the extremes we can appreciate Blake's demand for a poising of the self between its self-insistent tendencies and the reconciliation of the carelessly arrogant tendencies of things in the world.

Blake's equal resistance to overrepetition and to disconnection documents itself in "The Mental Traveller." Against overrepetition he writes:

And if the Babe is born a Boy
He's given to a Woman Old,
Who nails him down upon a rock,
Catches his shrieks in cups of gold.

She binds iron thorns around his head,
She pierces both his hands and feet.
                [8-14]

Here is a superfluity of rigidity and repetition, binding piled upon nailing, Christ's suffering upon that of Prometheus. But Blake sees through to the fact that this is the obverse of randomness and disconnection, which he equally condemns. The Woman Old continues working on the Boy Babe:

She cuts his heart out at his side
To make it feel both cold and heat.
Her fingers number every Nerve
Just as a miser counts his gold.
                [15-18]

The individual Babe is obviously essentially and ultimately less than the sum of his parts, if those parts are separated and numbered. He may be wealth ("gold") to her, but becomes nothing in himself.

This graphically demonstrates a romantic uneasiness with *mere* fragmentation. Actaeon could not be taken as the representative figure, or even Orpheus, because they are torn apart *and remain so*. Shelley reintegrates Orpheus into the romantic scheme by terming language "a *perpetual* Orphic song," thus overcoming the piecemeal temporal effect of the root story. No, fragmentation is problematical even at the level of synecdoche; when Coleridge complains in "Dejection: An Ode" that he is disoriented and dispirited because "that which [in his being] suits a part infects the whole," he is showing us that synecdoche—the part for the whole—both represents and represses what it stands for. It admits the existence of the rest, but by a coercive homogeneity denies the range and character and substance of what goes beyond it. At bottom, Blake's "The Tyger" works as a poem about the poignant insanity of a man who truly sees nothing but parts, whose vision is a fearfully unqualified and unrelieved synecdoche, affecting alike the Creator and the Tyger: hand, eye, wings, shoulder, feet, and smile are the parts for the Creator, and for the Tyger, sinews of the heart, brain, eyes. The fragment, in short, is not being held up for itself and in isolation, but as a signpost—so to speak, an index finger—bearing toward an ultimate whole.

It is wholly in keeping with this principle that we recognize an ambition of the infinite in the way the romantic poets handle the long poem. It is clear in Blake and Shelley that the long poem (taking *Prometheus Unbound* as a poem in dramatic guise) is meant to encompass infinity, and the form of the works images this fact. *Jerusalem* ends at the ninety-ninth plate, but it makes no bones about the fact that the ending is a poetic fiction and an authorial convenience. Enitharmon advises Los that the poet, Blake, is about to wind up the project they are living, and so the action, the poem, moves into a landing pattern. Accordingly, we have not so much a conclusion as a resolution of the poem, which might have flown on forever and which conceptually does fly on forever, since the human states or Zoas with which it deals are timeless. Much the same effect is achieved in *Prometheus Unbound*, where the sober, if not somber, injunction of Demogorgon to struggle against relapse suggests a perennial tension, if not an everlasting cycle.

The Prelude may also be instanced as a poem boasting a sense of resolution rather than a strict conclusion; the princi-

ples of "something evermore about to be" and the contention that "our home is with infinitude" both convey a
reaching toward as governing the emergencies of the poem's
action, and that action, though so lucid and so comprehensive in the Snowdon episode, still remains open and unpredictable. Assurance is given, reliably so, but how to live up
to this assurance will have to be discovered. Just as in "Resolution and Independence," a given solution is perennially
to be tested and challenged by some inevitable, though
unnameable, emergency. *The Prelude* itself constitutes a
resumption and a recognition of its own action,[3] with every
suggestion of an everlasting cycle, in Wordsworth's mind,
analogous to the everlasting cycle set up between William
and Dorothy at the end of "Tintern Abbey." More than
this, the poem's beginning in discrete fragments and its
gradual, as well as endlessly self-modifying, crystallization in
Wordsworth's mind make it resemble *Don Juan* stage for
stage.

In the case of *Don Juan*, then, it would seem timely to
ask: is it in the singular romantic sense an infinite poem,
or did it only stand in danger of growing physically interminable?[4] First let me say there is in the abstract no reason
why we should not greet an interminable poem with perfect
equanimity: it is nothing to us if we choose to ignore it.
But benign neglect did not seem a possibility with *Don
Juan* in 1824 and is not now a century and a half later; the
projected interminability of the poem accordingly threatens
us, as an extension of the fact that the poem itself threatens
us, at any length. I venture to say *Don Juan* threatens the
reader as no comparable poem does—*Paradise Lost* and
Jerusalem and *The Prelude* are actually consolatory efforts,
and Swinburne's *Atalanta in Calydon* and Hardy's *The
Dynasts* prove, though forbidding, less than inescapable in
vision.

Given that it is too much and too good to ignore, what
makes *Don Juan* a threatening poem? Certainly not its

theme of liberty, a very shibboleth of British self-opinion. And not the sexuality of the poem, where it falls far short of Fielding or even in some respects Goldsmith and Gay. Nor should it have been the multifariousness of the poem; an episodic structure is characteristic of epic and picaresque forms, as well as traditional in the Don Juan stories, and Fielding and Sterne would both stand as precedents for a multifarious form; Sterne indeed amuses the reader with his projection of the *opus sine fine*:

> I am this month one whole year older than I was this time twelve-month; and yet have got, as you perceive, almost into the middle of my fourth volume—and no farther than to my first day's life—'tis demonstrative that I have three hundred and sixty-four days more life to write just now, than when I first set out; so that instead of advancing, . . . on the contrary, I am just thrown so many volumes back. . . . It must follow, an' please your worships, that the more I write, the more I shall have to write—and consequently, the more your worships read, the more your worships will have to read. [*Tristram Shandy*, chapter 13]

And yet in a way all three factors—liberty, sexuality, and multifariousness—help to make *Don Juan* threatening because of the peculiar and unconventional use Byron makes of them. For *Don Juan* first of all confronts us with a state of dissolutions. Within a brisk four cantos it dissolves the premier genre of Western literature, the epic, with a few perversely dextrous, or perhaps I should say sinister, strokes: the opening phrase, "I want a hero," is a scandal to the tradition and a far cry from Wordsworth's anxious reverent pondering and Milton's "long choosing and beginning late"; and by the same token the insistence on beginning at the beginning and on proceeding without a Muse, that panacea against poetic disability, helps to destroy any sense of orientation or coherence in a story whose center, the hero, is already "wanting." Here is an epic, that noble and conventional form, in which anything can happen. The extent to which Byron undoes our expectations and threatens our assurance may be inferred from the fact that his greatest epic catalogue occurs in a private letter as a litany of his recent conquests, and his finest descent into the underworld occurs on the morning when he awoke and found himself in a crimson-curtained bed with Annabella Milbanke, and gave voice to the ungallant outcry "Good God, I am surely in Hell." Meanwhile, in his ongoing epic, he proceeds to dissolve our towering estimate of Plato ("Oh Plato! Plato! you have paved the way,/ With your confounded fantasies, to more/Immoral conduct . . .), and to dissolve the marriage of Donna Julia and Don Alfonso, Juan's ties to his homeland, our faith in the covenant of the rainbow and in man's humanity to man, and one entire Aegean island:

> That isle is now all desolate and bare,
> Its dwelling down, its tenants pass'd away;
> None but her own [Haidée's] and father's grave is there,
> And nothing outward tells of human clay;
> Ye could not know where lies a thing so fair,
> No stone is there to show, no tongue to say
> What was; no dirge, except the hollow sea's,
> Mourns o'er the beauty of the Cyclades.
>
> [4, st. 72]

And having as it were immersed us in the mourning of the sea, while disingenuously denying the existence of any elegy, he is off again ad lib: "But let me change this theme which grows too sad. . . ."

The fact is that, as much as Keats would oppose this, Byron is his consummate chameleon poet, changing themes and schemes quicker than the mind, let alone the eye, can follow. And this is what poses a threat. Byron strips us of all forms of assurance, from the generic to the linguistic to the religious, offering us in place of this slavery of custom a freedom of the moment that is inseparable from its perils. He, however, having voluntarily cast off form and custom, proceeds effortlessly on his way ("Carelessly I sing"); we struggle up behind. He keeps his footing wherever he goes, even into the pitfalls of skepticism; we do not and cannot. In short, *Don Juan* threatens us because it does not lend itself to plotting and bounding, and as we trail after it we experience not only the exhilaration of its freedom, but also the embarrassment of its unfamiliar power and ways. We might delight in its unplotted ease, indeed we do so, until there comes home to us a sense of its unboundedness. It is hard not to pull back at the intersection of spontaneity and infinity.

It has been observed that every risk entails an opportunity; no doubt every threat also disguises an invitation. It seems to me that *Don Juan* poses an invitation to explore the problem of spontaneity in romanticism; it is only the most vivid instance of a phenomenon we can recognize in poems as diverse as *The Prelude* and *The Fall of Hyperion*, namely, a structure of collision and surprise experienced by writer and reader alike. Such a structure exhibits the kind of development where a ride in a rowboat, an all-night party, reading a book by Cervantes, or climbing the Alps or Mount Snowdon will lead to effects entirely unforeseen and unforeseeable. Significantly, this structure affects both the speaker and the reader; the poet who, say, enjoys a draught of vintage, is as subject to collision, as taken by surprise as we. Perhaps Byron for his part displaces his surprise, but he does not dissimulate his vulnerability:

> But let me change this there which grows too sad,
> And lay this sheet of sorrows on the shelf;
> I don't much like describing people mad,
> For fear of seeming rather touch'd myself.
>   [4, st. 74]

Or again we have his avowal that, strive as he may to become a "Stoic, Sage," "The wind shifts, and [he flies] into a rage" (17, st. 10).

On the strength of such indications let me suggest that spontaneity is not all freedom and arbitrary lines. At bottom, indeed, spontaneity and a fatalistic tendency or bent run together, as do spontaneity and sheer local reaction. The things we describe as spontaneous, as opposed to laborious, are the things that coincide with our preferences, which after all constitute limitations as much as strengths; what the Spaniards call a "querencia"[5] nicely suggests the rigid and bovine quality of a preference. Furthermore, we need to recall that the art of improvisation, which Byron so admired, is a highly trained art, and that, within the realm of conventional literary expression, romance flourishes on the art of *divagation*, of taking off in unforeseen directions. Allowing for the charm of a variegated energy, then, we must note that incoherence is anathema to the human mind. Closely looked at, how spontaneous is spontaneity? It seems crucial to stress the peculiarly romantic practice of clinging to random incidents as though for dear life, and of finding in them a cumulative pattern of meaning and value. For this becomes the basis and the purpose of the long unfinished or, as we may say, the infinite poem in the romantic scheme: to go over, and over and over, some material that we cannot let go, and to go into, and ever further into, the possibilities of that material, which becomes at once obsession and careful choice, fixation and source of revelation. And one is struck to find the same determination to encompass all acts and states, along with the same inability to leave anything alone—in short the same willed and obsessive spontaneity—in Goethe's *Faust* and Rousseau's *Confessions*.

What I am proposing boils down to this: *Don Juan* builds itself on the pattern of repetition and reflection and variation, of subtle repetition and oblique reflection and intricate variation, of the simple single action of the initial Juan-Julia episode.[6] This multiform episode becomes the poem's central figure, or at least configuration: *Don Juan* revolves around a complex of human behavior rather than an individual character, and the poem's beginning becomes at once perpetual and final—if we knew enough of the exfoliating form of this episode, we would have to go on no further. Of this, more anon. It is well here to recall the positive implications of the avowal "I want a hero," which advises us of a need and active desire, as well as a brute deficiency. In other words there is an affirmative thrust toward reconstitution underlying the overt dissolution of the hero in the poem. In this dispensation Juan must choose to be a hero, and of what stripe; he will not find hero status thrust upon him.

The factor of choice in *Don Juan* is easy to overlook, but it is pervasive and can readily be invoked to show the reflexive complexity of the poem's design. Let us first recall its pervasive presence; Juan must choose—that is, he cannot, if he is to survive, choose but choose—how to respond vis-à-vis Alfonso and Lambro; it is fight or die. I would refrain from praising him merely for fighting here, especially since he does not do it well, and that only for the simplest sort of survival. But his fighting seems to anticipate and to be consonant with two other choices Juan does *not* have to make, in the shipwreck and the harem episodes. The latter choices, not impetuous but deliberate, not convenient but contradictory to survival, seem to me to enunciate a standard and principle of human dignity that the hullaballoo with Alfonso and Lambro somewhat beclouds. To choose not to die drunk and not to eat human flesh as a means of staying alive, and to declare to the smitten and nervous Gulbeyaz, "love is for the free": these are not the marks of a sensual or indifferent nature. Not that Byron goes overboard and sacrifices Juan's human plausibility to the pieties of heroism; the lad does at last, and despite "some remorse,"[7] allow himself a paw of his father's spaniel, and does treat himself to an incipient dalliance with Dudú. In a sense Byron seems to say that Juan's heroism, if it is to come about, must come from a personal and moral act of his nature rather than from an aesthetic definition of character established by genre or authorial fiat. Thus the choices he continues to be faced with convey intuitions or intimations of deeper being; the act of saving Leila momentarily stems the tide of his commitment to the inhuman siege; the choice of becoming the Empress Catherine's plaything—a far cry from his defiance of the more sympathetic Gulbeyaz—proves a choice of spiritual and physical dissipation.

The final choice of the poem as we have it involves a recapitulation of the individual moments we have seen Juan in before: the bossy Lady Adeline Amundeville, the sensual Duchess of Fitz-Fulke, and the refined and lovely Aurora bring back Gulbeyaz-Catherine, Julia, and Haidée respectively. Juan has a second chance, with the intensities and precipitancies of first experience now tempered by reflection and comparison, to choose what kind of man he will be, in terms of what kind of woman he will identify himself with. Such a choice has been adumbrated in the harem episode, where Lolah, Katinka, and Dudú lend themselves to distinction, *mutatis mutandis*, according to degree of bossiness, sensuality, and serene loviness (see especially canto 6, sts. 40-54).

I would go so far as to suggest that the strategic placement of the female trios in *Don Juan* symbolizes the three modes of relationship that the protagonist may experience with women and through them with the world. Depending on the choice he makes, women (and his life) may become for him an experience of the graces, of the fates, or of the furies. In more abstract terms, Haidée-Aurora, suggesting the graces, would represent a timeless world formed of compassion, candor, and love; Julia-Fitz-Fulke, suggesting the fates,[8] would represent a sensual world marked by brute repetition and monotony; and Gulbeyaz-Catherine-Lady Adeline, suggesting the furies, would represent an unfeeling but insatiable world characterized by exhausting duty and punishment. There is some indication that Juan feels he is put to choosing among the three women at Norman Abbey, and there is every indication that the narrator has a stake in the choice Juan makes; "I want a hero" is a tacit threat, though not a threat of force. Certainly the narrator chides Juan for finally choosing war over compassionate love, and slights him as the Empress Catherine's love-object, and confronts him with an explicit and unprecedented social-moral disapprobation after his sleeping in with the opportunistic Duchess.

This last episode generates a veritable hubbub of resonances. It not only shows Don Juan falling into the casual ways of the flesh, but shows this in the midst of one of his battles against superstition and terror (shades of the shipwreck episode). Where he should be wrestling with spirits, if not angels, he gets entangled in flesh. He is left unfit to meet the new day (Aurora) or even the ordinary world (A-mundeville), having quite spent himself on the false spirit of darkness and concealed indulgence, and having left himself, as the poem observes with a telling Spenserian resonance, with "eyes that hardly brook'd / The light. . . ." The "air rebuk'd" in which the Duchess is seen also picks up the vocabulary of "virtue" and "vice" which Byron resorts to in this scene; its evaluative tone emerges markedly where Byron calls it an occasion for "Man to show his strength / Moral or physical." It is striking that where imagery of the Fall abounds in all previous love episodes,[9] it is actually withheld and even opposed at this stage. For Byron carefully associates Aurora with a seraphic state and a possible recovery of Eden: "She look'd as if she sat at Eden's door./And grieved for those who could return no more." It need not surprise us that she induces in Juan an unwonted "contemplation." She is, if Byron's pun may be spelled out, a cultivated Aurora who restores Haidée[10] in a viable social mode, and not an idyllic, and perhaps idolatrous, isolation. She affords Juan the chance of a full new beginning, bringing to the poem "an ideal of womanhood attainable *within* society, though free from all its vices and illusions."[11]

Two points may be brought into focus here. The first is what I would call the realistic humanism of this singular "non-epic" epic, which cannot consummate itself without a hero but whose hero, given opportunity and choice, seems to balk at a systematic heroism. Occasional heroism he is

capable of, but he is betrayed into realism by his very capacity for heroism. To grapple with the Friar is to fall into the
clutches of the Duchess of Fitz-Fulke. And we must observe
that the narrator, though seeming to hope for more of his
protagonist, knows human failing at first hand:

If such doom [to be thought "Bores"] waits each intellectual Giant,
We little people in our lesser way,
In Life's small rubs should surely be more pliant,
And so for one will I—as well I may—
Would that I were less bilious—but, oh, fie on't!
Just as I make my mind up every day
To be a *"totus, teres,"* Stoic, Sage,
The wind shifts and I fly into a rage.

[17, st. 10]

Narrator and protagonist are not just separate figures in *Don
Juan*, they are set at odds, one aspiring to stoicism and the
other wavering between Aurora's purity ("beyond this
world's perplexing waste") and the availability of her Frolic
Grace, Fitz-Fulke. But both come together in being tripped
out of the ideal. The "I want" which begins *Don Juan* and
whose epic resonances may echo in the *cri de coeur* of Saul
Bellow's Henderson, finally means both "I fail to discover,
anywhere," and "I fail to become, anyhow" a hero. But it
also means we are made to encounter, instead of the lyrical
epic of Wordsworth's *The Prelude*, another innovation taking
the form of an epical elegy tinged with a mythical or trans-
lunary vision. As Haidée and the Tartar Khan and even
Aurora Raby show, we may not realistically expect a relation
of more than nostalgia with that high world, of love and sacrifice and "a depth of feeling to embrace / Thoughts, bound-
less, deep, but silent too as Space." A shy leitmotif of elegy
sets one of the amplitudes of *Don Juan*. The poem can make
comedy of gothic terror, as in the Black Friar episode. But
Byron is not kidding when he says that he laughed in order
not to weep. The realistic humanism the poem displays is in
this sense an achievement, not a dubious compromise. The

poem constitutes the only place, between the procrustean
magnitudes of traditional heroism and the procrustean di-
minishments of industrialism and imperialism, where mortal
individualism has any play. "Between two worlds," Byron
anticipates Arnold in saying

> life hovers like a star
> 'Twixt night and morn, upon the horizon's verge.
> How little do we know that which we are!
> How less what we may be! The eternal surge
> Of time and tide rolls on, and bears afar
> Our bubbles. . . .
>
> [15, st. 99]

To stay afloat is credit in itself, and in successive moments
to defy the demon rum and deny a cannibalistic definition
of human survival, and then to meet and mate Haidée constitute a life's achievement not to be sneered at. After this,
of course, much is forgotten, even lost, and elegy supervenes
on aspirations; but elegy, after all, is the tribute that mortality pays to the immortals of the erstwhile epic. And
besides, it remains consolingly possible, with a sly shift of
emphasis, "to laugh and make laugh."

The second point to focus on, in connection with the twofold pressure *Don Juan* exerts toward man's showing his
strength, moral or physical, and his showing in the field of
idealism and heroism, concerns less the tone of the poem
than Byron's apparent freedom from formal or conventional
constraints within it. I would like to suggest that every way
he turns Byron manages to go in one direction. The way and
the destination become, with each succeeding episode, increasingly difficult to sum up in a nutshell, but variations on
the theme of physical and moral strength appear throughout.
With this explicit theme, and with the narrator's infiltration
into the poem's action, *Don Juan* becomes a generic hybrid
of confession and satire, in epic guise. Confession and satire
muffle each other, but both are based on a common preoccupation with the shortcomings of heroism. The play and the

interplay of war and love, tyranny and individual fulfillment become the root concerns of the poem—its variety is tonal and modal, rather than substantial. Things and people do not stay long enough in the poem to change, it is true; instead they become one another, as war and love do in the person of the Empress Catherine, as Spanish, Turkish, Russian, and English worlds become versions of one another, as love becomes the god of evil, as Donna Inez becomes Lambro becomes Gulbeyaz becomes Suwarrow becomes the Empress Catherine becomes Lady Adeline Amundeville, or as the Fall becomes a matter of Newtonian physics and humbler physiology and sexual rhythm (see canto 9, sts. 22, 45, 55), as well as wry allusion and social fortune and undifferentiated theology. And linking and imaging all this Don Juan becomes a part of all he sees and encounters.

In light of this mutual presence of classifiably separate things in each other, we may see a principle of association or ramification within the surface spontaneity and versatility of *Don Juan*. In fact we may argue a principle of unity based on obsession: Byron keeps coming back to one issue in various guises. The idea of obsession, startling though it may seem in relation to so sportively mannered a composition, does help to account for the reflexive repetitiousness of the poem, and may be necessary to account for any form of spontaneity, which after all expresses the unlabored capacity of a finite organism for response and action. One does most freely what one most fundamentally is bent to do. In literary terms we may see this also in Wordsworth's "spontaneous overflow of powerful feelings" that are carefully cultivated and also strongly, independently resurgent.

But the psychology of spontaneity and the quality of *Don Juan* require that more than this be said. The recurrence of obsession comes out here without its stagnancy and arrest. We can identify a pattern of enclosures in the poem and see that Don Juan falls deeper and deeper into prison or rather a realization of prison; his position changes though his situation remains roughly similar from his mother's house to Julia's tumbling bedroom to the ship *Trinidada* to Haidée's cave and Haidée's luxurious bedroom and the slave ship and the harem. Even this cursory catalogue makes it clear that Byron does more than repeat a certain setting and situation; he explores its forms and implications, and makes it into an instrument for apprehending and elucidating a human motif.[12] In other words, as he goes back to it obsessively, he goes into it creatively; setting becomes an evolutionary symbol. Thus we can appreciate the irony of Juan's defying Gulbeyaz with his profession that love is for the free, and then literally fighting his way into the moral and physical subjection and exhaustion of the Empress Catherine's boudoir. The text moves from action to reflection to abstraction, though the protagonist may fail to keep pace.

In connection with this pattern of unfolding, enlarging, and altering identity in *Don Juan*, it should be of advantage to recall two cathedrals that figure prominently in the architectural symbolism of the romantic period: Wordsworth's "Gothic Cathedral" and Byron's "St. Peter's Basilica." The metaphor of Wordsworth's entire work as a Gothic cathedral conveys, beyond the immediate occasion of the preface to *The Excursion* (1814), his conception of all things as part of one; this is the conception that makes beginnings so difficult for Wordsworth ("Who knows the individual hour in which/His habits were first sown, even as a seed . . . ," when the mind, in "The words of Reason deeply weighed, / Hath no beginning"?).

It also makes ends chancy and imprecise for Wordsworth; the contribution any part makes to the whole stands beyond dispute, the vagueness or failure of every guide in *The Prelude* leaves every end in doubt and makes the poem nothing better than an exercise in frustrated teleology.

The metaphorization of St. Peter's in *Childe Harold*, canto 4 also serves to reveal, for the mind as well as for poetry, a process of indefinite epistemological development; like Zeno's traveler, one gets closer to a total comprehension of things met piecemeal, without ever quite getting there.[13] "Thou movest," Byron writes of the reverent visitor whose mind "Has grown colossal":

>   —but increasing with the advance,
> Like climbing some great Alp, which still doth rise,
> Deceived by its gigantic elegance;
> Vastness which grows, but grows to harmonise—
> All musical in its immensities;
> Rich marbles, richer painting, shrines where flame
> The lamps of gold, and haughty dome which vies
> In air with Earth's chief structures, though their frame
> Sits on the firm-set ground—and this the clouds must claim.
>
> Thous seest not all; but piecemeal thou must break
> To separate contemplation the great whole;
> And as the ocean many bays will make,
> That ask the eye—so here condense thy soul
> To more immediate objects, and control
> Thy thoughts until thy mind hath got by heart
> Its eloquent proportions, and unroll
> In mighty graduations, part by part,
> The glory which at once upon thee did not dart,
>
> Not by its fault—but thine. Our outward sense
> Is but of gradual grasp: and as it is
> That what we have of feeling most intense
> Outstrips our faint expression; even so this
> Outshining and o'erwhelming edifice
> Fools our fond gaze, and greatest of the great
> Defies at first our Nature's littleness,
> Till, growing with its growth, we thus dilate
> Our spirits to the size of that they contemplate.
>
>   [4, sts. 156-58]

It would seem fair to infer, on the strength of these two cathedral metaphors, that the character of infinity does not belong to the poem as physical object, but rather to the pursuit of the object—the world and our experience of it—which the poem embodies. And it is important to acknowledge the obverse of the ever-expanding circuit of Byron's

interest, namely, his own awareness of the tremendous intricacy of what seems small. Such intricacy results in a kind of
expansion inward; as Byron writes in "The Dream," "in itself a thought,/A slumbering thought is capable of years,/
And curdles a long life into one hour." This principle of
immense miniaturization is illustrated in *Don Juan*, canto 8,
stanzas 56-59, where Lascy and Juan reenact the Tower of
Babel; Byron summarizes as follows:

And therefore all we have related in
Two long octaves, pass'd in a little minute;
But in the same small minute, every sin
Contrived to get itself comprised within it.
The very cannon, deafen'd by the din,
Grew dumb, for you might almost hear a linnet,
As soon as thunder, 'midst the general noise
Of Human Nature's agonizing voice!

The passage has a severely cryptic quality and is full of
images yearning to be heard, like Juan or a linnet; but we
may note that a cannon and an agonizing voice, though
these are at top decibel, also fail to be heard, indicating a
moral rather than an acoustical problem. The little minute
contains more than every sin; it contains everything by
implication, and it would seem that the poem gets larger,
as by authorial commentary, not only to encompass a poly-
glot universe in a single aesthetic space, but also to enunciate
the wealth of implication in that universe's single objects.
The use of allusion, so prevalent in the poem, thus deserves
special notice as a form of bringing various worlds, of time
and thought and value, into concert around a given, ostensibly
isolated moment.

The mode of development of *Don Juan*—"now and then
narrating, / Now pondering"—clearly reinforces the techniques
of turning obsession into a disciplined instrument of creative
insight. The action themes of war and love consort with
the contemplative motifs of skepticism and humanism. In
short, the poem is thinking its action, through itself, fusing

obsession and philosophy, incident and teleology. We should note that, after the adventitiousness of the shipwreck and arrival on Haidée's island, the sequence of incidents right up to the landing in England is very closely linked together, almost becoming a causal chain in the teeth of the casual emergency system that seems to prevail.

It is necessary to go beyond the patterning of moments and characters if we are to realize the full aesthetic discipline and shapeliness underlying the free play of *Don Juan*. There operates in the poem in idiocratic (or self-determining) action and rhythm, whereby it becomes remarkably consistent and lucid and weighty and significant in form. This action and rhythm may well derive from Byron's life, and to that extent may resemble a helpless or mechanically obsessive occurrence, but it is generalized and abstracted to meet extra-biographical, catholic needs, and so must be taken as a matter of artistic choice and deployment.

This is, of course, the action and rhythm that we recognize in all the major episodes of *Don Juan*; it first appears in the Juan-Julia episode, which I have accordingly signalized as prototypal, and it comprises five main elements:

1. an authority figure (Donna Inez, Lambro, Gulbeyaz, the Empress Catherine, Lady Adeline Amundeville) who more or less directly contributes to the development of a profane or wrong action;

2. initial passivity or dependency on the protagonist's part, though he exerts a powerful attraction and possesses great potential energy;

3. a clandestine affair of love softly, almost inadvertently, begun, and with strong hints of exaltation;

4. a realistic redefinition of that love, with a burst of violence and a threat to the protagonist's life;

5. the protagonist's renewed subjugation, to force rather than to authority, and his ensuing exile, a period of reflection and evaluation.[14]

The elaboration of this idiocratic structure in *Don Juan*

affords a sense of stability in the poem, but would be harm-
ful if it implied any sort of stagnation. Rather the dynamism
of the poem is invested in this structure, which grows increasingly subtle and reverberative and revelatory of the poem's
values. Thus, for example, the exile from Haidée's island
constitutes more of a spiritual loss than the initial exile
from Spain, though Spain is technically home (the homeless-
ness and nostalgia running through the poem are not geo-
graphical but spiritual); the superior value of Haidée's world
to Julia's is manifest in Juan's naturally and nobly remembering Haidée's, as opposed to the fate of the missive with
which Julia pursues him.

In short the contours, the textures, the values of the elements in the idiocratic structure of *Don Juan* significantly
alter as we proceed. Perhaps the most elusive and most complicated instance occurs at the Russian court, which will
repay a closer scrutiny. This is some justice in beginning at
the end of canto 8, where Juan makes a vow "which,"
Byron emphasizes, "he kept," to shield the Moslem orphan,
Leila. She, like Aurora to come, is one of the homeless in
the text, but we may see more significance in the ways she
calls Haidée back to mind; for, like Haidée's, Leila's entire
world, her family and her very place of birth, have "perished." But she survives, and Juan, albeit purblindly, may
be regarded here as preserving something which the poem at
any rate associates with Haidée. It is an authentic act, but it
continues to exist in the framework of Byron's earlier question: "What's this in one annihilated city?" The dominant
energy resides with war, not compassion, and Juan approaches
the Empress Catherine's court as a man capable of occasional
good but, as Vergil says of warriors, intoxicated with blood.

It is ominous that Donna Inez reenters the poem here for
the first and only time, to give her maternal sanction to
the "maternal affection" the Empress Catherine bears Don
Juan, just as she had earlier fostered Donna Julia's "platonic"
affection for him. In fact the confusion of love and bad

poetry and humor and war that exists in Catherine's soul (and which stands embodied in Juan artificially accoutred as "Love turned a Lieutenant of Artillery") is compounded by the identification of the domestic and political power and by the disguise of raw imperious lust in the cloak of benevolence. A kind of metaphysical chaos is dissimulated by the splendor of the court and the recent victory, but its perversity finally appears in the very form of its disguise—if the Empress Catherine is maternal, she is the mother who consumes her own children, and consumes them incestuously. This, of course, focuses her in opposition to Haidée, the "mother" who saves Juan and whose dreams, however harrowing to herself, imply an infinite capacity for saving, if not giving, life. A further sign of chaos resides in the fact that when all is said and done, the Empress Catherine functions at once as Donnz Inez, as Donna Julia, and as Don Alfonso—as instigator, paramour, and punisher in this escapade. The height of Juan's reputation becomes the height of confusion and, indeed, of degradation. It is not surprising that "he grew sick," in body and spirit. Catherine of course tries to save him, and we have the final irony and confusion of the entire episode, namely, that the purported cure is designed to prolong the disease and may endanger his life. A gracious but effectual exile ensues.

Juan here reaches the nadir of his career. But there are good, or at least hopeful, signs. Leila, with all the benevolence that she attracts, firmly frames the episode at the Russian court, and as she heads for England over land and sea with Juan a significant positive temper springs up in him. I have suggested above that the exile scenes serve as intervals of reflection and evaluation. In each Juan has one main companion: Pedrillo, the tutor manqué; Johnson, the worldly-wise man whose wisdom is not à propos and whose skin is really saved by Juan; and now Leila. With Leila there is no uncertainty as to who is protecting whom. Juan, coming off his worst subjugation and most essential defeat in the poem, begins to recover himself as a magnanimous man. Clear and viable relationships begin to crystallize again, and even as the English scene looms ahead, wheeling like swords about his so-called virgin-face, it seems that in Aurora Raby he can find the three crucial relationships Comte says man bears to woman: that of veneration, as for a mother; of attachment, as for a wife; of benevolence, as for a child. Here is the relationship of wholeness that opposes the relationship of chaos we have seen in the case of the Empress Catherine. These relationships have partially existed, or perversely appeared, before. Now, having gone through them, however imperfectly, and having reflected on them, however incidentally, he is in a position to commit himself and satisfy the soul of the man who cannot but "want a hero."

It is only by the structure of the poem, with its discovery of the critical value of obsession and of self-discipline in an unconventional spontaneity, that such a position has been reached.[15] And it is in turn what I have called the realistic humanism of the poem—a compound of plangent skepticism and sardonic merriment and undying dreams of human magnificence—that makes this position so hard to resolve. The poem falls somewhere between the picaresque and the *Bildungsroman*, and so, perhaps, Don Juan becomes, more even than Wordsworth, the romantic hero of everyday, whose occasions and whose aspirations lead him to a transcendental Haidée and Aurora, while yet his occasions and his impulses involve him with hoary Empresses who stand for old Glory and indiscriminate primitive modes of love.

Postscript

Prose in the Romantic Period

"All that is not prose is verse; and all that is not verse is prose."
Molière

Within a scant three decades in the nineteenth century there occur two critical junctures in the fortunes of expository prose. First DeQuincey challenges the hereditary right of poetry to the realm of passion and power, and commences to annex and delineate the kingdom of "impassioned prose." This in 1821, in the *Confessions of an English Opium-Eater.* It was a gesture very much in keeping with the tendency of the times to relieve formal constrictions and break down boundaries between genres and modes (epic and autobiography, lyric and ballad), or between states (dreaming and waking); as such it could almost be taken as a liberal literary counterstatement to the system of land Inclosure that recrudesced during the Industrial Revolution and the Napoleonic Wars. But even in the field of literature an open dynamics was not easy to bring about. In the 1830s the influential rhetorician, Wilhelm Wackernagel, was proclaiming that "prose is the direct, as it were the polar, opposite of poetry." Wackernagel's pronouncement harks back to Thomas Gray, who in the 1760s condemned a line of one of his Odes with the comment: "It is flat, it is prose."

The second crisis for prose effectively impugns the gains of the first. In 1853, with a display of severe if also sententious logic, Matthew Arnold turns away from poetry as something whose melancholy (a single manifestation of passion and

242

power) he cannot keep in bounds, and takes up the more decorous form of prose. Arnold's action has been considered from the vantage point of biography, and of poetry; its significance for prose also deserves to be scrutinized, for it constitutes an abrupt deglamorization of prose, a virtual repudiation of the experiment DeQuincey had undertaken. The inspector of schools puts an end to the dropout's pursuit of novelty and ecstasy; accordingly prose, which had taken flight, seems again a service vehicle, caught in the post-romantic retrenchment of Arnold's mind and time.

But how do we assess DeQuincey's experiment in itself? He, for his part, seemed unable to sustain it, and fell into the worst artificiality, that of self-imitation, in the revised *Confessions*. In its brief season, though, "impassioned prose" brings the romantic revolution into this seemingly staid area of literature and highlights a more general change in the period's conception of the essential values of prose. Perhaps we may think in terms of the radical mission of prose, for DeQuincey. His missionary activity on behalf of the true church of opium has an analog in his own prose and many analogs in the prose of the romantic period, as it implicitly pushes the legitimacy of new forms such as autobiography, of new definitions of old concepts like pleasure and imagination, of new principles of criticism (the underlying burden of the *Biographia Literaria*, as well as much of Hazlitt's work). Roland Barthes puts this impulse to verbal and conceptual change into perspective for us: "Nothing is more basic to society than its organization of language. Change that organization, displace the word, and you precipitate a revolution" (*Critique et Verité*).

English romantic prose becomes in essence a major medium for exploration and establishment of the timelessness of the new. As Hazlitt says, "Genius . . . is, for the most part *some strong quality in the mind, answering to and bringing out some new and striking quality in nature.*" In effect we are dealing with a susceptibility to the radiance of a moment,

almost perhaps a philosophy of the moment, encompassing
at once Leigh Hunt's "A 'Now': Descriptive of a Hot Day"
and Wordsworth's "Preface to *Lyrical Ballads*," as micro-
scopic and telescopic versions of the inclusiveness of what
stands before us. Schopenhauer complains that "Life nowa-
days goes at a gallop" and that "the way in which this affects
literature is to make it extremely superficial and slovenly"
("On Style"). But it is momentous that DeQuincey, looking
at the same phenomenon in *The English Mail Coach*, finds
not an impairment of the old orthodoxies but an "opening
of apocalyptic vials":

These mail coaches . . . had . . . [a very large] share in developing the
anarchies of my dreams; . . . they through the conscious presence of a
central intellect, that in the midst of vast distances—of storms, of
darkness, of danger—overruled all obstacles into one steady cooperation. . . . But, finally, that particular element in this whole combination
which most impressed myself, and through which . . . [the] mail-coach
system tyrannizes over my dreams by terror and terrific beauty, lay in
the awful *political* mission which . . . it fulfilled. The mail coach it was
that distributed over the face of the land, like the opening of apocalyptic vials, the heart shaking news of Trafalgar, of Salamanca, of Vittoria,
of Waterloo.

Here prose both practices and captures the drama of all-
inclusiveness, which requires focus ("central intellect") if it is
to avoid chaos, and at the same time demands all possible
room ("vast distances") if it is to avoid preoccupation. What
DeQuincey has done is to bring analysis and apocalypse into
one synergistic system. A cool sorting of elements (first,
secondly, thirdly, fourthly, finally) merges into the incantatory naming of vials: "of Trafalgar, of Salamanca, of Vittoria,
of Waterloo." Breaking the barrier between analysis and apocalypse is a technical trick, but one with far-reaching implications for the innermost activity of the essay, which makes the
mail coach its occasion rather than its subject. Its subject, I
would propose, is the capacity, perhaps the necessity, of the
mind to accommodate exorbitant worlds. It need hardly be

said that the vial metaphor makes Waterloo, for example, into the equivalent of laudanum for the reader, and so removes another barrier between what we formally think and what we implicitly know. This effect is repeated in the phrase, "terror and terrific beauty," with its abrupt and yet grammatically simple, immanent re-vision of terror into "terrific" as a quality of "beauty."

How much DeQuincey includes in this one deft maneuver becomes apparent if we sort out the turns he makes off Burke's *Inquiry concerning the Origins of the Sublime and the Beautiful.* The direct involvement and apprehension that Burke says will impede a sense of the sublime is expressed in DeQuincey's use of the word "terror." But he refuses to observe a disjunction between subjective terror and perceived sublimity, and at the same time breaks down Burke's distinction between sublimity and beauty. The phrase "terrific beauty" reconciles beauty and sublimity, and fuses those attributes of the "object" with that "terror" in the observer which should block their being registered. DeQuincey, interested as he was in the literature of *power*, did not go headlong for the sublime. Rather he caught and rendered the rapid complex in experience where terms that are capable of separation in thought play across and at once confound and compound one another. Feeling terror, he remembers beauty, and with a singular romantic capacity for reunifying exclusive phenomena calls us to witness "terrific beauty."

DeQuincey is all but explicit about his intention of making prose into a medium of *insight.* "Modern nations," he observes in his protracted discussion of "Style," suffer from "an excess of external materials" that "has sometimes oppressed their creative power, and sometimes their meditative power." This, he says, leads to a virtual abolition of style, as an "exuberance of *objective* knowledge" that maintains itself at the cost of inhibiting the particular character of the holder and user of knowledge. The adage that "the style is the man" seems inadequate for DeQuincey's purposes; the implications of his position would have to be expressed in the form: "style is man," style is the manifestation of intrinsic humanity. "The problem before the writer," he declares (speaking of poetry but at least equally cognizant of prose), "is to project his own inner mind; to bring out consciously what yet lurks by involution in many unanalyzed feelings; in short, to pass through a prism and radiate into distinct elements what previously had been even to himself but dim and confused ideas intermixed with each other." Style thus becomes the instrument whereby "detention or conscious arrest is given to the evanescent, external projection to what is internal, outline to what is fluxionary, and body to what is vague." More than the salient overthrow of the grammarian's barrier between "arrest" and "evanescence," or between the definite (having "outline") and the "fluxionary," we need to note here DeQuincey's characteristic movement into precision and at the same time all-inclusiveness. The image of the prism, like that of the mail coach, defeats chaos and preoccupation by bringing everything into play, with nothing going out of control.

We may recognize in DeQuincey's statements much that is valuable for our study of romantic literature, and a capsule statement of the mission of romantic prose. The aesthetics of autobiography, which (not without resistance) the romantic period raised into an independent and permanent form, can be elaborated from DeQuincey's remarks. More than this, one may also see in those remarks the foundation for an aesthetics of the romantic essay. It is old hat to treat the dual purpose of romantic poetry, to elicit the fascination of everyday and to establish the relevance of the fantastic. This dual purpose is maintained by those uneasy Siamese twins of the spirit, Wordsworth and Coleridge. Without making invidious comparisons, we may note that DeQuincey recognizes and maintains it in and by himself: "secretly I was struck with awe at the revelation of powers so unsearchably new lurking within old affections so familiarly known as cold. . . . If cold could give out mysteries of suffering so novel, all things in the world might yet be unvisited by the truth of human sensations." Here analysis of everyday becomes apocalypse, and awareness of singularity becomes a promise of catholicity.

I do not mean to rest the weight of my argument exclusively on DeQuincey. A solicitation of the truth of human sensations can be documented also in Coleridge, who likewise showed an impulse or need to establish as a common principle what originated in private perception. His criticism of Shakespeare is marked by the art of transmuting impressionism into critically valid propositions. His *Biographia Literaria* is a quest for the imaginative meaning and value of his life, and its subjectivity is nowhere more manifest than in its absorption of the exuberance of *objective* knowledge—to wit, earlier critics—into what he insistently termed *"my own"* life. As Hazlitt astutely observes, "Mr. Coleridge talks of himself, without being an egotist for in him the individual is always merged in the abstract and the general."

But neither do I wish to argue an apocalyptic subjectivity in romantic prose from the work of the two significant writers who happened to be afflicted with an opium addiction (though DeQuincey, as well as Jung, might remind us of the kinship between such addiction and the states of childhood or dreaming). Very few people have charged Charles Lamb with an apocalyptic subjectivity, but even he shows germane interests in his prose. His essay on "The Sanity of True Genius" makes him a spokesman for such subjectivity, as he turns what society might see as eccentric lines of personality into the most fundamental pattern of human potentiality. In this light we might also see in the "Dissertation on Roast Pig" a light-hearted instance of the romantic taste for new developments or new revelation.

Beyond Lamb, it is possible to recognize a general sense of an altering character for prose in the romantic period. There is little reason to associate him with the form, but Keats in a letter to Reynolds envisioned an evolution of "distilled prose." The phrase brings to mind the ultimate essence of the "draught of vintage" in the "Ode to a Nightingale"; implicitly it clears away the encrustations of custom and generic rigidity in the area of prose, whose inner essence we are invited to trust and to pursue.

The inner essence of prose, of the individual, and of society may be seen as versions of one another. Wordsworth for poetry, DeQuincey for prose, and Blake for the soul: all had the same liberating mission. In a palpable way Lockhart's *Life of Scott*, going beyond the bounds of what his age thought fitting, is akin to DeQuincey's *Confessions*, and seems the more resolute and venturous in view of the fact that Alexander Chalmers had parodied Gibbon in "A Lesson in Biography." Richard Price's *Discourse on Love of Country* offers a revolutionary rather than a passive, blind patriotism. The rights of men—and the rights of women—occupy Godwin and Mary Wollstonecraft and Percy Bysshe Shelley. The revolution that romanticism attempted in the structures of conduct is expressed and conditioned by a revolution of understanding and value; and for this, prose proves more than a utilitarian vehicle. It emerges as an exemplification in form, a carriage redesigned for a redefined personality.

The irreducible, inalienable personality of this prose manifests itself even where it might seem most businesslike in carrying out a teaching function. From Dryden to Johnson neoclassical prose exhibits a teaching interest; so much we take for granted. But it is obvious that romantic prose keeps right on teaching. The "Preface to *Lyrical Ballads*" is nothing if not a teaching document; the same must be said of DeQuincey's *Confessions* and of Landor's *Imaginary Conversations*, Shelley's *Prefaces*, and even Dorothy Wordsworth's *Grasmere Journals* (Dorothy is not the profoundest, but she is in her way the most radical teacher, instructing us how to see). What then is new? First, what is taught, and second, the way it is taught. Addison teaches the known, as one who enables the public to look into the window of a normal or normative house. Hazlitt teaches the knowable, always with an emphasis on his own as well as our discovery, as one who enables the reader to look into the window of his significant soul. We may find with surprise that the first person singular pronoun abounds in, say, Dr. Johnson's life of Gray, and observe that Hazlitt "egotizes" rather less. Yet it is Hazlitt who devises room, and indeed defenses, for the eccentric personality, Hazlitt who redefines the arcs of the circle to accommodate eccentricity, whereas Johnson brings his personal authority to bear on Gray's eccentricity with crushing centripetal force.

It is tempting to call neoclassical prose Aristotelian and romantic prose Platonic, in view of Aristotle's position that in cultivating rhetoric one develops "a faculty of discovering all the possible means of persuasion in any subject," whereas Plato, in *Phaedrus*, calls on rhetoric to define "the nature of the soul." Certainly Plato's transcendence of local occasions and his radical all-embracing investigation of the soul makes him seem more akin to the romantics than Aristotle. But this is to fall into a species of compartmentalism and exhibit a tic of oppositional thinking quite at odds with the romantic adventure. Wordsworth's reference to things like hedgerows ("hardly hedge-rows, little lines of sportive wood run wild") as *beauteous forms* both shows the romantic attachment to Plato's basic concepts and their deviation and admission into dimensions of experience, under Plato's aegis, that could never meet with his approval. With the phrase "hardly hedge-rows," not a material object but an unconvincing instance of its class is offered as *an embodiment of a platonic ideal.* This does not happen in defiance of Plato; rather it makes for a correction of the cast-eyed view of reality he has generated (just as, taking a more inclusive position on platonic love, Byron laments that Plato has become the pimp of all posterity).

When Matthew Arnold retreats from passion into prose, then,

prose returns to a systematic mundaneness and reasoned safety that may be taken to declare the end of the romantic experiment. We can virtually see the change in the way the figure of Wordsworth, incorporating the Grande Chartreuse in his unguaranteed, unorthodox, intrinsically unlimited pursuit of his memory and his future in *The Prelude*, is replaced by the figure of Arnold enclosing himself, securing himself vis-à-vis the lack of guarantees and reliable bounds, in "Stanzas from the Grande Chartreuse." But it is to be remembered that the act of inclusion proves neither easy nor free. Its primary form and ultimate symbol perhaps is the taking in of food, and we have the figure of Keats eating "deliciously" of the remnants of the Garden of Paradise (from which to that extent we are not excluded), only to find it an "overwhelming" experience. It was the wisdom of the romantics that they knew the act of inclusion included the surprise of its consequences, and their virtue that they faced and often proved equal to the redefinitions thereby implied.

Notes

CHAPTER 1

1 "A Letter to the Publisher" of *The Dunciad*, in *The Poems of Alexander Pope*, in one volume, ed. John Butt (New Haven: Yale University Press, 1963), p. 320. Cleland, if not a front for Pope, certainly speaks in his idiom.

2 *Comedy*, ed. Wylie Sypher (Garden City: Doubleday Anchor Books, 1956), p. 155. Elder Olson makes a comparable point when he says that "comic plays depend upon the minimizing of [those actions which give an action its importance] to the point where the amazing and the ridiculous can work upon us" (*Tragedy and the Theory of Drama* [Detroit: Wayne State University Press, 1961], p. 164).

3 Northrop Frye, dealing with the "moral ambiguities" of comedy, observes that "insisting on the theme of social revenge on an individual . . . tends to make him look less involved in guilt and the society more so." Frye is well aware of the potential cruelty of comedy, but sees recognizable cruelty as art's "lower limit in actual life," as a "condition of savagery, . . . in which comedy consists of inflicting pain on a helpless victim"; his emphasis falls on the socially restorative, reconstitutive aspects of comedy (*Anatomy of Criticism* [Princeton: Princeton University Press, 1957], p. 45).

4 We may usefully recall here that the Dorians of Greece, claiming to have invented the form, traced the name back to "their habit of strolling from village to village *(komai)* when . . . forced out of the city" (Paul G. Ruggiero, "Introduction: Some Theoretical Considerations of Comedy in the Middle Ages," *Genre* 9, no. 4, p. 280). A kind of changing of ground affects the form as well as the performer.

5 *Anatomy of Criticism*, pp. 44, 163 f.

6 George Bernard Shaw must have seen *Coriolanus* as failing to survive that risk. In the "Preface" to *Man and Superman* he dubs it a

"comedy." Of course the play is not a comedy in any arguable generic or literary sense, but it does give rise to the generically unsettling question whether the hero, with his singularistic ways, can be taken seriously from a mature social standpoint.

7 It is interesting here to consider Karl Marx's dictum that history repeats itself—occurring the first time as tragedy, the second as farce.

8 In a letter to George and Tom Keats. *The Letters of John Keats, 1814-1821.* 2 vols. Ed. Hyder Edward Rollins (Cambridge, Mass.: Harvard University Press, 1958), 1: 191.

9 It is fitting to quote Blake, in *Milton*: "And Satan not having the Science of Wrath, but only of Pity:/Rent them asunder, and wrath was left to wrath, & pity to pity./He sunk down a dreadful Death, unlike the slumbers of Beulah/The Separation was terrible" (1.9, 46-49); and again in *Jerusalem*: "What is a Wife & what is a Harlot? What is a Church? & What/Is a Theatre? are they Two & not One? can they Exist Separate?/Are not Religion & Politics the Same Thing?" (3.57.8-10).

10 C. Kerenyi uses the phrase in a context which adds evocative dimensions to the theme, combining nature, science, myth, and theology in one picture. "Every natural law," he writes in his essay "Kore," is "a balanced aspect of the world and is immediately intelligible as the mathematical formulation of a border-line situation." He continues: "So it is with the figures of the gods. In *Apollo* sublimest clarity and the darkness of death face one another, perfectly poised and equal, on a border-line; in *Dionysus*, life and death, in *Zeus*, might and right. . . . In relation to the cosmos as a whole, these divinities are merely certain aspects of it; in themselves they are wholes, 'worlds' which have aspects in their turn, and contradictory aspects for the very reason that their structure combines contradictions in perfect equilibrium. Such gods can only be understood as *spiritual ideas*; in other words, they can only be known by immediate revelation" (in *Essays on a Science of Mythology: The Myth of the Divine Child and the Mysteries of Eleusis*, trans. R. F. C. Hull [Princeton: Princeton University Press, 1969], p. 104).

11 *Fallible Man: Philosophy of the Will*, trans. Charles Kelbey (Chicago: Henry Regnery Co., 1965), p. 9.

12 Monroe K. Spears, quoted by Leonard Feinberg, *The Satirist: His Temperament, Motives and Influence.* (New York: Citadel Press, 1965), p. 35.

13 Alvin B. Kernan, *The Plot of Satire* (New Haven: Yale University

Press, 1965), p. 14. It is useful to recall also Dryden's judgment
that "the original" of "satire . . . was nature, and that depraved"
("A Discourse Concerning the Original and Progress of Satire").

14 *The Affecting Presence: An Essay in Humanistic Anthropology*
(Urbana: University of Illinois Press, 1971), p. xviii.

15 *The Archaeology of Knowledge*, trans. A. M. Sheridan Smith
(New York: Harper Colophon Books, 1972), p. 143.

16 One quick example will suffice to show the danger and the absurdity of the practice. We call "near" the antithesis of "far," and
assign emotional values—unreachability, danger, etc.—to "far," as
opposed to "near." But surely we are dealing with a continuum in
space, with degrees of distance, when we speak of "far" and
"near." A "near" oasis and a "near" copperhead don't evoke the
same response, and help thereby to show that the issue is radically
one of degrees of intensity of reaction, rather than opposition of
being. At all events, if a "near" oasis is a furlong away, a "far" one
a league away, we certainly wouldn't call a furlong the antithesis
of a league. By the same token, an oasis is not the antithesis of a
copperhead. We may usefully recall here Ricoeur's argument that
"anguish," far from being in a "clash" with "Beatitude," is
"only its underside of absence and distance." The interrelation
of "absence and distance" is strikingly apropos. As Ricoeur observes, "man is capable of Joy, of Joy in and through anguish"
(*Fallible Man*, p. 16). The reader will find it interesting to compare
Jacques Derrida's undoing of the opposition between good and
bad writing, in *De la Grammatologie* (Paris: Les Editions de Minuit,
1967), pp. 30–31, 68, 92, 222–23, 228; and also Mircea Eliade's
discussion of the *coincidentia oppositorum* in *Traité d'Histoire
des Religions* (Paris: Payot, 1964), pp. 351–52.

17 Whether one takes singular and plural arithmetically or platonically,
they share in each other's existence: one of many, or one as the
source and end of many. Similarly preterite and present are part of
one continuum of time, and cannot be opposed unless time is opposed to itself. One may as soon call these pairs polar bears as
polar oppositions.

18 Near the end of *The Raw and the Cooked*, Lévi-Strauss in effect
concedes the freedom of culture from "rigid relations" and invariable manifestations. This is tantamount to freedom from the laws
that may have governed any earlier behavior. The point is of great
importance, and is worth pondering in Lévi-Strauss's summation:

It is a question rather of long-term pressures, within the limits of which the mythological system can, in a sense, argue with itself and acquire dialectical depth: that is, be always commenting on its more direct modalities of insertion into reality, although the comment may take the form of a plea in favor or denial. It is thus very rare for a mythological system, if it is at all resourceful, not eventually to exhaust all the possible codings of a single message, even if this is achieved through the apparent inversion of certain signs.

The same community—or communities that are geographically, linguistically, or culturally close to each other—sometimes invents myths that systematically tackle a given problem by envisaging, in one variant after another, the several different ways in which it may be solved.

. . . Each version provides a particular image of reality: social and economic relations, technical activities, relation to the world, etc.; and ethnographic observation must decide whether this image corresponds to the facts. External criticism thus allows us, *at least as a working hypothesis,* to *replace the relational* orders we have already obtained *by an absolute* order, constructed according to the rule that the myths, whose subject matter expresses directly observed reality, are myths of the first rank, the others being myths of the second, third, and fourth ranks, etc., and further removed from the type that is logically the most simple (since there is no question here of historical priority) in that they *have to be subjected* to a *greater number of transformations*—unwound, as it were—to be brought back to the simple type. (Trans. John and Doreen Weightman [New York: Harper and Row, 1969], pp. 332-34; italics added.)

On the question of the intrinsic functional ties between the parts of systematic antitheses, the reader may also with profit refer to Ludwig Feuerbach's *The Fiery Brook: Selected Writings* (trans. with intro. by Zawar Hanfi [Garden City: Doubleday Anchor Books, 1972], pp. 232 f.).

19   For Nietzsche, who ultimately saw health and grace in a fusion of Apollo and Dionysus, see *The Twilight of the Gods* and also Arthur Danto, *Nietzsche as Philosopher* (New York: Macmillan, 1965). For Arieti, see *Creativity: The Magic Synthesis* (New York: Basic Books, 1976), p. 157; for Perry, see *Roots of Renewal in Myth and Madness* (San Francisco: Jossey-Bass Publishers, 1976), pp. 50-51.

20   A certain temptation arises to make much of the two blank arcs— between "revulsion" and "realism" and between "reconciliation" and "scorn." But it need not prove surprising that imminent

"reconciliation" and "revulsion" should be relatively inarticulate. The closer one approaches to "substitution," the greater the urgency of speech, in the mode of criticism (satire) or prophecy (the word means "to utter in advance," being made up of *pro* and *fatus*). In a sense speech at this end of the continuum fills a dualistic gap between actuality and desire. When there is reconciliation the gap disappears and the harmony residing in the succession of moments renders itself in silence. Similarly "revulsion" throws one back into oneself, stemming communication and causing silence. The interesting phenomenon in the ring is the proximity and concentration between prophecy and satire, and their forming a base for a triangle with elegy as its apex.

21 In *The Rambler*, 156. The redefinition of genres and the general habit of redefinition in romanticism have been touched on in my study *The Romantic Will* (New Haven: Yale University Press, 1976), pp. x, 26.

22 William K. Wimsatt, Jr., and Cleanth Brooks, *Literary Criticism: A Short History* (New York: Vintage Books, 1967), p. 320.

23 "Romantic Verse Form and Metrical Contract," in *Vision and Resonance: Two Senses of Poetic Form* (New York: Oxford University Press, 1975), p. 200. Of course the background of the elegy enlarges upon the metrical contrast. Hermann Frankel describes the "proper purpose" of traditional classical elegy as "admonition, instruction, reflection" (*Early Greek Poetry and Philosophy*, trans. Moses Hadas and James Willis [New York: Harcourt, Brace, Jovanovich, 1973], pp. 132 f., and esp. 151-59); and Albin Lesky suggests that while lamentation over the dead *could* have been the "original function of elegy," when it "first becomes known to us, [it] has subjects of a very different kind" (*A History of Greek Literature*, trans. James Willis and Cornelius de Heer [New York: Thomas Y. Crowell, 1966], pp. 117-21). Ovid makes a spontaneous association of elegy and lamentation in *Heroides* 15, where, recognizing his "carmina" as "lyricis . . . magis apta modis," he nonetheless proclaims "flendus amor meus est—elegiae flebile carmen."

24 The subject of "She Dwelt Among the Untrodden Ways" is of course "Lucy," but this name seems more an interpretive and symbolic instrument than a pointing to any identity external to the poems. The title "a maid" conveys a more concrete basis for identity than the name "Lucy" in this particular piece.

25 In the spirit of the poem as written and not, of course, in biography. The assumption of the elegiac persona and its evolution

from initial recognition scene to final protestations involves the
speaker in ways that seem to enliven the convention, if at some
cost of credibility. The problem is at bottom that no convention
is ever adapted impeccably, or as it were merely conventionally.
There is always an investment and an opportunism in taking up a
convention, and these remain liable to internal challenges as well
as eligible for formal privileges. It seems to me that Pope's fourth
pastoral, "Winter; or Daphne" shows what problematical riot-
ousness can result from the appeal to so-called *pure* convention.
In keeping with the practice from Theocritus on, Pope has "Nature's various charms decay" upon Daphne's death; in keeping
with the practice that Bion originated in his "Lament for Adonis,"
Pope sets mourning aside and cries up a glad renewal: "But see!
where Daphne wond'ring mounts on high/Above the clouds,
above the sky!" But then Pope also invokes the topos of waste-
ful, all-conquering Time (out of St. Augustine and the Spenser
of the "Mutability Cantos," rather than the pastoral tradition),
and concluding that "we must Time obey" bids "Daphne, fare-
well; and all the world adieu!" It is hard to ignore the fact that
Pope is exploiting the conventions and the reader's responses,
moving ad lib from effect to effect, giving and taking away with
more external legerdemain than internal legitimacy. One almost
wonders if the concluding dark apocalypse (Time conquers all . . .)
does not spring from a peculiar bias that Pope will only integrate
with his subject and his system of understanding in the fourth
book of *The Dunciad*. The convention is his pretext, not his
purpose here.

26 Elegy always implies an antagonist in the sense that every lament
about something approaches a complaint against something or
someone else. When the object of opposition becomes definite,
satire is imminent. When its appearance is rejected and transcendence is sought, prophecy is afoot.

27 On the classical elegy, the reader may with advantage consult not
only Lesky and Frankel, cited above, but also Georg Luck, *The
Latin Love Elegy* (Oxford: Oxford University Press, 1938); C. M.
Bowra, *Early Greek Elegists* (Cambridge, Mass.: Harvard Univer-
sity Press, 1938); and A. R. Burns, *The Lyrical Age of Greece*
(New York: St. Martin's, 1960).

28 Virginia Woolf draws a distinction, pertinent here, between "convention" and "intellect." The former she signalizes in the person
of George Duckworth, who "accepted Victorian society so implicitly that . . . like a fossil he had taken every crease and wrinkle

of the conventions of 1890–1900. He was made presumably of precisely the right material. He flowed into the mould without a doubt to mar the pattern." Convention, in short, fossilizes. By contrast "intellect" makes experiments, departures, extensions. As she says, "Vanessa and I were explorers, revolutionists, reformers" (*Moments of Being: Unpublished Autobiographical Writings*, ed. with an intro. and notes by Jeanne Schulkind [New York: Harcourt, Brace, Jovanovich, 1976], pp. 130, 126–27).

29 Mantuan and Petrarch had earlier taken the turn into pastoral satire, and Spenser had modified this to church satire in *The Shepheardes Calender*. Milton takes a distinctive step in this line of development by employing specifically elegiac satire.

30 Respectively, "*Lycidas*: Poet in a Landscape," in *The Lyric and Dramatic Milton*, ed. Joseph H. Summers (New York: Columbia University Press, 1965), p. 72, and *John Milton: A Sketch of His Life and Writing* (New York: MacMillan, 1964), p. 62.

31 *The Motives of Eloquence: Literary Rhetoric in the Renaissance* (New Haven: Yale University Press, 1976), p. 16.

32 The reader will find it valuable to consult C. Kerenyi, *Archetypal Images in Greek Religions*; vol. 2: *Dionysos: Archetypal Image of Indestructible Life*, trans. Ralph Manheim (Princeton: Princeton University Press, 1977).

33 Thomas Perrin Harrison, *The Pastoral Elegy* (Austin: University of Texas Press, 1939), p. 4.

34 Quoted from Harrison, p. 37.

35 "*Lycidas*: Poet in a Landscape," pp. 67, 77.

36 *Milton's Poetry of Choice and Its Romantic Heirs* (Ithaca: Cornell University Press, 1973), p. 149.

37 *A Study of Shelley's Poetry* (Albuquerque: University of New Mexico Press, 1967), p. 276. It is also well recognized that Shelley drew on the classical elegists Bion and Moschus, the former being the originator of the *Lament for Adonis* and the latter, in mourning Bion's death, the originator of the link between lamented poet and Adonis. A neat commentary of the Shelley-Bion parallels is provided by Carlos Baker, though at the same time Baker observes that Shelley did not hesitate to alter "the Greek story wherever it suited his . . . purpose" (*Shelley's Major Poetry: The Fabric of Vision* [New York: Russell and Russell, 1961], p. 240); on the use of classical material the reader should also consult Harrison, *The Pastoral Elegy*, p. 22. Shelley's readiness to go his own way, using anterior work as a springboard, is important to the understanding of *Adonais*. For extended discussion of the relation of

Adonais to the original myth, the reader may with profit consult Edward B. Hungerford, *Shores of Darkness* (New York: Columbia University Press, 1941), pp. 216-39.

38 Earl R. Wasserman offers a cogent reading of this development in *Shelley: A Critical Reading* (Baltimore: Johns Hopkins University Press, 1971), pp. 465 ff.

39 Reiter, *A Study of Shelley's Poetry*, p. 276.

40 The same synaesthesia, rectified and creative, recurs in the ineffectual spring of stanza xvi *et seq.*

> The leprous corpse, touched by this spirit tender,
> Exhales itself in flowers of gentle breath;
> Like incarnations of the stars, when splendour
> Is changed to fragrance, they illumine death.

41 This line actually echoes Bion's *Lament for Adonis*. It may be noted here that the sensuous interests of Urania seem modest beside the outcry of Bion's Venus: "O stay, Adonis, ill-fated Adonis, stay, that I may possess thee for the very last time, that I may embrace thee and mingle lips with lips. . . . kiss me as long as a kiss may live, until from thy soul into my mouth, even into my very heart, thy breath may flow, and I may drain thy sweet love charm" (42-47).

42 It is telling that her appeal, "Stay yet awhile" (xxvi), should seem so pathetic, when its model statement in Goethe's *Faust* is so heroic. On the other hand, her regressive tendencies have a momentary promise when in response to Misery "She rose like an autumnal Night, that springs /Out of the East" (xxiii). The autumn-spring movement intensifies the overt statement of renewal in the lines.

43 But note that he has raised the metaphysical issue himself in the passage on the ineffectual spring: "Whence are we? and Why are we? of what scene /The actors and spectators? (xxi). These, as Byron says in *Don Juan*, are questions "answerless and incessant."

44 Urania's approach to satire is easy to miss, because it poses itself as idle speculation, an "if only" that on one level simply aggravates the condition of grief; but on another level it conveys rage and scorn for the culprits: "hadst thou waited," she advises the dead Adonais, "Thy spirit should have filled its crescent sphere, / [And] the monsters of life's waste had fled thee like deer" (xxvii; see also xxviii).

45 On this subject the reader should also consult Brian Wilkie, *Romantic Poets and Epic Tradition* (Madison and Milwaukee: University of Wisconsin Press, 1965), chap. 6; and Jerome J. McGann, *Don*

Juan in Context (Chicago: University of Chicago Press, 1976), pp. xi-xiii; chap. 5.

46 "Touched" implies madness as its primary value, but it also conveys the idea of being moved, involved in the exorbitant effects of Haidée's death. The word suggests an identification of madness and grief, thus reinforcing the notion that the dominant voice of satire is adopted in the interest of sanity.

47 *Anatomy of Criticism*, p. 50.

48 Ibid.; italics added.

CHAPTER 2

1 Trans. with an intro. and notes by J. B. Baillie (New York: Macmillan, 1949), pp. 242-43.

2 Morse Peckham, *The Triumph of Romanticism* (Columbia: University of South Carolina Press, 1970), p. 78.

3 *Wordsworth's Poetry: 1787-1814* (New Haven: Yale University Press, 1971), p. 159.

4 *Amor and Psyche: The Psychic Development of the Feminine*, trans. Ralph Manheim (New York: Harper Torchbooks, 1956), pp. 69, 71.

5 Hartman, *Wordsworth's Poetry*, p. 159.

6 It is of interest that Goethe, in his *Gesprache*, sees "consequence" in a positive and personal light, as something which gives every person the hope of bringing about the heart's desire in time. Using as his definition the "consistent pursuit of a goal," Goethe says that "consequence, unyielding, strict consequence, can be applied even by the most insignificant, and will seldom fail of its purpose, since its silent power grows without ceasing over the course of time. When I cannot act with consequence, cannot exert continuous influence, it is advisable not to seek to act at all." Perhaps that last phrase, suggesting the impotence if not the treachery of action, makes room for consequences in the sense I am calling typical in romanticism. That sense goes beyond the underlying weakness that we declare when we speak of the defect of an excellence. It recognizes that commendable desires and virtues which we treat with praise effectively undermine our lives—desire becomes disaster, and virtue is in effect as good as vicious.

7 Though the notion of saving, *soteria*, originated as a local and practical matter of "deliverance from perils by sea and land and disease and darkness and false opinions," without theological implications and without spiritual overtones (A. D. Nock, *Conversion* [New York: Oxford University Press, 1961], p. 9).

8   Scientific inquiry still surrounds itself with an aura of "purity"—
    an aura, one might say, of inconsequence—but its bearing on the
    totality of human experience gives increasing concern. Ecology,
    for instance, has come to the fore as a science of evolving relation-
    ships among the residents of the earth, including man. It is im-
    plicitly the science of consequences.

9   *Problems of Dostoevsky's Poetics*, trans. R. W. Rostel (Ardis,
    n.d.), p. 45.

10 In *The Short Novels of Dostoevski*, trans. Constance Garnett (New
    York: Dial Press, 1945), p. 133.

11 *The Brothers Karamazov* dates from 1879-80, *The Portrait of a
    Lady* from 1881.

12 Alexandra F. Rudicana offers a perceptive analysis of Dostoevski's
    "vision of the Fall and Redemption as applied to modern man," in
    her study "Crime and Myth: The Archetypal Pattern of Rebirth in
    Three Novels of Dostoevsky," *PMLA* 87 (October 1972): 1065-74.

13 Quoted by Eva le Gallienne, intro. to *Six Plays of Henrik Ibsen*
    (New York: Random House, 1959), p. xix.

14 Ibid., pp. xix–xx. One may also recall that Catherine Morland, in
    Jane Austen's *Northanger Abbey*, calls marrying for money "the
    wickedest thing in existence."

15 E. T. Donaldson, ed., *Chaucer's Poetry: An Anthology for the
    Modern Reader* (New York: Ronald Press, 1958), p. 872.

16 *Mimesis: The Representation of Reality in Western Literature*,
    trans. Willard R. Trask (Princeton: Princeton University Press,
    1953), pp. 8–11.

17 Morton W. Bloomfield, "The Man of Law's Tale: A Tragedy of
    Victimization and a Christian Comedy," *PMLA* 87 (May 1972):
    384, 389. Bloomfield cites also *The Clerk's Tale, The Physician's
    Tale, The Second Nun's Tale, The Man of Law's Tale*, and *The
    Prioress's Tale*.

18 Donaldson, *Chaucer's Poetry*, p. 924.

19 "Chaucer and Medieval Allegory," *ELH* 30 (June 1963): 180n10.

20 *Conversion: The Old and the New in Religion from Alexander the
    Great to Augustine of Hippo* (New York: Oxford University Press,
    1933), pp. 99, 100.

21 On the question of shame, see Stanley Cavell, "The Avoidance of
    Love: A Reading of *King Lear*," in *Must We Mean What We Say: A
    Book of Essays* (New York: Chas. Scribner's Sons, 1969), pp. 277-
    78, 286-87, and also René Descartes, *The Passions of the Soul*,
    article cxvii, in *The Philosophical Works*, trans. Elizabeth S. Hal-
    dane and G. R. T. Ross (Cambridge: Cambridge University Press,

1911). The basic difference between dread and shame, the ontological character of the one and the social character of the other,
can be descried in the response of the wife of the Bishop of Wor-
cester when she heard of the theory of evolution: "Descended
from apes! My dear, let us hope it is not so; but if it is, let us hope
that it does not become generally known." The first hope arises
from dread, the second from shame.

22 *A Preface to Chaucer: Studies in Medieval Perspective* (Princeton:
Princeton University Press, 1962), p. 27. The reader will also be
interested in Frances Leonard's extension of the redemptive idea
into comedy, in "The School of Transformation: A Theory of
Middle English Comedy," *Genre* 9, no. 3: 179 f.

23 *The Waning of the Middle Ages*, trans. F. Hopman (London: Edward Arnold and Co., 1927), pp. 4–5.

24 Robertson, *A Preface to Chaucer*, p. 281.

25 *Waning of the Middle Ages*, p. 18; and see pp. 1–21 in general.

26 The redemption is not of the king himself, but of the situation he
has precipitated. His emotional idiosyncrasy regarding the terms of
succession proves to be ultimate political madness, and sets in motion a juggernaut of consequences. Edmund's late change of heart
and the unexpected triumph of Albany's forces reverse the dismal
tendency of things and, though singularly wanting in jubilation,
institute the redemptive situation.

27 *The Yale Review* 61 (Summer 1972): 530–43. Attention should
also be called to Helen Gardner, "Milton's Satan and the Theme of
Damnation in Elizabethan Tragedy," *Essays and Studies* 1 (1948):
42–61.

28 "Conclusion" to *The Renaissance* (New York: Boni and Liveright,
1919), p. 197.

29 *The Common Liar: An Essay on "Antony and Cleopatra"* (New
Haven: Yale University Press, 1973), p. 12.

30 Ibid., pp. 24, 27.

31 Julian Markels, in *The Pillar of the World: Antony and Cleopatra
in Shakespeare's Development* (Columbus, Ohio: Ohio State University Press, 1968), makes many valuable comments on the play's
language (chap. 6 passim). But since the conditions of Antony and
Cleopatra's transcendence seem to me inimitable, I would have
reservations about Markels's claim that they "are creating by their
action a new, coherent, and protean life that guarantees man's
moral freedom and his power to create endlessly a unique identity"
(p. 154). It seems sounder to support the distinction Bergson
makes in his essay on "Laughter" between a universal phenomenon

and a singular phenomenon that gains universal acknowledgement. Surely the case of Antony and Cleopatra is of the latter type.

32 Ted Honderich, *Punishment: The Supposed Justifications* (Baltimore: Penguin Books, 1971), p. 32.

33 *The World as Will and Representation,* trans. E. Payne (New York: Dover Publications, 1966), 1: 334.

34 Both philosophy and psychology, from Plato to Jung, support this general treatment of the symbolism of the horse, and it is dramatized not only in the story of Phaeton "wanting the manage of unruly jades," but also in that of Neptune, whose horse surges, as a kind of primordial form, out of the chaos of the sea.

35 See Michael Foucault, *Madness and Civilization: A History of Insanity in the Age of Reason,* trans. Richard Howard (New York: Pantheon Books, 1965), pp. 11, 38-64, 202-09, 250-58.

36 *Politics and English Romantic Poetry,* p. 18.

37 The breakdown of a theological sense of human behavior in the romantic order (perhaps this constitutes the beginning of the disappearance of God) has been cited in individual cases: Northrop Frye, in *A Study of English Romanticism,* sees Mary Shelley's *Frankenstein* occurring in "a world where the only creators . . . are human ones" (New York: Random House, 1968, p. 45); and Leslie Tannenbaum sees in the same text "a world apparently devoid of divine agency" ("From Filthy Type to Truth: Miltonic Myth in *Frankenstein,*" *Keats-Shelley Journal* 26 [1977]: 101). This atheological vision appears again in *Don Juan,* where man's Fall is not an event but a primary datum of autogenetic character, and in *The Fall of Hyperion,* with its curious sense that a compassionate redemption may be necessary though no Fall as such is visible. The shift away from theological accountings warrants further attention, as occurring with, and not just in, the romantic scheme.

38 See *The Romantic Sublime: Studies in the Structure and Psychology of Transcendence* (Baltimore: The Johns Hopkins University Press, 1976), pp. 167 f. Interest must also attach to Victor Turner's general anthropological comments on "liminality" in *Dramas, Fields and Metaphors: Symbolic Action in Human Society* (Ithaca: Cornell University Press, 1974), pp. 231 f.

39 Goethe's *Faust,* which is supposed to have influenced *Manfred,* also reveals a pattern of development from a Christian, retribution-and-repentance scheme of values to a concern with consequences and, finally, a kind of post-Christian humanism. In Goethe this humanism is creative-communal, in Byron stoical-individualist.

40 See Michael G. Cooke, *The Romantic Will,* pp. 30-39.

41 "I cannot tell" may, of course, also express a chosen or an imposed silence, rather than simple ignorance; such a reading reinforces the point.

42 Thel's illustrative relation to things out of nature has a striking anticipation in the seventeenth century, where Margaret of Newcastle bitterly sums up the lot of the female of the species: "Women live like Bats or Owls, labour like Beasts, and die like Worms" (quoted by Virginia Woolf, *A Room of One's Own* [New York: Harcourt Brace & World, 1957], p. 64). Thel focuses on her own condition, Margaret Cavendish on the experience of the class, but at bottom a sense of waste and gloom links the two positions closely.

43 Because the "daughters of Mne. Seraphim," Thel's sisters, fall short of her in reflective power, it may seem that she is justified in leaving their world for a larger vision. But they obviously also surpass her in realized power, and her withdrawal comes to resemble a withdrawal from reality into speculative pathos. She reminds one of the virgin in "Ah, Sunflower" as "she in paleness sought the secret air," and this damaging analogy is confirmed if we associate the "sunny flocks" with the rampant power of male sexuality (a reading supported by Greek mythology and modern psychology alike).

44 An interesting extension of the subject of silence appears in Susan Hawk Brisman's article "'Unsaying His High Voice': The Problem of Voice in *Prometheus Unbound*," *Studies in Romanticism* 16 (1977): 51-86.

45 In *The Archaeology of Knowledge* Foucault writes: "Identity is not a criterion even when it is exhaustive; even less so when it is partial, when words are not used each time in the same sense, or when the same nucleus of meaning is apprehended through different words" (trans. A. M. Sheridan Smith [New York: Harper Colophon Books, 1972], p. 143).

46 The difference between the "defiled bosom" and the "pure breast" goes beyond wilful semantics or the fudging of shock and grief. The "bosom" should be taken in a physical sense, the "breast" in a spiritual one (but, in the plural, "breasts" has a physical signification, as when Oothoon puts the plucked flower "to glow between my breasts"). Physical and spiritual senses should be joined indissolubly; they are so when Oothoon goes out to find Theotormon, before Bromion "rends" her and them. The imagery of the flower is candidly sexual, as is Oothoon's "exulting swift delight" and her "impetuous course." But all this bursting prompt-

ness expresses, along with a desire of the body, an impulse and choice of Oothoon's spirit: "I . . . put thee here to glow between my breasts/And thus I turn my face to where *my whole soul seeks*" (1. 12-13; italics added). The problem of the poem is whether this innocent unity of body (bosom or breasts) and spirit (soul or breast) can be restored after the Bromionic rending.

47 The tableau of course represents an arrested and degenerating prothalamion. The wedding couple, allegorized as "terror and meekness," are "Bound back to back in Bromion's cave" (2.5); here is per-*vers*ity indeed! The poem's refrain also contains a secondary echo that conveys a failure in relation to marriage. As the Daughters of Albion "hear [Oothoon's] woes, & eccho back her sighs," they darkly reminisce the refrain of Spenser's *Epithalamion*: "That all the woods may answer, and your echo ring."

48 One may read this line to say that Oothoon has had less sense than a chicken, in not knowing enough to shun Bromion. But the paramount value of the line is to point to a sense beyond the senses, a pristine intuition graphically and fruitfully working everywhere in nature, and why not then in man (and woman).

49 The gain in complexity and pith from the first analogies (2. 23 f.) to the present series (3. 2 f.) is instant and striking. Not only is Oothoon forcing inference upon the listener in the second series (where she has pointed to likenesses before), but she also resorts to involved comparisons (ass, camel, wolf, and tiger) and to overt logic (No. for these . . . have) to refine a point that scores with the initial simple question about the chicken and the hawk.

50 She is still correcting, as with a rod, the definition of "sense" inculcated in her defenseless youth.

51 As Blake says in *Milton*: "If you account it Wisdom when you are angry to be silent, and /Not to shew it: I do not account that Wisdom but Folly" (1. 4. 6-7).

52 An obvious exception is *The Rime of the Ancient Mariner*, but this is a slight for which Coleridge amply makes up in *Christabel, Dejection: An Ode*, and "Kubla Khan."

CHAPTER 3

A note on the chapter title: The word *value* occurs, among other contexts, in mathematics, as "the quantity, magnitude or number an algebraic symbol or expression is supposed to denote"; and in phonetics, as "the special quality of the sound represented by a written character." Both senses may apply here, but I wish to emphasize its usage in the graphic arts, to indicate "the relation of the elements of a picture, as light and shade, to one another, especially with reference to their distribution and independence."

1 In *The Case for Wagner* Nietzsche writes of "love as *fatum*, as fatality, cynical, innocent, cruel—and precisely in this a piece of nature. That love which is war in its means, and at bottom the deadly hatred of the sexes" (in *The Birth of Tragedy and The Case for Wagner*, trans. Walter Kaufmann [New York: Random House, 1967], pp. 158-59). The identification of love and the battle of the sexes, in the closing phrases, warrants the association of sex and "a piece of nature."

2 Bruno Bettelheim presents a crucial and, given its premises, compelling argument for fairy tales in *The Uses of Enchantment: The Meaning and Importance of Fairy Tales* (New York: Alfred A. Knopf, 1976). Eric Rabkin's study of *The Fantastic in Literature* (Princeton: Princeton University Press, 1977) is also of interest.

3 I draw on the version of the story recorded by the Brothers Grimm. It is in effect the "standard" version; but those by Basile and Perreault have distinctive and powerful features which merit special attention (see Bettelheim, pp. 227 f.).

4 Interesting variants and analogs, as well as a valuable suggestion that the transformation is seasonal (winter-spring), may be pursued in Eric D. Brown's study "Transformation and the *Wife of Bath's Tale*: A Jungian Discussion," *Chaucer Review* 10 (1976):303-15.

5 In some versions he changes when the princess petulantly dashes him against the wall.

6 For further elaboration of this point, see Bettelheim, pp. 288 f.

7 See H. R. Hays, *The Dangerous Sex: The Myth of Feminine Evil* (New York: Putnam's, 1964), pp. 88-95.

8 That is to say, as a story of how the Agora was formed, and how the jury system originated.

9 Aeschylus, *The Oresteia*, trans. with an intro. by Richard Lattimore (Chicago: University of Chicago Press, 1953): *The Eumenides*, 11. 900-12, 984-85, 1003-11, 1025-42.

10 The fact that she is born full-grown from the head of Zeus appears to minimize her female connections, and to return both priority and birth-giving to the male. But her birth can with cogency be read as a raising of male interests from Jovian power (the hands, and thunder) or sex (the loins, and license) to wisdom (the head, and creativity). That wisdom takes a female form would suggest then a sense of male limitation—the male is responsible for and yet not ready to embody this highest virtue which is, symbolically,

born of the head. On the other hand, Sarah B. Pomeroy bluntly presents Athena as a manly goddess (*Goddesses, Whores, Wives and Slaves: Women in Classical Antiquity* [New York: Schocken, 1975], pp. 4f.).

11 The male-female (sex) conflict which the scene builds on is compounded by a racial conflict, with the Oriental standing for effeminacy and decadence to the Greek mind.

12 A different view of this god, not specifically pegged to *The Bacchae*, is afforded by Walter Otto, who writes that Dionysus is "a warrior and a hero who triumphs. . . . His manhood celebrates its sublimest victory in the arms of the perfect woman. This is why heroism *per se* is foreign to him in spite of his warlike character" (*Dionysus: Myth and Cult*, trans. Robert Palmer [Bloomington: Indiana University Press, 1965], p. 175).

13 In this connection, one should consult Pomeroy, *Goddesses, Whores, Wives and Slaves*.

14 See discussion of Pope's "Elegy to the Memory of an Unfortunate Lady," above, pp. 23-30.

15 In *Eighteenth Century Poetry and Prose*, ed. Louis I. Bredvold, Alan D. McKillop, and Lois Whitney, 2d ed. (New York: Ronald Press, 1956), p. 154. See also Myra Reynolds's edition, and Reuben A. Brower, "Lady Winchilsea and the Poetic Tradition of the Seventeenth Century," *Studies in Philology* 42 (1945):61-80. But Virginia Woolf has hit on Anne Finch's sense of frustration with considerable accuracy and force, in *A Room of One's Own* (New York: Harcourt, Brace and World, 1957), pp. 60 f.

16 The word *forest* is derived from the Latin *foris*, designating the undomesticated area beyond the demarcations of civil residence. A sense of the opportunity and of the problems of the "forest," occurring as early as *The Bacchae*, develops into a crucial perception for romanticism. It comes out in Rousseau, Schlegel, Wordsworth, Keats, and Coleridge, to name just a few prominent writers.

17 Quoted by Virginia Woolf, *A Room of One's Own*, p. 65.

18 Memorably, Hester Thrale summed up his style: "all he did was gentle, if all he said was rough." (in *Anecdotes of the late Samuel Johnson, LL.D., during the last twenty years of his Life. By Hesther Lynch Piozzi*, ed. S. C. Roberts [Cambridge: Cambridge University Press, 1925], p. 141).

19 In Abelard's defense, one revises the old maxim: once castrated, twice shy.

20 Sir Thomas Wyatt's "Whoso List to Hunt" unreflectingly assumes that such values alone may be realized by a woman. The poem

turns bitter irony on the female lover for not being tame but "wild for to touch," and never acknowledges for her a scope and independence of action beyond the speaker. The ultimate irony is that she may not imagine anything more for herself. She goes from the speaker's protection to that of a mightier man: "Caesar's I am." Though "wild" to the speaker, she remains tame in her basic position, tame in the system.

21   As opposed to a quality of weakness. In the matter of weakness we are dealing less with a descriptive than a political formulation. Johnson illustrates this political bias in his comment to his friend John Taylor, whose wife not only abandoned him but also continued to badger him for support: "You are, in my opinion to consider yourself as a man injured and instead of making defence to expect submission. . . . You enquire what the fugitive Lady has in her power. She has, I think, nothing in her power but to return home and mend her behaviour.). . . . Nature has given women so much power that the law has very wisely given them little" (letter of 18 August 1763, in *The Letters of Samuel Johnson*, ed. R. W. Chapman [Oxford: Clarendon Press, 1952], p. 157).

22   This phenomenon is exemplified in Keats's "On First Looking into Chapman's *Homer*" (where "Cortez" lucidly faces the overwhelming Pacific), and is discussed as a general feature of romanticism in my study *The Romantic Will*, p. 203.

23   Michel Foucault, *The Archaeology of Knowledge*, pp. 44-45. The extended quotation is worth perusing: "It is not easy to say something new: it is not enough for us to open our eyes, to pay attention, or to be aware, for new objects suddenly to light up and emerge out of the ground. But this difficulty is not only a negative one; it must not be attached to some obstacle whose power appears to be, exclusively, to blind, to hinder, to prevent discovery, to conceal the purity of the evidence or the dumb obstinacy of the things themselves; the object does not await in limbo the order that will free it. . . . It exists under the positive conditions of a complex group of relations."

24   Wordsworth was acutely aware of the fact that the new might be something old and unnoticed and not new in itself. Thus the new would prove to be immemorial if we could succeed, as he put it in the "Essay, Supplementary to the Preface (1815)," in "breaking the bonds of custom, . . . overcoming the prejudices of false refinement, and displacing the aversions of inexperience." He goes on to associate this effect with genius, of which he says "the only proof is, the art of doing well what is worthy to be done, and what

was never done before. . . . Genius is the introduction of a new element into the intellectual universe."

25 Isabella Fenwick, in a note to *William Wordsworth, The Poetical Works*, ed. from the MSS with textual and critical notes by E. DeSelincourt and Helen Darbishire (London: Oxford University Press, 1947-49), 2: 504.

26 Among the few exceptions to this statement one should cite Alan Grob, "Wordsworth's 'Nutting'," *Journal of English and Germanic Philology* 61 (1962): 826-32; David Perkins, *The Quest for Permanence: The Symbolism of Wordsworth, Shelley and Keats* (Cambridge, Mass.: Harvard University Press, 1959), pp. 14-16; and David Ferry, *The Limits of Mortality: An Essay on Wordsworth* (Middletown, Ct.: Wesleyan University Press, 1959), pp. 22-28.

27 Fenwick, see note above.

28 The irony of course is that he himself, in his private act of ravage, has ripped in the hazel cover the holes that allow the sky's intrusion.

29 It is well to acknowledge that the rapacious boy could not, *as such*, have written the poem. He is too secretive, too obsessed with mere action, which as Wordsworth himself says "is transitory, a step, a blow, the motion of a muscle this way or that." As poet he includes but also far surpasses action.

30 For more along this line of discussion, see chapter 4, "The Mode of Argument in Wordsworth's Poetry."

31 But if the "cheek on . . . green stones . . . fleeced with moss" suggests Hamlet's "head in the lap" and the *mons veneris*, the fleece also anticipates a scene of pastoral innocence, with "stones . . . scattered like a flock of sheep." The point of the poem is that different possibilities inhere in one phenomenon, one scene, and the poem works out, among these embodied possibilities, a choice of the fullest and the best.

32 Apart from the one recognized by the "ribald of Arezzo," Aretino, who observed in his *Dialogues* that literalness affords no variety and may be tedious in itself.

33 For an extended discussion of rape, the reader may consult Susan Brownmiller, *Against Our Will: Men, Women and Rape* (New York: Simon and Schuster, 1975).

34 Friedrich Schiller, *On the Aesthetic Education of Man, in a Series of Letters*, ed. and trans. by Elizabeth M. Wilkinson and L. A. Willoughby (Oxford: Clarendon Press, 1967), XXVII, p. 213.

35 The "Maiden," as such, obviously also repairs at the human level

the rape which the hazel-bower has suffered at the youth's hands; at the natural level, the bower takes care of itself, while at the psychological-symbolic level the man is clearly following a course of atonement and reverence that may slowly make up for the harm done.

36 I quickly co-opted this term, but it is clear that it would not have suited my pedagogical purpose had I thought of it on my own.

37 The bleeding youth is here a kind of false Orc, an embodiment of energy that fights oppression without participating, even indirectly, in any positive revolution.

38 The form of the poem is not cyclical but rather spiral, in that at the end we return to the opening position on a different plane.

39 Cobbett said that Bentham made the whole idea of universal suffrage absurd by proposing to include women.

40 Introduction to Schleiermacher's *Soliloquies*, trans. with a critical introduction and an appendix by Horance Leland Friess (Chicago: Open Court Publishing Co., 1926), p. xxii.

41 *Essays*, trans. T. Bailey Saunders [in three separately numbered sections]. (New York: Willey Book Co., n.d.) sec. 3, pp. 76, 79, 79-81, 82, 84.

42 Schopenhauer's essay of course traces back to the anti-feminist tradition that so galled Chaucer's Wife of Bath; he is well aware of the tradition, and gives citation from it (pp. 80 f.). But his concession of "natural rights" and implicitly natural dignity for women puts him on another plane, even if he leaves men greater rights. Pope, for example, conceded that one woman was an exception to all the unfavorable things he had to say about the sex (*Moral Essay*, III), but nowhere approaches the concept of a general good belonging to and inhering in every woman.

43 In *The Philosophy of Schopenhauer*, ed. with introduction by Irwin Edman (New York: Modern Library, 1928), pp. 337-76.

44 In *The Radiance of the King*, by Camara Laye, Diallo is an artisan whose axes are much admired but who laments his creative deficiencies, insisting that he could never make an axe worthy of so much as a glance from the King. His is clearly the platonic idea of the axe.

45 The qualities that are peculiar to the male sex are uniformly in keeping with this judgment, "manly structure of the skeleton, broad shoulders, slender hips, straight bones, muscular power, courage, beard, etc." (p. 355).

46 In fairness it should be noted that *The Metaphysics of the Love of the Sexes* has its moment of startling atavism. Schopenhauer sees

it as the "aim of nature" when the male "looks about after other women" and the female "sticks firmly to one man." From this he concludes that "faithfulness in marriage is with the man artificial, but with the woman it is natural, and thus adultery on the part of the woman is much less pardonable than on the part of the man, both objectively on account of the consequences and also subjectively on account of its unnaturalness" (p. 352).

47 In their study *Modern Woman: The Lost Sex* (New York: Harper and Row, 1947), Ferdinand Lunberg and Marynia F. Farnham provide interesting sidelights on the psychology that may be involved here ("Mary Wollstonecraft and the Psychopathology of Feminism," pp. 144-45).

48 *A Vindication of the Rights of Woman*, ed. Carol H. Poston (New York: Norton, 1975), pp. 11, 12.

49 Wollstonecraft, perhaps anticipating Jane Austen, fears to acknowledge "sensibility" because it was not only associated with women but thought their only quality (pp. 43-44, 60-61, 63, 64, 188, et passim).

50 In his *Memoirs of Mary Wollstonecraft* Godwin says she thought of women as "labouring under a yoke which . . . had degraded them . . . almost . . . to the level of the brutes" (ed. W. Clark Durant [New York: Greenberg, 1927], pp. 53-54).

51 But note that, again like Schopenhauer, Rousseau gives glimpses of a higher vision in the midst of his selfish outlook in *Emile:* "Women have most wit, men have most genius; women observe, men reason: from the concurrence of both we derive the clearest light and the most perfect knowledge, which the human mind is, of itself, capable of attaining" (trans. Barbara Foxley [London: J. M. Dent & Sons, 1950], p. 350).

52 See Lionel Tiger, *Men in Groups* (New York: Random House, 1969).

53 But note that both community and institution may deny or satisfy the individual, just as both lend themselves to maintenance of the social organization. They differ in mode and emphasis; no simple or radical opposition arises between them.

54 The text steadily treats pleasure as a lesser form of happiness, and seems to anticipate Friedrich Schiller's dictum that "pleasure may be stolen," while "happiness must be earned."

55 It is fashionable to say, "biology is destiny." But then it becomes necessary to ask, "what is biology?"

56 What I would call a secondary incarnation takes place in Tenny-

son's *In Memoriam*, where the male poet plays the feminine role to
the "canonized" masculine hero. It is in a way exciting to see the
Victorian male make himself so at home with the feminine (Swinburne evinces an obsessive interest that seems to spring from raw
terror). But it is at bottom a disturbing phenomenon, not only for
its presumption, but for its reactionary *role-bias*. The "feminized"
poet is a cento of stereotyped traits: passivity, sensibility, dependence, loyalty. . . . Despite his choice of Don Juan as a protagonist,
Byron gives the feminine in itself and in relationship to the masculine a much truer and fuller portrayal, as I try to demonstrate in
chapter 5, "Byron's *Don Juan*: The Obsession and Spontaneity of
Self-Discipline."

57 "Introduction" to *Lucinde and the Fragments* (Minneapolis: University of Minnesota Press, 1971), p. 24. Lucina is of course Juno
in her manifestation as goddess of childbirth. Schlegel sets up
Lucinde as an enlarging, revelatory figure in the realm of creativity, just as Keats in the *Fall of Hyperion* sets up Moneta (Juno in
her capacity as counsellor, source of judgment) as an enlarging and
revelatory figure in terms of spiritual growth. Both are expatiating
on the value of the feminine. Where the Augustans defer to classical antecedents, the romantics—as Keats and Schlegel do—typically
naturalize them, bringing them to immediate full life in an emulous
contemporary form.

58 Perhaps we are too hasty in regarding *couvade* as a primitive derangement, when it might represent an ultimate identification and
participation, in essence, by the masculine figure in the activity the
feminine figure sustains for him.

59 At an apocalyptic moment in the "Allegory of Impudence," Julius,
hearing the inspiring phrase, *"the time has come,"* says he "reached
for weapons in order to leap into the warring tumult of the passions, who use prejudices as weapons. I wanted to fight for love
and truth: but there were no weapons to be had." It would seem
that battle has no place in his world, except as a source of im-
poverishment. As his "friendly companion" remarks, he must
"Create, discover, transform *and retain* the world and its eternal
forms in the perpetual variation of new marriages and divorces"
(p. 58; italics added).

60 "Let love itself be," he requests, ". . . not more rational than great
Plato and holy Sappho" (p. 63).

61 *Madame Bovary*, ed. Paul DeMan, Norton Critical Editions (New
York: Norton, 1965), pp. 340 f.

CHAPTER 4

1 This quotation from the "Ode to the West Wind" is often devastatingly increased by a single uncanonical phrase, "I die!" That is gratuitous and impossible for a first-person speaker, as Shelley would have known infallibly.

2 "'Unsaying His High Language': The Problem of Voice in *Prometheus Unbound*," p. 86.

3 *Complete Works*, ed. P. P. Howe, after the ed. of A. R. Waller and Arnold Glover, vol. 5 (London: J. M. Dent & Co., 1930), pp. 161, 163.

4 *The Art of Wordsworth* (Hamden, Ct.: Archon Books, 1965), p. 131.

5 *Complete Works*, 9: 86.

6 Samuel Taylor Coleridge, *Biographia Literaria*, 2 vols., ed. with aesthetical essays by J. Shawcross (Oxford, 1907), 1: 134.

7 For Wordsworth clearly assumes what De Quincey later enunciated, the dichotomy between the literature of knowledge and the literature of power.

8 This point of view resides in "the fourth class of defects" drawn up against Wordsworth's poetry in the *Biographia Literaria*, where Coleridge criticizes "an intensity of feeling disproportionate to *such* knowledge and value of the objects described, as can be fairly anticipated of men in general . . . and with which therefore few only, and those few particularly circumstanced can be supposed to sympathize" (2: 109). It occurs ubiquitously now, as in Raymond Dexter Havens, *The Mind of a Poet: A Study of Wordsworth's Thought* (Baltimore: The Johns Hopkins University Press, 1941), I; 4; G. Wilson Knight, *The Starlit Dome: Studies in the Poetry of Vision* (Oxford: Oxford University Press, 1941), pp. 22, 36; Norman Lacey, *Wordsworth's View of Nature and Its Ethical Consequences* (Hamden, Ct.: Archon Books, 1964), pp. 122, 126; Geoffrey H. Hartman, *The Unmediated Vision: An Interpretation of Wordsworth* (New Haven: Yale University Press, 1954), pp. 4, 6, 8; Henry John Jones, *The Egotistical Sublime: A History of Wordsworth's Imagination* (London: Chatto and Windus, 1954), pp. 2, 15, 35; M. H. Abrams, "Wordsworth and Coleridge on Diction and Figures," *English Institute Essays, 1952*, ed. Alan S. Downer (New York: Columbia University Press, 1954), pp. 171-72; Donald Davie, *Articulate Energy: An Enquiry into the Syntax of English Poetry* (London: Routledge and Kegan Paul, 1955), p. 107; Josephine Miles, *Eras and Modes in English Poetry* (Berkeley and Los Angeles: University of California Press, 1957), pp. 125, 131-36; R. A. Foakes, *The Romantic Assertion: A Study in the Language of*

Nineteenth-Century Poetry (London: Methuen, 1958), pp. 80, 115; Anthony E. M. Conran, "The Dialectic of Experience: A Study of Wordsworth's *Resolution and Independence*," *PMLA* 75 (1960): 70; David Perkins, *The Quest for Permanence*, pp. 91, 100; Edward E. Bostetter, *The Romantic Ventriloquists: Wordsworth, Coleridge, Keats, Shelley, Byron* (Seattle: University of Washington Press, 1963), p. 5; Harold Bloom, *The Visionary Company: A Reading of English Romantic Poetry* (Ithaca, New York: Cornell University Press, 1963), p. 141. Perhaps the most sweeping presentation of the charge of "assertion-making" comes from a non-Wordsworthian, R. L. Drain, who writes: "It was Wordsworth . . . who smuggled over the stormy borderline between the centuries just those conceptions ['law of nature,' 'right reason,' 'the moral sense,' 'natural rectitude'] Bentham worked so hard to destroy. He did so in a way that it baffled even Benthamite analysis to stop. A comprehensive intellectual refutation of materialistic fallacies . . . had no part in it. The day was won not by intellectual strength but by intellectual weakness. . . . The message . . . slipped by the reader's logical defenses not by overcoming the critical intellect, but by offering it no hold" (*Tradition and D. H. Lawrence* [Groningen: J. B. Wolters, 1960], p. 6).

9   Quotations of Wordsworth's poetry are taken from the *Poetical Works*, ed. with intro. and notes by Thomas Hutchinson, new ed. rev. by Ernest DeSelincourt (New York: Oxford University Press, 1959). Concerning this question of "art," Helen Darbishire sees in Wordsworth an opposition between "impulse and intuition" and "careful art" (*The Poet Wordsworth* [Oxford: Clarendon Press, 1950], p. 4). This conjures up the image of Wordsworth warbling his native woodnotes wild, and denies what Wordsworth knows, namely, that careful art is the handmaiden of impulse and intuition. Miss Darbishire later appraises Wordsworth's art at a higher rate, especially when contending against the treatment of him as a doctrinaire poet (pp. 65-66, 193).

10 The word *dialectic* occurs widely in criticism of Wordsworth and of romanticism (see, e.g., Bloom, *The Visionary Company*, p. 143; Conran, "The Dialectic of Experience: A Study of Wordsworth's *Resolution and Independence*," passim; Colin Clarke, *Romantic Paradox: An Essay on the Poetry of Wordsworth* (New York: Barnes and Noble, 1962), p. 12; and Geoffrey Hartman, "Romanticism and 'Anti-Self Consciousness,'" *Centennial Review* 6 [1962]: 556). It is used to describe perhaps the sort of life situation or process or structure that would give occasion for argument,

a situation marked by contraries and working toward an equipoise or resolution. It has not heretofore been carried to the point of identifying the rhetorical procedures or strategies whereby, in portraying the dialectical situation, the poets convey and earn distinctive philosophical positions, except negatively by F. R. Leavis when he says, "Wordsworth's verse . . . goes on and on, without dialectical suspense and crisis or rise and fall" (*Revaluation: Tradition and Development in English Poetry* [New York: George W. Stewart, 1957], p. 162).

11 D. G. James, *Scepticism and Poetry: An Essay on the Poetic Imagination* (London, 1937), p. 273.

12 The chronology of the poem's composition fairly bears out this point (see Darbishire, *The Poet Wordsworth*, pp. 87-88, 90-91); the toning down of intimacy in the revised references to Coleridge (pp. 121-22), if anything, promotes this effect.

13 *Romanticism* (Adelphi: Martin Secker, 1927), p. 183.

14 As in 1.14-15, 329-30, 404, 445, 475, 500, 554-58, 591, and further selectively in 2.140, 306, 312; 3.157, 158, 169-70, 193; 14.308, 358, 414. In *The Egotistical Sublime* John Jones says that "Wordsworth carries his delight in negatives to the point of tiresome mannerism: there are too many double negatives" (p. 204). I. A. Richards, in turn, calls the double negatives in Wordsworth "opacities" (*The Portable Coleridge* [New York: Viking Press, 1961], p. 36). It needs to be recognized that with his double negatives, as with the less common "not . . . but" constructions, Wordsworth adds general definition, not just idiosyncratic delight, to what he says.

15 Robert Langbaum, "The Evolution of Soul in Wordsworth's Poetry," *PMLA* 82 (1967): 268.

16 *Lucinde and the Fragments*, p. 61.

17 On romantic nature imagery, see W. K. Wimsatt, Jr., *The Verbal Icon: Studies in the Meaning of Poetry* (Lexington: University of Kentucky Press, 1954), pp. 103-16; for a discussion of the "vague" and "dreamlike" qualities of romantic poetry see F. L. Lucas, *The Decline and Fall of the Romantic Ideal* (New York: Macmillan; Cambridge: The University Press, 1936), chap. 1, pp. 1-54, and also W. T. Jones's discussion of "soft-focus" imagery in *The Romantic Syndrome* (The Hague: Mouton, 1961), pp. 121-25.

18 The use of argument in this poem is touched on by this writer in *The Blind Man Traces the Circle* (Princeton: Princeton University Press, 1969), pp. 62-63.

19 *The Egotistical Sublime*, p. 207.

20 Carlos Baker, ed., *The Prelude, with a Selection from the Shorter Poems . . .* , rev. and enlarged (New York: Holt, Rinehart, 1954), p. xii.

21 "When only one is shining in the sky" must of course be read as *limiting* the function of the image exclusively to that time. It goes outside the compass of the poem, and counter to the restricted applicability of the image as image, to fill the heavens with stars and depreciate Wordsworth's subject. If anything, we should imagine a second sky elsewhere, full of undistinguished stars. The same limiting use of the conditional "when" occurs in "The White Doe of Rylstone," 2. 60-62.

22 Perkins, *The Quest for Permanence*, p. 91.

23 *The Starlit Dome*, p. 38.

24 One can observe two further instances of an intellectual falling-back which costs Wordsworth's poetry some of its vibrancy, some of its special power to be both natural and new. In the poem "Suggested by a Picture of the Bird of Paradise," which indeed reaches for argument tardily and lamely after giving vent to a quasi-puritanical bile, concrete idealism becomes a conventional idealism, or platonism (2. 33 ff.). More striking yet, the second of the "Miscellaneous Sonnets," pt. 2, shows Wordsworth taking fright and shrinking from a wood wherein "thoughts, link by link/Enter through ears and eyesight, with such gleam/Of all things that at last in fear I shrink/And leap at once from the delicious stream." This is not just the "avoidance of apocalypse" that Hartman posits in *Wordsworth's Poetry: 1787-1814* (New Haven and London: Yale University Press, 1964, pp. 17-18, 45 ff., passim); it is avoidance of experience itself, and of experience which has constituted the anchor and nurse of apocalypse for Wordsworth.

25 *The Unmediated Vision*, p. 38.

26 *The Limits of Mortality*, p. 24.

27 Darbishire, *The Poet Wordsworth*, p. 133.

28 See *The Blind Man Traces the Circle*, ch. 6, pp. 175-213.

CHAPTER 5

1 See A. C. Bradley, "The Long Poem in the Age of Wordsworth," in *Oxford Lectures on Poetry* (New York: St. Martin's Press, 1955), pp. 177-208.

2 Vol. 1 of *The Collected Works of Samuel Taylor Coleridge*, ed. Barbara E. Rooke (Princeton: Princeton University Press, 1969), p. 449.

3 Geoffrey Hartman discusses recognition in relation to poems as diverse as *The Prelude* and "Resolution and Independence" in his *Wordsworth's Poetry.*

4 It is possible in theory that the poem, for all its activity, could betray a real aesthetic or conceptual impasse for Byron. But that kind of impasse, seen in *Christabel* or *The (First) Book of Urizen* or *Hyperion,* usually results in a suspension or abandonment of the text. *Prima facie* Byron's continuing with his magnum opus is a sign of viable substance.

5 From *querer,* to desire or love. The term is used in bull-fighting to describe a position in the arena to which the bull repeatedly and as it were instinctively returns.

6 Most critics of the poem take up the subject of its form. None to my knowledge has worked it out as I am attempting to do here, but it would be churlish and misleading not to cite the major critics who have contributed significantly to my responses: George M. Ridenour, *The Style of Don Juan* (New Haven: Yale University Press, 1960); P. G. Trueblood, *The Flowering of Byron's Genius: Studies in Don Juan* (1945; rpt. New York: Russell & Russell, 1962); Jerome J. McGann, *Fiery Dust: Byron's Poetical Development* (Chicago: University of Chicago Press, 1968); Alvin B. Kernan, *The Plot of Satire* (New Haven: Yale University Press, 1965); Leslie A. Marchand, *Byron's Poetry: A Critical Introduction* (Boston: Houghton Mifflin, 1965); Andrew Rutherford, *Byron: A Critical Study* (Stanford: Stanford University Press, 1961); Edward E. Bostetter, *The Romantic Ventriloquists* (Seattle: University of Washington Press, 1963); Truman Guy Steffan, *The Making of a Masterpiece,* vol. 1 of *A Variorum Edition of Byron's Don Juan* (Austin: University of Texas Press, 1957); M. K. Joseph, *Byron the Poet* (London: Victor Gollancz Ltd., 1964); Ernest J. Lovell, Jr., "Irony and Image in *Don Juan,*" in *English Romantic Poets: Modern Essays in Criticism,* ed. M. H. Abrams (New York: Galaxy Books, 1960); E. D. Hirsch, Jr., "Byron and the Terrestrial Paradise," in *From Sensibility to Romanticism,* ed. Frederick W. Hilles and Harold Bloom (New York: Oxford University Press, 1965).

7 If there is an etymological pun here on "chewing again" (*re-morsus*), we may the better appreciate Juan's difficulty in stomaching this brute necessity of self-preservation.

8 Byron calls Lady Adeline "fatal," but it is the Duchess of Fitz-Fulke who proves so, insofar as she bodily stands in the way of his return to wholeness and innocence, on a mature footing with Aurora.

9   Even the Haidée episode, but there Byron is careful to shield
     Haidée from its severer implications, just as he shields her from
     the luxury of her surroundings and the corruption of her ances-
     try: she remains "as pure as Psyche ere she grew a wife," and if
     she is as stubborn as her father, her stubbornness as devoted to
     preserving freedom and love, not curtailing them.

10 Haidée of course contains both heyday and high day. Aurora, the
     dawn goddess, may be repeated in the surname "Raby" (ray be).
     The critical thing, in any case, is to see that Aurora reminisces
     and also revises Haidée; she is herself a gem, while Haidée seems
     alien to the bejewelled state of her apartment. Aurora's power and
     perfection in the form come from her escaping single definition
     and becoming an instance of geniune wholeness: she is not only
     dawn, and gem, but also budding flower. The gem of course picks
     up the dawn's light, while the dawn is analogous to the opening
     of the flower. For a more extended, biographical view of Aurora's
     name, the reader should consult Thomas Ashton, "Naming Byron's
     Aurora Raby," *English Language Notes* 7 (1969): 114-20.

11 Rutherford, *Byron: A Critical Study*, p. 203.

12 In small compass, the snake image used of Haidée may be cited to
     illustrate the minuteness of the technique in the poem, and also
     perhaps to meet a difficulty in construing her character. She is at
     first a snake possessing venom and implying death, and later *not* a
     snake that loves a long and dreary length of life. It seems that the
     second image controls the application of the first. Byron makes the
     snake oppose itself, as a brief incandescent intensity and a drag-
     ging monotony are opposed. But both "snakes," in relation to
     Haidée, say the same thing: she is not long for this world. The
     images together make for a highly controlled effect and must be
     seen as drastically curtailing, if not eliminating, the negative
     associations we tend to have upon first encounter with the snake
     that "casts at once its venom and its strength."

13 But as Jerome J. McGann has privately observed for the benefit of
     this writer, the likeness between Wordsworth and Byron is not
     complete, as Wordsworth is "caught" by Gothic, Byron by Ba-
     roque architecture.

14 It is possible that the exile should be treated as a separate element;
     certainly the shipwreck episode and the war cantos, reminders of
     The Odyssey and *The Iliad*, are parallel in *Don Juan*, and the ship-
     ping to Turkey and to England may stand as lesser echoes of the
     exile theme, much as the harem trio suggests the English trio of
     ladies.

15 The manipulation of the *ottava rima* stanza offers a concrete
summary of the poem's joining of the modes of necessity and
surprise. In itself the stanza is precise and invariable, but in effect
in Byron's hands it proves disconcerting and treacherous (see,
for further elaboration of this point, my *The Blind Man Traces the
Circle*). It may be worth noting that *Don Juan* formally prepares
for the maintenance of the long poem in the English tradition,
with writers as various as Tennyson, Pound, Lowell, Ammons,
and Ashbery drawing on its resources.

Index